ROMANCING
YOUR CHILD'S HEART

BY MONTE SWAN

WITH DR. DAVID BIEBEL

LOYAL

WWW.LOYALPUBLISHING.COM

DEDICATION

To my wonderful parents, Emery and Betty Swan.
Your lives wrote this book.

CONTENTS

ACKNOWLEDGMENTS

Peter Hiett, my pastor: Much of this book flowed from your messages. They broke spiritual dams, while anchoring me, biblically, and helped me see the larger Story and the romance more clearly.

Dr. David Biebel: Without you, my friend, brother, and fellow archer, this book could not have been written. In reality, I sang melody and you sang harmony.

Thanks to:

Matt Jacobson, my publisher, for believing in this vision and being my friend.

Margaret Sharpe, my editor, who took what was a pearly Colorado sky and turned it into a clear blue Colorado sky.

Kathy von Duyke and Tia Ciferno, for their continual prayer and encouragement and deep creative thought they gave throughout my research and writing.

Wade and Jessica Hulcy and the KONOS family, for their moral support and kindred-spiritship as I began this project.

Dr. Joe Wheeler, who helped me strengthen my idea of story: It is an honor to know you.

Stan Keith, for challenging my ideas and preventing me from taking myself too seriously.

Those who read my manuscript or discussed the idea of romance at various stages, encouraging me to write this book, including: Gene Swanson, Bruce Cripe, Jodi Hogle, Jim and Marty Johnson, Becki Anderson, Philip Yancey, Ray and Trish Cone, Kevin Keating, Levinia Hayes, Gina Braun, Laurie Bailey, Bob and Tina Farewell, Chris McCluskey, Chuck Bolte, Vicky Goodchild, Gayle Graham, Dr. Larry Crabb, Dave and Joan Exley, Dr. Ted Tripp, Bob Cryder, Dr. Ruth Beechick, Lisa Jacobson, Carol Bartley, and all the others who have sat around our dining room table.

My brothers and sisters-in-law: Mike and Linda, Skip and Cindy, and Scott and Chris. I am sure you are what God envisioned when He imagined family.

Heather, Travis, and Dawson, for your unconditional love, and for gladly giving Papa permission to use you as illustrations.

And Karey, the "fairest of ten thousand." You are my coauthor.

STRAIGHT AND TRUE

He was an arrow in our quiver,
Then we held him in our hand.
Soon the bowstring held the arrow,
And the aiming part began.

For as long as I can remember, I've been enchanted by the flight of an arrow. By age four, inspired by legends of heroic knights in days gone by, archers whose fame would live forever, I was making my own bows from alders by the creek, and arrows from the straightest sticks I could find. I smuggled strings for my bows from my mother's sewing cabinet, and pieces of cloth to make a proper archer's attire.

Even today, when I pick up a bow, I'm suddenly transported back to the woods behind our home in Wisconsin, where for hours on end I was Robin Hood leading his merry men. I can see the green leaves of springtime, smell the flowers of summer and the burning leaves of autumn as I crawl along the musty earth, trying to ambush one of the "king's" deer, or anything else with fur or feathers. Even though I never hit a single bird or beast, my joy was undiminished, because I was living a fairytale, participating in a story in which the adventure was everything. My boyish soul was caught up in the romance of it all.

Early one morning about ten years ago, when my children were still young, I arose before dawn. Life was so wonderful at that time, in tune just as it had been for me as a young child. But an adult anxiety gripped me: *I want this day to last forever. I wish that time would slow down. I have these arrows in my quiver, but they need to be sharpened, and properly fletched, balanced, and perhaps even straightened before they can be released.*

With these thoughts in my head, I sat down and penned a song I called "Arrows." The chorus went like this:

And time seems to fly
Oh, the years pass so quickly now,
Like sand through your fingers
You hold it once and then it's gone.

The children keep changin'.
They grow as the years rush by.
Like arrows in a quiver,
They're made to someday fly.[1]

More recently, our oldest son, Travis, joined my wife Karey and me in singing for a group of parents. As Karey and I sang "Arrows," it suddenly struck me: *The future has arrived.* Travis was already in college, a balanced arrow, strong and sharp. But which way would he fly? How straight? How true?

When we finished singing, the audience wanted to question Travis. This was not something we had anticipated or rehearsed.

Is there any greater love story than the one of God's love for us?

We soon realized that people were not so interested in our parenting philosophy, methods, or advice as they were in knowing Travis's heart. Karey and I stood behind Travis, waiting for our "report card" to be read in public. For us, the suspense was intense. All we could do was silently pray, watch, listen, and hope.

For Travis, it was no problem at all. The first question was: "Do you feel that your parents over-sheltered you as you grew up?"

"Not at all," he replied. "I did not feel so much sheltered as strengthened."

It happens to every parent: one day our child is safe in the quiver; then, we hold the arrow in our hands, and the next day the arrow is on the string, the bow is bent. The child is released, and flying into the future, toward some target beyond our world. Much of the flight we will not even be around to see.

Like most Christian parents, Karey and I had read the parenting handbooks and taken to heart the advice of experts concerning biblical training and truth, scriptural disciplines and knowledge. For years it was tempting to focus on Christian behavior, development of talents, and quality of education, all the time knowing that Travis's heart was the real prize. I assumed he would follow Christ and become a man after God's own heart. It seemed to be a given.

Many parents cruise along for years, thinking they have all the time in the world, all the while overlooking the simple truth that their child must embrace Christ for himself, from the depths of his own heart. Ultimately, the direction his heart turns is the key. Thankfully, the One Who gives Travis the choice, when He says, "Follow Me," is also the One Who has been at work, drawing Travis to Himself, creating a desire in Travis's heart for Himself, whether through us as parents, through others, or through the beauty of His creation.

You see, God has more at stake in the contest for our child's soul than we do. Our heavenly Father knows the terrible cost of a heart won by the other suitor, Satan—the deceiver who can make his way appear so delightful. He is engaged in a supernatural rivalry, an eternal competition for the heart of every child. Parents may be unaware that there is a contest. When they do join in the fight, their preoccupation with the battle on the front lines allows Satan opportunity to sneak in on the flank or the rear, enticing and drawing their child away.

God places before every human being the choice either to love Him or reject Him, because only uncompelled love is real, authentic, deep and strong. God desires this kind of love from His children. When He gave us this choice, He decided to pursue us, woo us, and draw us to Himself—in a word, He "romances" us.

"What?" you protest. Twenty-first century Christians don't normally associate the word "romance" with love for God, much less in the context of parenting. Perhaps this is because we've allowed the other suitor and his surrogates to seduce our minds, convincing us that romance is solely the domain of pop music, movie theaters and dime store novels. We have cheapened the true meaning of love—love that, when it is given freely to God and not to the pretender, becomes the ultimate gift any human can offer.

Is there any greater love story than the one of God's love for us? He loves us even though we don't deserve it—in fact, He loved us before we were born. He loved us with a love marked by heroism, wonder, beauty, extravagance, sacrifice, and suffering. The story of God's love for His people is real "history"—His Story as recorded in His Word, from its beginning to its ultimate happily-ever-after ending. And at the center of His Story is Romance—an affair of the heart. It emanates from God Who, since before time began, has loved us deeply and desired our love in return.

Our role as parents is far more than to provide food, clothing, and shelter for our children. It is ultimately about facilitating and fighting—facilitating the spiritual choices they will make, while fighting the influences of an imposter who would steal their affection, devotion, and passion, and direct it toward their own destruction.

In my "Robin Hood" days, when the world began to woo me, my mother and father chose to fight for my heart—not by building a wall around me, but by out-romancing the competition. They knew that the vast and lush beauty of nature had always mesmerized me, so they gave me freedom to explore it. From the start, I had always sensed something both magnificent and amazing in creation. A sense of wonder burned strong in my heart.

I know now that it was God drawing me to Himself. As a little boy, I spent countless hours in the creek or hiking through hardwood forests and boggy marshes near my childhood home. I loved the rocks, chased the dragonflies, and climbed the hills. I became intimate with the work of God's hands, and this made me desire to know Him.

My parents provided a safe place for me to grow—a home where fairytales really did come true. Their relationship provided the solid bedrock upon which my security was built. Although their life together included its share of adversity and tragedy, they continued to trust God, and they never lost heart. They pressed on, protecting me with a hedge of hope and joy, and a genuine vision for God's larger Story. Unconditional love, grace, and their faith in me quenched any rebellion before it arose in my heart. This was a crucial element in their wooing me to God. And then there were the family stories and the books they shared—all filled with adventure, mystery, and happy-ever-afters. My parents' hearts were irresistibly beautiful.

The image of God, projected through their true blue life together, naturally drew me to my heavenly Father. My parents inspired me; they nourished my dreams, aspirations, and visions by protecting and cultivating my creativity. When they encouraged me to design, to bring order from disorder, and to make things, I sensed a camaraderie with my Creator. I felt His image coming alive within me. I built tree houses, sculpted dinosaurs from creek clay, and whittled animals from black walnut. I played the trumpet, built my own basketball court, and fished with homemade tackle. My childhood was a whimsical romance in which my parents, through much sacrifice, won my heart for God.

When I became a parent, I began the same process with my own children. We all dream of our children flying straight and true when we launch them into the world. But shouldn't we aim a notch higher, beyond our human vision? The trajectory God has planned for our children may take them flying high and far, beyond what they or we can possibly imagine. Somewhere out there, in their future, perhaps even beyond our lifetimes, God will use our children to penetrate deep into enemy territory, to engage in battle and romance other hearts to Himself.

PART I:
THE IDEA OF ROMANCE

I see His blood upon the rose,
And in the stars the glory of His eyes.
His body gleams amid eternal snows;
His tears fall from the skies.

I see His face in every flower;
The thunder and the singing of the birds
Are but His voice—and, carven by His power
Rocks are His written words.

All pathways by His feet are worn,
His strong heart stirs the ever-beating sea,
His crown of thorns is twined with every thorn,
His cross is every tree.

- Saint Patrick

1

ONCE UPON A CHILDHOOD

He's found riches in rocks and ropes and rain
And in bugs and bark and bones.
He's got a treasure trove that money can't buy
And his own goldmine in his boyhood blue sky.

Once upon a time, there was a little boy who lived in the north
woods of Wisconsin.

The boy lived in a log cabin that his father built, decades after
the last stands of great virgin white pines had been logged off.
Homesteaders had followed the loggers, but by the time the boy
was born, most of them had moved elsewhere. Abandoned
homesteads and overgrown fields whispered tales of hard labor,
lean times, and courageous men and women who had struggled
to cultivate this land of stony soil and short summers.

The boy's grandfather, the son of Swedish immigrants, told him many stories of those early days "vhen da pines gruew so tall dat da highest branches seemed to vreach da stars, and vhen you valked amoung dem it vas like valking truew a catedral." Sometimes, the old man's voice quavered with emotion. A faraway look in his gray-blue eyes would pull the boy back to those days, and suddenly he was there, in the story with his grandfather, wandering through an enchanted forest created by God.

The cabin symbolized his parents' dream of establishing a simple home in a beautiful place, close to nature and family. It stood at the edge of a deep, clear lake, seven miles east of town, on a country road that wound through hardwood hills and hollows and scented cedar swamps. There was a porch for sitting, and a fireplace sculpted of fieldstones collected from the rock pile of an abandoned homestead. The forest that surrounded it possessed a timeless serenity and stillness that touched the souls of all who passed by.

On summer days, the lake came alive as the sun made diamonds dance on the water. The lake was also alive with fish, which the boy's mother loved to catch. On one sunny day when the boy was three, his mother returned from fishing holding up a stringer of bass she had caught across the lake. She claimed that she could set her watch by those bass, because they fed every day at exactly the same time. The boy's father came down to see the fish, but when they turned to show their son the catch, he had disappeared.

Their first thought was the lake. But it was calm, and they had heard no splash, or cries for help. They looked in the cabin. In the quietness their panic grew. They scanned the woods, where the sanctuary of dark green hemlock and cedar, with roots entwined, had become a maze that seemed to block their way.

They were about to head into the forest when they saw the boy, sitting on the soft moss at the edge of the trees, trying to hug the ancient, charred stump of a white pine. He was making friends with the stump, which was just his height. It captivated him as he used all his senses to study this sentry of the woods. He was a "tree hugger" before tree hugging was cool.

The boy never forgot how that stump looked, smelled, felt, tasted—even what it said, directly to his soul, in that magical moment—a story of days gone by, of the million hours of sunlight it had drunk in, of primeval land that had not felt a ploughshare or heard the ring of an axe. Something, or rather Someone, was wooing his heart. He was in a state of pure wonder.

As you have probably guessed, that boy was me. Looking back, it seems both poetic and prophetic that this—my earliest memory—involves God romancing my heart to Himself.

My parents never forgot that day. In the years to follow, as they watched me battle with other suitors for my heart and soul, they often recalled that picture of their son's first encounter with God's creation.

After the old-growth hemlock and hardwoods of northern Wisconsin had been logged off, my father found work in the carpentry trade in southern Wisconsin. There, he built another house for his family, next to a stream that I called "the crick."

The crick drew me with irresistible force. It held a mystical quality unlike anything I had known before. Beyond the flowing water, which would have called to any boy my age, the stream possessed an identity of its own. Its face changed with each new day; every changing season provided chapters that were like newly penned stories, written just for me.

At first, my parents did not allow me to go near the crick. The waters seemed dangerous, even if they were quite shallow. But it wasn't long before they were convinced that it was in my best interest to begin my "schooling" there. For several years the crick tutored me in biology and geology, engineering and architecture. Fort building was mandatory; rope swinging was my favorite extracurricular activity. I repossessed many rafts, skiffs, and canoes left abandoned in the field behind our place by the spring runoff, and floated them down the crick, ducking bridges and balancing precariously as I ran mini-rapids.

My guardian angel worked overtime in those years. One day I saw a head sticking out from under a submerged rock. Assuming it was a mudpuppy, I reached into the water to capture this treasure. I pulled and pulled, tried to pry open its mouth, even felt its star-like eyes, but it would not budge. I wondered if it was petrified. Later, having watched a snapping turtle splinter a broom handle, I shuddered as I realized that my "mudpuppy" had been a huge snapping turtle.

One Easter, I fell in the crick while trying to cross a two-by-four "bridge" before church. The worst that happened then was that my new Sunday suit got soaked. Another time, while I was hammering a nail into one of my more elaborate tree houses—complete with an intricate network of rope swings—the main supports broke. It fell—along with me—into the crick. I did a full gainer and ended up sticking my head into the mud three feet under water. I swallowed about a quart of water before figuring out which way was up and finding the surface. But that challenge was nothing compared to my mother's efforts to empty my stomach, and clean my body and clothes.

A dedicated rock-hound neighbor, noticing my passion for nature, planted wonderful mineral and fossil specimens along the crick bank for me to find and collect. These "discoveries" ignited the flames that later fueled my interest in geology, and led to my life's work.

Only when I became a man did I realize that God is like that neighbor, hiding treasures for us to find as He draws us to Himself.

Toward the end of the summer, with the water low, I branched out into engineering, constructing dams out of rocks and blue-black mud from the banks of the crick. Sometimes these dams would stop the flow of water long enough for me to run downstream

God, like that neighbor, hides treasures for us to find as He draws us to Himself.

to collect fish and crawdads. The flashfloods that rushed down the crick bed when the dams broke were a sight to behold, inspiring sensational tales for my parents' enjoyment at the dinner table.

The geologist in me regularly dug underground forts. In each "dig" I measured and recorded the various soil layers, and longed to read the story behind the stratigraphic record.

Once, after intersecting a pure gray clay layer, the amateur paleontologist in me swung into action with a burst of creative energy. I sculpted every type of dinosaur known at the time, and exhibited these works of art on the front porch of our house. This did not exactly match my mother's decorating scheme, but she tolerated, and even praised, the gooey display.

Some days I became a zoologist, capturing many creatures to keep as pets. They all fascinated me. I wanted to get closer to them, to touch them. The chase and capture were challenging, exciting means to this end. But I had a tender heart for living things and actually wished they would escape from their cages and aquariums—which they always did. My favorites were baby snapping turtles and little fish—one of which my youngest brother eventually trained to jump into his hand.

I kept salamanders in the basement, in a hole near two well pipes. The little beasts liked the arrangement so much that they made it a family affair, reproducing until there were nearly a dozen of them living a lizard's utopian dream. They waited patiently for me to feed them the juicy night crawlers I gathered after summer rains. Although my mother dreaded walking across that section of the basement to get to the root cellar, she never asked me to remove the creatures, or my father to cement the hole.

As a botanist in training, I developed a taste for the wild berries and apples that grew near the crick, though I was often more interested in studying than in eating them. The black raspberries seemed like miraculous treasures that Someone had created just for me. It was hard to imagine how God had packed so much juice and joy into such a tiny package. When I found some by chance, I picked them, not eating even one, and proudly presented them to my mother in a pouch made with the bottom of a previously white tee shirt. Instead of scolding me, she thanked me for my generosity—though she later supplied me with a berry bucket.

One day, Mom found fishing worms floating to the surface in her washing machine. I had figured out that my jean pockets were the best place to carry angleworms, which I dug as I fished. After the initial shock, she just laughed and laughed. Later, though, she shed a tear or two, as she realized that someday there would no longer be fish bait floating in her wash, and she would miss the child who had grown up.

Autumn along the crick was vintage nature. As the leaves began to fall and the Winesap apples cured to a rich flavor, I became a little pioneer, wandering further and further each year, following the crick both upstream and down toward the horizon. One year I discovered, in a grove of huge hardwoods, a tree house so high it took my breath away. The image of that enchanted tower, and so many other experiences like it, fueled my imagination. I spun dozens of yarns for my mother and father, who always listened as if they'd never heard such tales before. During those special weeks of the year, as the days grew shorter, Robin Hood lived in my heart as I hiked through fallen oak leaves, shooting hundreds of arrows at flying pheasants without ever bringing one down.

In winter, the crick became a wonderland. As I skated on the ever-changing topography of the ice, the young physicist in me was fascinated by the transformation of water to ice, and back again. I would lie on it, slide on it, jump on it—and fall through it—always trying to know it more intimately. Early in the winter, I saw fish through the ice, and chased them up and down the stream. When the water froze solid in the dead of winter, I sometimes skated for miles, jumping logs and sliding down frozen rapids.

One winter afternoon, just at dark as I was crossing the crick, the ice broke in a large sheet, throwing me headlong into the water. It was ten degrees below zero, so my clothes froze immediately. To my surprise, this insulated me from the cold. Excited by this discovery, I ran all the way home, with my nearly frozen dog beside me. As I marched through the doorway, my parents said I looked like a knight in transparent armor. They ignored the dripping water as they listened to my tale of yet another adventure.

This magical, adventurous childhood seemed to go on forever—until I turned seven, and had to go to school. After just three days, I was already lost in a wilderness of vowels, consonants, and rules. The *Dick and Jane* primers told no tales like those I had read in the trees and rocks. My body, used to being in constant motion, desperately wanted to escape the confines of the metal desk. Only the respect for authority I had learned from my parents held me there. I watched the giant wall clock slowly tick away the tedious time. And the strain showed on my face, as I developed embarrassing facial tics that could only be controlled through concentrated effort. When I tried to read, my mind wandered. My eyes focused on the farthest horizon of the countryside outside the schoolroom window, which connected me to the crick, and beyond that to a cabin "up north" where I yearned to be.

My family often made trips back up north to visit the old homesteads and family. As the years passed, these trips became more and more important to me. Even today, the words "up north" transport me back to dark green cedar swamps and maple forests stretching for miles, where as a boy I was Davy Crockett, coonskin cap and all, "King of the Wild Frontier."

I anticipated the trips up north with such passion that thoughts of them occupied my mind for days before and afterward. Tears filled my eyes when it was time to travel back south, and I watched the last of the old pine stumps disappear into the distance. The stumps were monuments to paradox—on the one hand they spoke of creation, beauty, and nature; on the other, of greed, fire, and civilization. Yet they were my link to the old times, a special bond I shared with those who had gone before. As I grew older, "up north" became a reference point, like the North Star, helping me regain my orientation when life didn't seem to make sense. Recently, while visiting my parents, I searched for just one stump to show my son. I soon realized that they are all gone.

In the summer I often stayed for extended periods at my grandfather's cabin. Life was simple there, mostly revolving around fishing, swimming, exploring, and storytelling. My grandfather told story upon story, connecting me to the old days when "up north" truly had been a wilderness. Our imaginations fed off each other. We were friends, roaming from place to place, each story leading to another, nurturing and reinforcing my sense of wonder. I wanted to know all about the trees, the fish, and my great-grandfather's world. My grandfather took me, in person as well as in imagination, to see all the places in his stories.

Even though I was often homesick during my stays with Grandpa, my experiences with him gave me a lasting passion for the outdoors—especially fishing for muskies, the "fish of 3,000 casts." By the time I was twelve, I had contracted a severe case of "muskie fever" from Grandpa that lasted several years. My parents helped me start a business delivering newspapers so that I could feed my fever. It took me a year and half to save enough money to buy the specialized equipment I needed, and then Grandpa took me out to buy it.

The very next day, my father and I set out to float the legendary Cumming's Oxbow of Jump River, in pursuit of my dream. The water was deep in this stretch of the river, and the cool early morning air created a mist that almost obscured the far bank. We had just pushed off when I made my first cast toward an old white pine that leaned out over the water. As I began my retrieve, my heart leaped into my throat as what looked like a log appeared and began to follow the lure. I plainly saw two eyes above the water's surface, and a V-wake trailing behind. Mesmerized by the huge fish, I reeled the lure faster and faster to make it look like a baitfish trying to avoid being inhaled. As I lifted the lure from the water, the muskie lunged and missed, striking the water with such force that my father thought I had fallen in. Then everything was quiet except for my passionate "wow!" that hung in the air for a long time.

When I was up north, I attended an old church built by Swedish immigrants, with huge stained glass windows and a beautiful maple floor. The vibrant congregation, led by strong men I looked up to and respected, served as a powerful influence in my life, an anchor for my faith when other voices beckoned me away from God. The building is gone now, but it still stands fresh in my memory, a place where I made lifelong friendships that helped me stand through doubts and temptations. Even today, when I hear "He Leadeth Me"—a hymn always played during the morning prayer—my soul still responds in reverence.

My early grade-school years were more than just difficult. Teachers thought I was willfully daydreaming as I stared out of the windows. But the real issue, apart from my yearning for "up north," was a problem with my eyes. Even though I had exceptional vision, when I looked at pages of words I saw double. My brain had to force the letters to come together. This caused painful neurological fatigue. The only relief I had came from gazing at the far horizon.

Many years later, an eye doctor diagnosed this condition as a simple convergent problem that could have been corrected with glasses or through eye exercises, had it been noticed earlier.

I compensated for my reading difficulty by putting great energy into show-and-tell and special projects, especially science and art-oriented projects, in which I excelled. During these years, my parents went out of their way to support my ideas, and most of all to believe in me. I responded so well to their encouragement that they were unaware of my struggles.

Two teachers in fourth and fifth grades took a special interest in me. They seemed to understand. Most importantly, they believed in me too. One gave me classroom time to pursue my projects; the other spent many hours reading books such as *The Mysterious Island* aloud to the class. This hooked me on the power of books, and to everyone's surprise I began to read passionately. Reading was still difficult, but I progressed to a point where I could get by.

Years later, I found a kindred spirit in the dedication of Charles Pellegrino's spellbinding archaeological book *Unearthing Atlantis*:

> To five who believed in a "retarded" boy who could not read, but thought he would. Mom, Dad, Adelle, Barbara, and Dennis, thank you for not believing in test scores, for not browbeating and for believing instead that you could bring the boy out by encouraging his love of science. Would that every school had five teachers like you.[2]

Loving parents, two teachers who believed in me, and the wonders of creation were God's instruments as He orchestrated a romance with a stressed-out, reading-impaired, hard-to-educate, dreaming-designing-digging-sculpting-building boy with crick mud on his britches. During those childhood days, my sense of wonder was ignited by a pine stump, fueled by the flowing water of an obscure little crick, and fanned into a blazing fire—the heat of which I can still feel today.

I believe that all of us—by using God's creation, and encouraging creative activities, while providing the security of unconditional love—can learn to ignite a similar fire in our own children.

2

FINDING THE SILVER BULLET

When she was just a little girl,
She'd dream of days gone by,
Of dashing Prince Charmings,
And castles in the sky;
Of a story told untold times,
Romantic words of love,
A haunting strain sung again,
A dance from above.

My parents continued to romance me through my adolescent years, but it became more challenging and complex, not only because my mind, emotions and will were maturing, but also because another suitor became openly aggressive in the competition. My parents knew that they could not protect me from the temptations teenagers face. So their strategy was simply to out-romance the competition.

During those defining years my parents loved me strategically, majoring on crucial matters of the heart, while keeping such things as behavior in proper perspective. Their hope was that when the time came for me to face the temptations that come with growing up, I would choose to keep walking with God.

They did this by providing me with as many options as possible, so that I could discover my talents, gifts, and natural inclinations. Whether this exposure was within the domains of music, art, cooking, fashion, trades, science, car buying, or athletics, they consistently went the extra mile to ensure that I would find the expression of God's creative image within me. They might not have been the "perfect" parents of today's parenting manuals, but the freedom they gave, within certain well-defined limits, expressed their respect for me as an individual, and earned my lifelong devotion in return. I know now that they won my heart through the irresistible force of their winsome, sacrificial love.

My mom, on reading this manuscript, said, "Monte, you enlarged what we did."

"Of course," I told her. "I was looking for the larger Story, and I found it."

My choice is to view all of life—the hardships, the trials, and the joys—as much as possible from an eternal perspective. I'm confident that, when I look back on my life from eternity, all my troubles will be forgotten in view of the grace that carried me forward. If I'm going to have that perspective when I've been made whole and every tear has been wiped away, it only makes sense to adopt it now.

While I was a graduate student at the University of Arizona, I supplemented my income by helping with the high school ministry at a church in Tucson. One weekend, the high school minister asked me to lead music and teach skiing for a retreat in the White Mountains of Arizona. During this retreat, I met my future wife,

With Karey beside me, it wasn't a hot bus anymore. It was heaven.

Karey. The first time I saw her, she was sitting in the ski lodge, strumming a guitar and singing. She definitely caught my eye, but since she was only in high school, I thought I was too old for her. Also, I figured I was just too "square."

Several years later, on a Sunday morning in the basement of the church, which we had remodeled with rustic barn wood, I was leading worship with my guitar for the college group when Karey walked into the room. She looked like an angel— long blonde hair to her waist, tan, sweet—in a word, WOW! I could hardly wait for the class to finish so I could talk with her. I invited her to go on our upcoming spring retreat to a beach in Mexico. She had other plans, which thankfully fell through, so she came. We sat next to each other on the packed school bus on the way from the campus to the beach.

One of the athletic highlights of my life happened on this trip. The little ski boat we had brought with us, strapped to the top of the bus, had barely enough power to get me up on skis if I started in the water. But we found that if I started at the water's edge, with about twenty feet of slack rope, and the boat accelerated to full speed, I could slingshot out onto the water. While skiing along the beach I became distracted by the thousands of college kids watching me, and I got too close to the shore. The tail end of the ski dug into the sand and I was catapulted straight up into the air. I should have broken my neck, but by some miracle I did a perfect flip and landed standing on my feet as if I'd done it a thousand times. Everyone cheered and clapped and I took a bow. Without a doubt, for me that Mexican trip was charmed from start to finish, and the magic could be traced to one source—Karey.

Since the midday sun was intense, each day I sat in the bus for a few hours, strumming my guitar. But when Karey quietly slipped in to listen—and to be with me—it wasn't a hot bus anymore. It was heaven. Eventually I talked her into singing a duet with me— the love song "Creators of Rain," which was sung by the Canadian duo Ian and Sylvia. For me, it was a moment of pure romance and harmony—the white sand, the blue ocean, the yellow sun, and Karey's green eyes.

After we returned to Tucson, I asked Karey out on a date. She was surprised when I dragged her up the north face of a mountainside to a crude, hand-sculpted bench where I had sat for ten days drawing a tree. We sat there for six hours, drawing together. During this time I sketched a single branch in photographic detail while Karey sketched rocks, trees, cliffs, and clouds. She also made a fire because she was cold—a huge challenge as she was a city girl and she'd never done it before. In the process, she told me later, she passed what she thought was a test. But testing her had never crossed my mind. I just wanted to be with her. That evening I cooked her a steak dinner and played her my Ian and Sylvia albums. Later I discovered she really didn't like Sylvia's vibrato. And she wasn't a steak person, either. But you would never have known, because romance was now affecting both of us.

One of my brothers came to Tucson that summer with a friend. Every weekend when we headed for the Graham Mountains to escape the Arizona heat, Karey came along. Her mother was overjoyed because we were clean-cut (i.e., old-fashioned) Christian guys—something Karey had never experienced before. One of our favorite pastimes was to cruise desert roads at night after heavy rains, hunting tarantulas and rattlesnakes. We kept the tarantulas in our house to control the cockroaches. The rattlesnakes we roasted over campfires, and ate with fresh corn and artichokes. Karey thought it was a real kick.

When Karey and I were together at her home, she played the piano and I sang. Once we attended a Gordon Lightfoot concert, after which we discussed theology for hours. During the Easter season we dyed eggs, Ukrainian style, while Karey's mom cooked aebleskivers. We ministered together through several musical dramas, shared cross-country ski trips, and backpacked all over Arizona. After a year or so Karey had become my best friend, and I realized that this was what I had missed in all my past relationships with girls—friendship.

On July 4, 1975, while standing on a cliff edge overlooking Skyrocket Creek—my home for that summer in Ouray, Colorado—I told Karey that I loved her. It was the first time I had ever said those words to a girl. Soon after that I sang my marriage proposal to her, while on my knees, accompanying myself with my guitar. It went something like this: "Karey Lynn, will ya marry me? Will ya say good-bye to your city life and all that strife, and come with me to the mountains free, and be my wife?"

She laughed. But the main point is that she said, "Yes."

We were married November 14, 1975 atop Mount Graham, an alpine island in the desert of Arizona, overlooking my thesis area, Stockton Pass. I had spent the previous few months alone, mapping the mountains above Red River, New Mexico, exploring for molybdenum. During that time I sent Karey maybe a hundred letters, cards, and many poems, which she saved—and we still have—in a special box. Her favorite card is one I wrote in bold crayons. On the cover it says, "I was going to make you a Valentine's card." When she opened it, there were squashed blobs of melted crayon inside, and the words, "But every time I think of you, my crayons melt." As I write this, I've been reading the letters and poems again, and I have to say, the crayons are still melting!

When the Red River aspens turned golden, I drove to Tucson, picked up a couple of friends and a minister, our gold nugget rings, and my bride-to-be, and we eloped—with the consent of all four parents, just as my own parents had done nearly thirty years earlier. The ceremony took place in a semicircle of aspen trees on a hilltop at the edge of a meadow. We have only one wedding photo, taken by the pastor—a silhouette of the bride and groom against a gold and crimson setting sun. To the east, over the pastor's shoulder, a crescent moon was just rising and a cool desert wind was blowing in our faces.

We honeymooned in a backpacking tent, which I figured would be good preparation for a geological prospecting trip on the horizon. My company was planning to send us to Hall's Creek in the northwestern desert frontier of Australia, to search for massive sulfide copper and gold deposits. In Australia we would be dry camping, hundreds of miles from the nearest town, among world-renowned desert death adders whose bites—I had heard—can kill a human in a matter of seconds. (I must admit, this was a little too "out west," even for me.) But that trip never happened; the price of copper plunged and the company abandoned metal exploration in that part of the world.

Instead, I continued my geological research in Arizona, with Karey by my side every step of the way. Some steps were more hair-raising than others. For example, not long after we learned that Karey was pregnant with our first child, we were guided on horseback to a copper prospect near Zane Grey's cabin in the Mogollon Rim country of Arizona. Our hosts provided Karey with a horse but failed to tighten the cinch properly. After a mile or so on the trail, the saddle slipped, and all of a sudden my bride was hanging upside down under the horse, clinging on for dear life! That night we were treated to a steak dinner, cooked over an open fire, accompanied by coffee made in an antediluvian pot with water scooped from a stagnant pool filled with fermenting oak leaves. I can still taste it—full-bodied, with a slight hint of oxidation and a tinge of tannic acid. Later we reclined in an old prospector's cabin on rusty bedsprings that had once been the insides of a mattress, and which the resident mice used as a jungle gym all night long.

After our first child was born, Karey and her father (who was an architect) designed a house, which I built with the help of my father in the mountains west of Tucson. Previously, Karey had grown a garden in planters on the patio of our little townhouse, and made awnings out of string bean plants. Now, with wide-open spaces all around her, she began to garden in earnest—growing grapevines, fig trees, artichoke plants, and a cherry tomato plant that lived several years, producing fruit the whole time.

Because of Karey's vision for togetherness in our marriage and family, she traveled with me through the great outdoors that was my workplace. Most geologists' wives soon grow tired of the novelty of living in cabins and tents without the comforts of civilization—such as telephones, televisions, hot or even running water, not to mention toilet seats. But Karey marched to a different drummer. She spent the late 1970s roaming the backcountry of the American West with two small children and one big one—her swashbuckling geologist. She was satisfied to set up housekeeping wherever we were—in a cabin, motel, tent, or the back of our four-wheel-drive vehicle.

The real world, they insist, does not produce whole families where peace, respect, trust, and unconditional love reign.

Why did she do this? Because she was determined to keep our family together. While I totally agreed with her motivation, taking everybody along on every trip was a colossal logistical challenge. When I look back on it now, I wonder why I didn't buy a trailer. Instead, I filled our four-by-four Chevy Blazer to the gills every trip. The space behind the rear bench seat was tightly packed with playpens, diaper pails, baby food, cribs, suitcases, toys, typewriter, sewing machine, and guitar. The packing process, which I did for more than ten years, was always a giant jigsaw puzzle challenge. Every surface was piled with paraphernalia, right to the bases of our children's well-used car seats.

Was it worth the effort? Absolutely. We would do it again in a heartbeat.

One memorable night, we were camped at eight thousand feet on an Arizona mountain in November, miles from the nearest paved road, with our four-month-old daughter, Heather. In the morning, when we awoke, we were struck by the perfect silence. A foot of fluffy snow covered everything, and a thick icy fog hung over the landscape. We were warm enough in the tent, with our down sleeping bags, down pillows, and down parkas, but the hike out was difficult as we tried to protect Heather from the cold.

Since Karey did not have the modern luxuries and entertainments her peers were enjoying, she read books purchased primarily at used bookstores in the out-of-the-way places we visited. In no time, books began to accumulate in the vehicle, in cabins, in tents, wherever we went. This further complicated my packing job, but it was well worth it because, as we traveled, we often discussed her latest reading.

I was only mildly infected with the used book bug until one fateful day when we attended an open-air auction in southern Wisconsin. We were just spectators enjoying the auction until a box of old books came up. When no one bid on them, we bought them all for seventy-five cents. Then we read them—all—and in the process became addicted to books, particularly old hardbacks and classics.

Some people, when they travel, can't pass an antique shop. For us, used bookstores whispered our names so tantalizingly that we simply had to stop. Once, I wanted Karey to experience an authentic Finnish sauna in Michigan's Upper Peninsula. In the cedar-scented lobby of the building that housed the sauna, old books were for sale—hundreds of them rescued when a nearby one-room schoolhouse had shut its doors forever. It was like Christmas in July, or finding buried treasure. We were drawn like mice to the cheese, like moths to the lantern, like trout to a worm…you get the point. I can't even remember if we made it to the sauna. But I do remember the books.

My bent toward research, combined with Karey's passion for reading—which she soon passed along to me—became a lifelong search for knowledge and truth through the written word. It's a little like searching for gold. And once we find a nugget of truth, or better yet, deposits of truth in a book, it's very hard for us to part with it. Maybe that's one reason we have over six thousand volumes nestled here and there in our home.

As our children neared school age, we met a homeschooling family, and were immensely impressed with their three girls. When these young ladies walked into a room, they were like a breath of spring air. All of them were three years advanced academically beyond the grade levels of their public school contemporaries. Then, at about the same time, my mother sent us some educational research stating that, due to childhood development patterns, it may be better to delay age segregation and structured academics until third grade. Considering these factors—along with our desire to continue our traveling lifestyle—we decided to homeschool. Actually, we decided to "road school." Integrating this with the parenting approach I had inherited from my parents made for an interesting combination.

This new challenge of raising children in a culture where Christianity has been marginalized motivated Karey and me to read far and wide on the subject. Those were the early days of parenting books, so much of what we read was hot off the press.

At times, we were challenged by our friends and relatives about our unique lifestyle, so we wanted to be able to defend our choices. As we formulated and then verbalized our "philosophy" of parenting, we began to receive invitations to speak and write on the subject, and I wrote a number of songs on this theme. Our immersion in the process fueled our passion to be the best parents we could be, and to try to help others do the same. Within a short period of time, thousands of people encouraged us, challenged us, and shared with us their insights into parenting. We soon discovered that many parents were anxious to learn from us, but we struggled for just the right words to communicate with precision what we knew in our hearts. As we did, it became increasingly clear to us that my parents knew something very few books touched upon.

So we went to visit them. We peppered them with questions, trying to find the elusive, mysterious ingredient that had made their parenting such a success.

"Did you ever go out on weekly dates like most modern marriage manuals recommend?" I asked.

They replied, "We did everything together as a family. We wouldn't think of going off alone without our boys."

So much for "date night."

"Did you treat each of us differently, or all of us the same?"

"We always tried to treat each son the same, while also trying to find what special talent each one had," they replied. "We believe that respect for each family member, no matter what their age, is extremely important."

The conversation went on for some time, but the magical ingredient did not make itself known to Karey and me that day. My parents were intrigued by the intensity of our search for their silver bullet, and nearly as mystified. As far as they were concerned, they had just done what came naturally—what had seemed right to them at the time.

As Karey and I discussed what they had said, we decided that the missing ingredient had to do with an integrated lifestyle that had pervaded their lives so completely that it was hard to define, even for them. Clearly, they had practiced many of the things we had found in parenting books. In fact, much of what they had done was on the leading edge a generation later. But still the key to their success eluded us.

By the spring of 1996, Karey and I had accumulated thousands of books—and one filing cabinet full of notes and articles—on parenting and related subjects. It seemed as if we would never be able to identify the elusive ingredient. Then, on Easter Sunday 1996, our pastor entitled his message "Romancing the Stones." He was thinking of the Pharisees and the hardness of their hearts toward the love and grace of God, especially as it was expressed in the person of Jesus.

As I listened, something happened in the part of my brain that was perpetually pondering the puzzle of parenting. As a result, the words "romance" and "child" came together, and they've stayed together ever since. Interestingly, Karey had already put these words together a few months earlier, but somehow I had not recognized their significance, and in her typical, unassuming way, she refused to throw ice water on my excitement. In her book *Hearth and Home* she had written, "Monte and I believe it is the heart that gains the heart. In our diligence to find access to [our children's] hearts, we believe if our heart and home is filled with God's love and words, our daily living will not be a hindrance but a help in leading their hearts heavenward. Like a courtship—we are romancing their hearts."[3]

I'm not saying that all of a sudden we were enlightened with everything every Christian parent needs to know about parenting. In fact, for several months we tried out the phrase "romancing your child's heart" on anyone who would listen. During this time we became increasingly convinced that it was not only a legitimate idea but also the ingredient that we had tried so hard to identify for all those years. It was a truly exhilarating time for us. Almost everyone we talked to about romancing a child's heart immediately knew what we meant.

It was exciting to realize that what my parents had done for me, intuitively, we had tried to do with our own children. Even more exciting was that we could now pass these ideas on to other parents. I'm not talking about another set of principles, or a list of rules, but an invitation to a new way of thinking about parenting—more, a new way of thinking about living.

Plenty of books out there offer cookie-cutter recipes for parenting. One reason Karey and I missed the point for so long was that we devoured these books—ad nauseam. We were thinking in the wrong realm—the realm of *doing*.

Effective parenting is partly about doing—and it starts even before the children are born. We talk about them, discuss how many we want, and how we will raise them. They occupy our vision, hope, and passion. We dream dreams, buy books, and pray prayers. We design our houses, select our vehicles, and even choose our careers with them in mind.

After their birth, much of our emotional energy is expended in conversations with or about them, and in their instruction, training, and discipline. We spend thousands of dollars and as many hours educating and mentoring them, driving them to music lessons and athletic events. We buy things—so many things, from strollers to playpens, to doll houses, to bicycles, and insurance policies. We buy swing sets, build tree houses and shelves, and we order truckloads of sand. We provide musical instruments, computers, and sports equipment. We want so much for them, and we give so much to them.

But what remains when, one day, they drive away? A garage full of tennis shoes, old blue jeans, car seats, rocks, broken toys, and baseball gloves…or a relationship, deep and strong, that will only get better over time?

We can do…do…do…until the cows come home—and still end up estranged from our children. The missing element in so many parent-child relationships is a matter of *being*, rather than doing.

Is this some pollyannaish primrose path to never-never land? Not at all.

Let's go back to Wisconsin for a moment—to another time, another little boy, and another grandfather romancing that little boy's heart.

Accompanied by his eighty-year-old grandfather, the boy is on a mission through his grandfather's Christmas tree farm. Their goal is to select two trees, one for the boy's parents and the other for his grandparents. As the two treasure hunters wander through world-class balsams, the boy's father follows at a distance, close enough to hear their dialogue, yet far enough away that he may as well be invisible.

In the dim silver sunlight of that December day, the treasure hunters examine hundreds of trees—lingering at one, circling

Romancing a child's heart has the potential to radically transform our lives as parents.

another. Like two children they meander through the lacy, fragrant boughs, judging and appraising each tree as if making the decision of a lifetime.

They are, but it's not about trees.

From their conversation, several things are apparent. There is no other place the grandfather would rather be. He is in no hurry, and he lets the child lead as they walk from tree to tree. He never forces or presses for a decision. Occasionally he does suggest a tree, but it is clear that he has no agenda. He patiently awaits the boy's verdict, weighing it with all seriousness and respect, even though the ten-year-old has little experience in such matters. Verbally and non-verbally, the old man makes it clear that no tree in this grove—which he planted before the boy's birth—is too good for his grandson. When the boy chooses a tree that is too tall, the grandfather doesn't focus on the waste. Instead, he says, "If we cut off the lower two feet it would be a great tree for you, and you could make wreaths from the extra boughs."

When they reach an impasse, the grandfather suggests that they jump on his four-wheeler, which he has taught the boy to drive, and off they go to a remote part of the farm, their hearts connected in the adventure. After several hours, they have each cut a tree. Later, the boy spends an entire day intently decorating the tree that was a special gift from his grandfather. The family is unanimous—there has never been a more beautiful Christmas tree than this one.

The boy in this story isn't me. He's my son. And the grandpa is my father. As I witnessed their Christmas tree hunt not so long ago, I was reminded of the unusual family to which I belong. Surely, such moments of romance are rare. Seeing the two of them together brought back memories of my own childhood. Sometimes people laugh and say that the family I describe could not possibly exist. The real world, they insist, does not produce whole families where peace, respect, trust, and unconditional love reign. Children will, without exception, rebel at some point. It is naïve to think that children could be their parents' best friends and willingly obey them.

Really?

In the summer of 2000, Karey and I spoke at a weeklong conference at Sandy Cove on Chesapeake Bay. The message of "Romancing Your Child's Heart" touched one of the fathers in a very special way. Toward the end of the week he shared his story with us.

"Until this week," Steve said, "I have misunderstood my father—never really appreciating him. He wasn't the kind of father who would play ball with me and do all those things the parenting books say a father should do. So I thought he had somehow failed me." As the tears began to flow, Steve continued, "But my father did pour his music into my life—it was all he knew. I never realized until now that when my father shared his first love—his passion—with me, he was romancing me to God the only way he knew how. He included me—trained me and taught me his music—and now he is so proud of my music. He was successful as a father because he won my heart for God by giving the finest part of himself to me."

Steve concluded, "I see it clearly now—the idea of the larger Story—the Romance—and I intend to do this for my children, to romance their hearts to God. I thought I was on track, focusing primarily on teaching them biblical truth and training them in proper behavior, but I was missing the true prize. I am from this point on going to enter the contest for their hearts."

Steve wrote a song that week and sang it for the conference participants:

Plans of the heart are made by man.
The Lord our God has given such to me.
Open my eyes, allowing me to see
The tender hearts You placed within my hand.
I can hear them screaming for romance.

CHORUS
Fairytales are more than fantasy.
I believe that they come true within a child's heart.
Their hearts can be both ravished and romanced.
Before mine are old I'm gonna take the chance,
And fill their hearts with fairytale romance.

Until today I thought my ways were pure.
Yet in my heart somehow I'm just not sure.
Will they believe the story my life tells?
O my God, I've wasted so much time.
One more chance—I will make their hearts mine.

Spirit, I pray You, bring from above
Strength to portray the Father's passioned love.
Let their hearts sail on a voyage filled with dreams,
And help me teach them to believe
What You have spoken, not just what they see.[4]

This concept of romancing a child's heart has the potential to radically transform our lives as parents, giving our children something to write, speak, or sing about, someday.

If it's written, the story may begin like this: "Once upon a time…" Everyone has a story; or rather, everyone is living a story, and that story is a part of the larger Story that God has been telling since forever. It is His Story, found in the pages of the Bible, a Romance describing how deeply, extravagantly, generously, and sacrificially God loves us and is pursuing and wooing us to Himself.

It is a story, for it starts: "In the beginning…"

It is theo-logical because it speaks of God.

God chose to use Story from the outset as a means of explaining Who He is and what He desires of us. More recently, in person, Jesus often used Story—in the form of parables—to speak of God, the deeper truths of His love and grace, and how to have a living, vibrant, dynamic relationship with Him by faith.

Our Christian faith is not so much about doing as it is about being—specifically, being in a relationship. And this must precede anything we try to do, or the romance we offer a child, or anyone else, will prove to be little more than pretence.

3

THE WAY OF WISDOM

If you knew you had one year
Left to live, left to love,
Would you live, to love?
What would you do
If you knew?

When our three-year-old son, Travis, had a bout with viral meningitis, I was in a desperate emotional state. He had a fever of 103 degrees for three weeks, and then developed an arthritic condition the doctors could not diagnose. He couldn't walk and was in constant pain. We visited numerous physicians, who ordered test after test. One of the most difficult was the spinal tap. We had to hold little Travis still while the doctor stuck a long, long needle between the vertebrae of his back. But I'll never forget how, when the fluid came out clear, the doctor said, "Praise the Lord. It's not bacterial." However, no one could explain what was causing our son's joints to swell.

The only thing that seemed to soothe Travis was the song "I Saw The Lord," by Dallas Holm. I played it over and over again for him. But I worried. *Will he survive? If he survives will he be disabled? If he is disabled will he be able to make it in life?* The questions seemed to go on forever. I was paralyzed by the scenarios that kept running through my analytical mind.

Finally, I reached a point of emotional exhaustion. All I could do was to cast myself on my face before God—which I did literally, under a pine tree behind the house where we were staying. I gave up hope from any human perspective, and surrendered to God. At that moment, I found peace in the knowledge that God has a good heart and that I could trust Him with our son's life.

Several weeks later, a team of five specialists at Denver's National Jewish Research Hospital reviewed all the tests and examined Travis. They told us that the arthritis was only a reactionary form caused by the virus leaving his body, and that it would burn itself out within a few weeks with no lasting effects. This was a relief, of course, but that encounter with God under the pine tree was the actual moment of relief for me—a time when I touched eternity. Such moments are, unfortunately, rare. Often it takes a crisis to help us see the larger Story, the reality behind the shadows—even the shadow of death.

Karey processed the whole situation differently. She felt a comforting sense of serenity—the peace that passes all understanding—and was able to guard her heart and mind during this whole experience because, while I was focused on the "if onlys" of the past and the "what ifs" of the future, Karey stayed focused on the present.[5] She calmly cared for Travis, hour after hour, day after day. She was able to live with the tension of not knowing how this particular chapter of Travis's story would end because she knew that in the larger Story—which includes our smaller stories, but never ends—all of us would live happily ever after.

> *The fact that there is a larger Story is known intuitively by all humans.*

While I had viewed Travis's crisis from a temporal perspective, Karey had seen it with the eyes of faith. This is one of the Bible's main points and the primary difference between secular and Christian worldviews.[6] It is why martyrs throughout history have chosen death, trading earthly life—the short story—for eternity. This is what missionary martyr Jim Elliot meant when he said, "He is no fool who gives what he cannot keep to gain what he cannot lose."[7]

One of the best biblical illustrations of this way of "seeing" is the story of Elisha and his servant Gehazi. Once upon a morning, the prophet awoke to find that an army of men had surrounded the city with horses and chariots. Gehazi trembled with fear at the sight of this enemy. In a state of panic he asked, "What shall be done?" Elisha said, "Those who are with us are more than those who are with them." You can imagine the look on Gehazi's face as he probably thought, *I don't see **anyone** with us.* Elisha asked God to let Gehazi see the spiritual reality—the larger Story. Then Gehazi saw the hills around them full of heaven's horses and chariots of fire. I can just picture his eyes opening wide and his jaw dropping in amazement. Immediately his whole outlook changed. Joy and hope replaced the fear and despair in his heart, as the invisible was made visible.[8]

C. S. Lewis was fond of using the metaphor "shadowlands" to describe this phenomenon of faith. He said that the natural world is the place where the shadows of the supernatural fall. While the shadows themselves seem real, our challenge is to trace the shadows back to the spiritual realities that are casting them. A classic illustration of this point is found in the closing paragraphs of *The Last Battle*, the final book of the Chronicles of Narnia, when Peter, Edmund and Lucy find out that they have died in a railway accident in England—our world, which Aslan, the great Lion and Christ-figure, calls the Shadowland—and they have come at last to the real Narnia. Lewis writes:

And for us this is the end of all the stories, and we can most truly say that they all lived happily ever after. But for them it was only the beginning of the real story. All their life in this world and all their adventures in Narnia had only been the cover and the title page: now at last they were beginning Chapter One of the Great Story, which no one on earth has read: which goes on forever: in which every chapter is better than the one before.[9]

The pure drama and deep truth of these few words are never lost on children. The larger Story is burned into their hearts, where it retains the ability to illuminate even their dark times with the light of eternal truth.

One of my friends remembers being overwhelmed with emotion as he read this passage to his son, who was at the time lingering between life and death (and whose younger brother had already died of the same mysterious disease). The father's emotion came from the contrast between the deep truth that the story expressed and his deep desire that this son would live—which he did, by the way. But the comfort the father experienced in that shadowland came not from a sermon or pious platitude. It came from a children's story reminding him that, even in the valley of the shadow of death, neither he nor his son need fear any evil, for the larger Story guaranteed that God was with them, and always would be.

My favorite description of the larger Story was written by George McDonald in 1893. C. S. Lewis regarded McDonald as his "master" and said that he had never known another writer closer to the Spirit of Christ Himself. McDonald wrote:

It will help much towards our understanding of the imagination and its functions in man if we first succeed in regarding aright the imagination of God, in which the imagination of man lives and moves and has its being.

[With this in mind] we discover…that where a man would make a machine, or a picture, or a book, God makes the man that makes the book, or the picture, or the machine. Would God give us a drama? He makes a Shakespeare. Or would He construct a drama more immediately His Own? He begins with the building of the stage itself, and that stage is the world....He makes the actors, and they do not act—they *are* their part. He utters them into the visible to work out their life—His drama....All the processes of the ages are God's science; all the flow of history is His poetry....Man is but a thought of God.[10]

The fact that there is a larger Story is known intuitively by all humans, as the apostle Paul explained to the pagan philosophers about their altar to the unknown god at the Areopagus (Mars' Hill) in Athens: "The God who made the world and all things in it...can be known. He, the Lord of heaven and earth, has established the nations and their boundaries and determined that all men everywhere should seek Him, for in Him we live and move and have our being. This God has fixed a day in which He will judge the world in righteousness through the man, Jesus Christ, whom He raised from the dead."[11]

In their book *The Sacred Romance*, Brent Curtis and John Eldredge use another analogy to make this point:

Our problem is most of us live our lives like a movie we've arrived at twenty minutes late. The action is well underway and we haven't a clue what's happening. Who are these people? Worse, we try to interpret the meaning of life with only fragments, isolated incidents, feelings, and images without reference to the story of which these scenes are merely a part....The plot of life is a tragedy, and we are playing the role of the victim of cruel circumstances. [We are] desperate for something larger to give our lives transcendence.[12]

Living this way is really living according to a non-Christian worldview—conforming to the fashions of morbidity, skepticism, and pragmatism—essentially in a state of moral anarchy. It is living in the random days of our lives, following daily soap operas scripted and choreographed by ourselves. Nothing hangs together, and there is no context. This produces lives characterized by isolated scraps of human experience—islands of information in a sea of ignorance.

We find it nearly impossible to see the big picture. It is the crisis of our age. Even the church, which is supposed to live out the larger Story, often gives its members only a three-point weekly script.

Some "Story-less" people go to a movie like *Titanic* six or seven times, looking for their script. Woven through all the special effects, the historical account, the cultural clashes, and the fornication, there is Story—a tale of the kind of bravery and sacrifice that are a picture of Christ's sacrificial love on Calvary. Hollywood cannot seem to keep this gospel out of its stories. Like the pagan philosophers of Athens, they are desperately building altars to an unknown god.

In Shakespeare's play *The Tempest*, Prospero alludes to a larger Story as he says: "Our revels now are ended. These our actors…The great globe itself…And like this insubstantial pageant faded. Leave not a rack behind….We are such stuff as dreams are made on; and our life is rounded with sleep."[13]

"Revels" are our lives, which are like a pageant played out on the stage of the "great globe"—the earth. This is the "real" world, but it is also an illusion, for it will crumble and dissolve, leaving not even a wisp of cloud ("a rack") behind. People are the "stuff" dreams are "made on," just as characters are the "stuff" plays are built on. Our little lives are like a brief dream in a divine mind "rounded with sleep." When we die, we awaken from the dream of life into true reality.

The Christian worldview clarifies this allusion to the larger Story. In it I am in relationship with God, my Creator—the author of the oldest Story in the world, yet a Story that is forever young, written by Someone Whose heart is eternally good—I can trust Him. In this context, the flow of history and the processes of the ages since before the beginning of time are a passionate drama—God's Story. Some may prefer to see this as primarily a cosmic conflict between God and Satan, good and evil—what the Greeks would call an epic. But it is also a love Story, made more powerful because it is told against the backdrop of spiritual warfare. Just as God could crush Satan at any time, He could force humans to "love" and serve Him.

Instead, He came to Earth in Person, to romance and rescue His bride, in a Story more magically romantic than any story ever told.

G.K. Chesterton in *Orthodoxy—The Romance of Faith* says, "I had always believed that the world involved magic: now I thought that perhaps it involved a magician....I had always felt life first as a story; and if there is a story there is a storyteller."[14]

Keats wrote: "A man's life of any worth is a continual allegory."[15] This is true because each man's life unfolds an eternal message while the person is confined in time and space. Not to live in the larger Story at the same time is, as the book of Ecclesiastes says, "pessimistic useless vanity."

As we live our life on earth we can only enter and participate in the Story in the present—the here and now—because Story is only lived in the present. The only moments in which we are totally alive are those in which we live in the present, savoring the moment. It is human nature to be distracted by the hustle and bustle, the responsibilities, and the self-imposed goals that fill our lives, so that often we become too occupied with what has happened, or may happen, to focus on what is actually happening. These distractions prevent us from living in the larger Story and being conscious of God's script.

C. S. Lewis develops this idea in the context of a senior devil, Screwtape, writing to a junior devil, Wormwood:

> The humans live in time, but our Enemy [God] destines them to eternity. He therefore, I believe, wants them to attend chiefly to two things, to eternity itself and to that point of time which they call the Present. For the present is that point at which time touches eternity. Of the present moment, and of it only, humans have an experience analogous to the experience which our Enemy has of reality as a whole; in it alone freedom and actuality are offered them. He would therefore have them continually concerned either with eternity (which means being concerned with Him) or with the Present—either meditating on their eternal union with, or separation from Himself, or else obeying the present voice of conscience, bearing the present cross, receiving the present grace,

giving thanks for the present pleasure....Our business is to get them away from the eternal and from the Present....We want a whole race perpetually in pursuit of the rainbow's end, never honest, nor kind, nor happy *now*, but always using as mere fuel wherewith to heap the altar of the Future every real gift which is offered them in the Present.[16]

If we as parents live in the larger Story, touch eternity in the present, and follow the script that God has written for us to live, it will have a major impact on our parenting. We will possess a framework for understanding all of reality. Our children will witness an eternal drama directed by God. Through Story we can transcend the experience of daily living. Inside Story we can accept pain, find justice, and recognize our motivation. The beauty in our lives will dazzle our children and woo them. They will see eternity in the way we invest our resources, talents, and time, and this will provide for them an ultimate reference frame—a transcendent purpose.

As our children see us bowing before God and serving others, tremors will pass down their spines, because they will begin to suspect that God really is real. The intimate presence of the Holy Spirit, unleashing the power of a personal God in our lives, will allow our children to witness awe-inspiring encounters. They will comprehend the passionate love God has for them, and will be irresistibly drawn to Him as they respond to the Romance. They will realize that they are made for a larger drama, as the disciples did on the road to Emmaus, when they said to one another, "Did not our heart burn within us...while He opened the Scriptures to us?"[17] Our children will greet each new day with wonder and joy as each new page of the Romance is turned. They will see that relationship is central in all we do.

Some people see me as a hopeless optimist, out of touch with reality. They call me "Pollyanna," which is okay with me, because I've read the book. It's a marvelous tale of how a little orphan girl, with every right to be bitter, transforms an entire New England town by teaching the "glad game" she learned from her minister father before he died. Essentially, the glad game turns the shadowland on its head, by finding a way to be glad for whatever happens.

One of the main characters in the book, Dr. Chilton, describes Pollyanna's remarkable positive effect on many of his patients, which he thinks to be "better than a six-quart bottle of tonic." His nurse asks, "Indeed! And what are the special ingredients of this wonder-working tonic of hers?"

"As near as I can find out," replies the doctor, "it is an overwhelming, unquenchable gladness for everything that has happened or is going to happen. At any rate her quaint speeches are constantly being repeated to me, and, as near as I can make out, 'just being glad' is the tenor of most of them....I wish I could prescribe her—and buy her—as I would a box of pills—though if there gets to be many of her in the world, you and I might as well go ribbon-selling and ditch-digging for all the money we'd get out of nursing and doctoring."[18]

Wouldn't it be wonderful if we who think the same way could effectively communicate such truth to our own children?

Why don't we? I think there are two reasons. The first may be that we fear being ridiculed by others who might label us as naïve, unsophisticated, unrealistic fools living in a make-believe, fairytale world. The second is that we too easily adopt secular patterns of thought.

As I see it, either there is a God, or there isn't. If there is no God, then there cannot be a larger Story because there is no Storyteller. Life truly is without purpose or meaning, full of despair, and happiness is just an illusion. Life is "but a walking shadow; a poor player, that struts and frets his hour upon the stage, and then is heard no more: it is a tale told by an idiot, full of sound and fury, signifying nothing."[19]

If, however, there is a divine Storyteller, there is a Story with a beginning and an ending—it's all going somewhere. Therefore, there can be purpose, meaning, and joy as our little stories meld into His larger one. To believe otherwise is to compromise our faith.

The reason so many religious and irreligious critics attack a pollyannaish perspective—that the larger Story is more important than their petty, pointless, purposeless lives—is that childlike faith is a powerful threat to the adultish or so-called sophisticated spirit of our age. It has become culturally incorrect to speak of such powerful realities as truth, joy, purpose and meaning.

The source of this power is the connection of childlike faith to the heart of God—the Source of truth, which shows the rest to be a lie—and wisdom, which is the ability to apply this truth to life.

Research has found that eighty-five percent of even the most severely rebellious prodigals return to their parents' basic religious faith and values by age twenty-four.[20] Most of the rest return as they grow older and wiser. I think of a prodigal as a youth who does not grasp the larger Story and is struggling—searching for meaning, purpose, a place in life, and the security that comes from "walls" that do not move. Thus, a prodigal is honestly seeking something better. He may have theoretical biblical knowledge and even be honorable, well behaved, and trained in biblical disciplines. But he lacks the ability to apply these as he steps out into the surrounding culture.

Knowing how to drive safely takes more than years of studying driving and the driver's manual. Even someone who obtains a perfect score on the written examination, knows an automobile inside and out, and has ridden many miles in a car, still needs behind-the-wheel experience in order to learn to drive safely. Similarly, knowing how to live life as a Christian is more than memorizing a manual of morality.

Children who grow up hearing and seeing stories are far better prepared to step into our culture. Stories give them "driving practice" for life. However—and this is crucial—we as parents need to select carefully the stories to which our children are exposed. The challenge is to find stories through which the larger Story runs like a thread— the biblical narratives, classics, great books and films, stories we

Children learn the way of wisdom best through stories.

create as we go, and family traditions. These include the gospel of Jesus Christ as lived out in our lives as parents.

Children by their very nature live in their imagination—in stories. Their worlds are large, filled with wonder, exploration, adventure, and drama. Wisely chosen stories take advantage of this natural attribute, and prepare them to participate wisely in the pageant called life. They know the props and set, and are experienced in following and improvising on the storyline through the use of their moral imagination.

For children raised this way, their whole childhood and adolescence has been a rehearsal for living as adults in our culture. They are practiced in the art of living in story—which we hope and pray will include the larger Story that is scripted and choreographed by God. They do not need to search for meaning—they have found it already. They become preoccupied, enthralled, fascinated, captivated by the larger Story, like deer panting after the water brooks—people after God's own heart.

Many factors outside our control can incline a child toward rebellion, including inherited characteristics and tendencies, their degree of intelligence, and physical limitations. What we can control is the teaching of the larger Story.

This desire and ability to live in the larger Story Is described in Proverbs as "the way of wisdom." This is the controlling principle of Proverbs: "The fear of the Lord is the beginning of knowledge."[21] This "fear" is a reverential awe and worshipful response of faith to God the Creator, Savior, and Judge. Wisdom is described as hidden treasure. "Seek her as silver," we are told. "Search for her as for hidden treasures."[22] Wisdom is "more precious than rubies, and all the things you may desire cannot compare with her."[23] Wisdom has great value: "My son, if you receive my words, and treasure my commands within you, so that you incline your ear to wisdom, and apply your heart to understanding; yes, if you cry out for discernment...then you will understand the fear of the Lord, and find the knowledge of God."[24]

"Wisdom," the author of Proverbs states, "is pleasant to your soul."[25] But wisdom is not static or an end in itself—it is gained as part of a process. Wisdom is described as a "good path," to be followed through resourcefulness: "Discretion will preserve you; understanding will keep you."[26] Biblical wisdom is a way of living. It is not something we finally achieve in our old age, nor is it the prize at the end of the race; it is living creatively and resourcefully in the larger Story.

The ability and passion to live in this way of wisdom are best taught to children through stories. Stories bring biblical knowledge, doctrine, character, and virtue to life—they are the process of applying these to life according to God's will. This is intimately connected with a dynamic living relationship *with* God, combined with a passionate desire *for* God, plus the desire to "press [on] toward the goal for the prize of the upward call of God in Christ Jesus."[27] This "pressing on" is proactive living in the way of wisdom.

John Eldredge, in his book *Wild at Heart*, speaks of adventure as "a deeply spiritual longing written into the soul of man. It is not just about having 'fun.' Adventure requires something of us, puts us to the test."[28] I believe he is referring to "the way of wisdom."

The way of wisdom is unique for every person. God has written a one-of-a-kind script for each of us. We should not be envious or judgmental of other people's stories, because we all have our own story, as do our children. For some it may mean facing high risks, for others daily discipline, for some suffering, or perhaps the challenges and dangers of wealth. For some it means the responsibility of leadership; for others it means service of a different kind.

The way of wisdom is not the way of the world. Usually the world does not understand the logic of the way we live in love with God and His ways. The way of wisdom makes little sense from a secular point of view. For example, was Christ reckless when He set

His face toward Jerusalem, against the advice of His disciples, knowing that He would be crucified there? Or was Jim Elliot foolish when he laid down his life for the Auca Indians of South America? Did Lilias Trotter squander her talent when she gave up her promising art career to become a relatively obscure missionary to the Muslims of Algeria? Is it foolish for Christian physicians and their families to turn their backs on significant wealth and prestige in order to serve the people of some underserved place?

The answer is a resounding "No!" As John Bunyan wrote: "A man there was, tho' some did count him mad, the more he cast away, the more he had."[29]

The way of wisdom is not a stuffy, boring religious concept. It is the literal and spiritual path that Almighty God has designed for each of us to walk through this life. As we walk, we should do so with bated breath and trembling excitement. We will look at the world with wide-eyed wonder and awe, and we will understand the implications of the central truth of the larger Story—that "in Him we live, and move, and have our being."[30]

4

THE IDEA OF STORY

Her work seems never to end,
And lately her days run together,
But she knows the page she'll write tonight
Will last forever.

"Mommy...Daddy...tell me a story."

We've all heard this from our children. Chances are, we haven't heard them beg, "Can I memorize one more sub-point of the long catechism?" Truth is conveyed most powerfully in stories, because stories carry the message, not just the information.

One Christmas Eve when I was very young, my mother's sister and her husband gave me a beautiful hardback book, *Marian's Big Book of Bible Stories*. My aunt had written these words inside the cover: "Tell Mommy to read you a story every day." She knew the power that stories have to touch a child's heart. The author, Marian

Schoolland, also knew this, as she said in the last sentence of the preface, "If this book leads some little heart and mind to know and love God it will not have been written in vain."

Every night for years my mother read to me from this book. As she turned the pages, I studied and savored the wonderfully colored pictures, and listened as she read my favorite chapters over and over again: "How the World Began"; "How God Made People"; "The Flood"; "We'll Build a Tower"; "The Walls of Jericho Fall"; "Samson the Strong Man"; "David and the Giant"; "Elijah Goes to Heaven"; "Jesus Walks on the Water"; "Early Easter Morning"; "Jesus Goes to Heaven."

Many entire books of the Bible are narratives, each revealing something special about God and His way with us. Think of Job, Hosea, Daniel, Joshua, Ruth, Esther, Acts, and others. Whole sections of the Bible are stories—from the history of Israel to the Gospels. And, in the Gospels, we see and hear Jesus, the best storyteller of all.

Scripture is one long story about Jesus. God's primary way of communicating to humanity His character, His love, and His will has been through stories—the only vehicle capable of carrying a significant cargo of truth to the human heart. This is how God designed us. As parents, we need to use the tool of storying to reach our children's hearts.

Let's go back to "Once upon a time...." A traditional fairytale involves clearly defined characters engaged in a conflict between good and evil. The story has a beginning, follows a linear arrow of time, and has an end. Good ultimately triumphs, and the characters live happily ever after. This pattern is "Christian" in contrast with the modern story that often follows a circular, relativistic path leading to non-resolution.

Children need fairytales as a part of their moral training, for this type of story mirrors the larger Story, and impresses that pattern in their minds as they participate in the story in their imagination. This is important practical training for the challenges they will face as adults. As adults we need fairytales, too, in order to keep alive the trusting child still within us—the part that allows us, according to Jesus, to enter into the kingdom of heaven. Remember the words of that old song: "Tell me the story of Jesus; write on my heart every word...."

> *A good story never has to say, 'Now the moral is . . .'*

The best test of a good children's story, according to C. S. Lewis—an expert at telling them—is whether adults as well as children enjoy them.[31] Fairytales stimulate what has been called a child's "moral imagination." A moral imagination enables people to think for themselves, to identify right from wrong, and discern what is truly good and righteous in the complex adult world where simple learned rules do not suffice—because they cannot anticipate every situation. It is applying biblical truth to life. It is the creative ability to walk in the way of wisdom.

In his wonderful book *Tending the Heart of Virtue*, theologian Vigen Guroian explores the moral and religious value of fairytales and other fantasy stories written for children. His goal is to "demonstrate how fairytales feed the moral imagination with the best food. There is no single solution to the moral crisis of childhood in our culture," he says. "But that something is seriously awry few would deny....Our children are in jeopardy and so is the future of virtue and human goodness as well."[32]

The solution to this crisis is not more religious education, with the goal of indoctrinating a child by hammering home yet more dry tenets of orthodox thinking. Nor is the solution to offer more courses, and at a younger age, in "values clarification." Children do not need a shopping list of character qualities or values from which to pick and choose. They need adult guidance in knowing how to live well.

Guroian serves as a wise and understanding guide for parents interested in teaching character and virtues with stories. He would say, however, that before you try to use such stories to teach others, you must *experience* them yourself—become as a child and let the stories touch and move your heart. He provides a fascinating cross-cultural, multi-generational literary smorgasbord, examining how life-impacting lessons permeate such stories as *Pinocchio, The Velveteen Rabbit, The Little Mermaid, The Wind in the Willows, Charlotte's Web, Bambi, The Snow Queen, The Princess and the Goblin, Prince Caspian,* and *The Lion, the Witch and the Wardrobe.* The original, unabridged versions of these stories are vastly different from their modern diluted and perverted video counterparts. They were written from a Christian worldview, and are filled with gospel imagery and themes. He sets these tales in the context of many other children's stories, incorporating the latter whenever they contribute to the topic he is addressing.

His chapter headings serve as a guide that I hope will whet your appetite enough to go out and get this book. They include: "On Becoming a Real Human Child"; "Love and Immortality"; "Friends and Mentors"; "Evil and Redemption"; "Heroines of Faith and Courage." Beyond his main headings, however, I offer this partial list of issues that the author finds (or he made me think of) in various children's stories: life and death; joy and sorrow; failure and resilience; a sense of mission and meaning; the natural and supernatural—visible and invisible; temptation, sin, forgiveness, and reconciliation; betrayal and loyalty; pain and pleasure; pride, prejudice, greed, envy, fear; romance, truth, beauty, and freedom.

In addition, Guroian identifies positive influences toward the development of character traits like courage, compassion, humility, kindness, self-control, generosity, patience, persistence, willingness to sacrifice, dependability, truthfulness, and responsibility.

At the end of the book, Guroian lists many other children's stories worth absorbing. These include *The Ugly Duckling, Where the Wild Things Are, Snow White and the Seven Dwarfs, The Reluctant Dragon, The Trumpet and the Swan, The King and the Golden River,* and *The Last Battle*—the final book of the Narnia Series by C. S. Lewis, from which I've already quoted. In relation to the entire Narnia series, Guroian shares one very telling story of his own. When his son, Rafi, was asked in a college application to name the books from his childhood that meant the most to him, he replied that "C. S. Lewis's Narnia Chronicles were the most memorable *because they left him with standards to live by.*"[33]

We all want that kind of transfer from the imagination to actual life for our children. But in order to achieve the goal, we must keep in mind that children learn almost nothing from abstractions and almost everything from stories. Abstractions are impersonal and detached. Stories are practical and personal. Children learn through stories because they internalize them—they *become* the characters in the story. When a story's conflict is resolved, new insight is gained. When a character fails, lessons are learned that will provide guidance when the child faces adult ambiguities.

When good triumphs over evil, a seed is planted that will someday grow into faith that God is good, and can be trusted. When the characters live happily ever after, the child is connected, if only for an instant, with the larger Story of which fairytales are but a mere reflection—the Story that promises eternal happiness for those who come to God by faith.

Perhaps to some modern Christian parents, fairytales and fantasies may not seem relevant or beneficial, because the stories are not "real." But this kind of story connects us with the most real things of all—a realm beyond our senses—the supernatural realm of God. Scientific realism (data and logic) is not enough.

The word "fantasy" comes from the Greek "a making visible."[34] Fantasies make the invisible, visible. Fairytales open the door to the supernatural, tapping a universal longing in the heart of every child and adult to connect with eternity. Frederick Buechner says, in his book *Telling the Truth: The Gospel as Tragedy, Comedy and Fairy Tale:*

> It is a world of magic and mystery, of deep darkness and flickering starlight. It is a world where terrible things happen and wonderful things too. It is a world where goodness is pitted against evil, love

against hate, order against chaos, in a great struggle....Yet for all its confusion and wildness, it is a world where the battle goes ultimately to the good, who live happily ever after, and where in the long run, everybody, good and evil alike, becomes known by his true name....That is the fairy tale of the Gospel with, of course, one critical difference from all other fairy tales, which is that the claim made for it is that it is true, that it not only happened once upon a time, but has kept on happening ever since and is happening still.[35]

A well-told story can be a phenomenal force that sweeps through the heart, rearranging the meaning of facts and ideas lodged in the mind as we react to the drama, the suspense, the anticipated outcome. The power of a good story lies in the "hook"—the conflict, the surprise, the unexpected twist in the plot—that causes palms to sweat and hearts to race. It's the "gotcha" that unseats pure logic to reveal the fallacy in and to our hearts. Like the parable of the man who was forgiven a million dollars but was unwilling to forgive a small debt, a good story portrays with power and insight the true nature and import of life. It has a much larger capacity to contain truth than does pure exposition.

One of the Bible's best-known stories takes place after King David committed adultery with Bathsheba, and then ordered her husband left alone in the thick of battle so that he would be killed:

And when her mourning was over, David sent and brought her to his house, and she became his wife and bore him a son. But the thing that David had done displeased the Lord. Then the Lord sent [the prophet] Nathan to David. And he came to him, and said to him: "There were two men in one city, one rich and the other poor. The rich man had exceedingly many flocks and herds. But the poor man had nothing, except one little ewe lamb which he had bought and nourished; and it grew up together with him and with his children. It ate of his own food and drank from his own cup and lay in his bosom; and it was like a daughter to him. And a traveler came to the rich man, who refused to take from his own flock and from his own herd to prepare one for the wayfaring man who had come to him; but he took the poor man's lamb and prepared it for the man who had come to him." So David's anger was greatly aroused against the man, and he said to Nathan, "As the Lord lives, the man who has done this shall surely die! And he shall restore fourfold for the lamb, because he did this thing and because he had no pity." Then Nathan said to David, "You are the man!"[36]

Nathan could simply have come to David and said, "You sinned. You did wrong. Make it right." But instead he told a story, on the wings of which the king became an active participant, and his anger burned against the miscreant. This made it so much easier for Nathan to make his point. His story went straight to the heart of the king. This reminds me of Hamlet, who said, "The play's the thing wherein I'll catch the conscience of the king."[37]

We can tell our children what to do, or how to do something. We can teach them morals and rules. But what we say is likely to go in one ear and out the other, unless we give them handles by which to grab the meanings we wish to communicate. Good stories carry the freight of truth without moralizing. The best stories show us God's reality, developing within us a thirst to experience it, not just know about it. Stories enable us both to feel and understand, and this empowers us to live well.

My friend Joe Wheeler describes how stories have a unique ability to touch hearts:

As if coated with Velcro, stories stick! And they don't go away. They, unlike ephemeral abstractions, doggedly dig into conscious memory and then keep digging until they reach our subconscious memory, not stopping until they tunnel into the subterranean bastion of our heart and the celestial eyrie of our soul. Once they reach these chambers, they dig no more, for henceforth they are part of us, part of our motivations, part of all that we think and say and do.[38]

Stories sneak past the screens and filters of our rational minds. Instead of being stored like bare facts in the files of our intellect, stories infect our spirit. They touch, open, and move our hearts, because they bring meaning to life, and meaning is essential to being truly human.

Norma Livo and Sandra Rietz, in their book about the process of storytelling, tell us that we remember events better when we shape our memories into stories—even though that shaping in itself may change the memory. And our "storied events" are "bigger" than the events themselves, because "they have been invested with the greater truth of 'story.'" Of all the ways we are able to express ourselves, stories are the most real because they are made up of the very stuff of life—"constructed of character, conflicts, and chronology."[39]

Sometimes a single symbol connects those who understand it with an entire "storied" event. For example, when the people of Israel had finally crossed the Jordan on dry land to claim the promised land, Joshua commanded a representative of each tribe to take a stone from the riverbed, which he then set up for them as a memorial, so that "this may be a sign among you when your children ask in time to come, saying, 'What do these stones mean to you?' Then you shall answer them that the waters of the Jordan were cut off before the ark of the covenant of the Lord....And these stones shall be for a memorial to the children of Israel forever."[40]

One of the greatest biblical symbols of all was the Passover, with its numerous elements—the doorframes marked with blood, the roasted lamb, the bitter herbs, and the unleavened bread. "And when your children ask you, 'What does this ceremony mean to you?' then tell them," Moses instructed, "'It is a Passover sacrifice to the Lord, who passed over the houses of the Israelites in Egypt and spared our homes when he struck down the Egyptians.'"[41]

Each of the elements of this observation pointed ahead to Jesus, the Lamb of God, the great King Who laid aside His throne, His robe, and His rights, Who celebrated the Passover with His disciples the night He was betrayed, imbuing it with new symbolism: "This is My body…" and connecting both Testaments in a liturgy that will last until He returns and an even greater feast begins.

Well-crafted stories ambush our hearts, and dazzle us with beauty and resolution.

In all these cases, an entire narrative is represented by symbols easy enough for a child to understand. When God wants us to remember something, He uses a story instead of a list of principles or rules. Even the Ten Commandments appear in the middle of a long story, and Matthew's account of Jesus' "Golden Rule," which summarizes the meaning of the Law and the Prophets, occurs in the context of a series of parables.

Is it not possible that God built the process of storying into human memory as the primary organizer of information and ideas? Plato recognized this initial partial organization of the brain, and the philosopher Immanuel Kant spent his life analyzing this concept—that we can recognize and assimilate experiences because of the underlying structure of our minds. We are not empty vessels into which perceptions passively pour; we have an inherent "operating system" through which we actively organize and structure our experiences. This inherent structure gives us the ability to think in context—ultimately so that we are to experience God's truth. Without it, all perceptive input would be nothing but noise, like static on a radio—as Kant said, "even less than a dream."

Recent scientific studies provide some insight into why God has chosen to reveal Himself and His will for us primarily through stories. Dr. Renee Fuller, a professor of physiological psychology, theorized from her work with mentally retarded students that mini-stories are the basic cognitive units of human learning—the deep structure of language. Dr. Fuller calls these units "story engrams," from the word used to describe the change in neural tissue that produces persistence of memory. They are comprised of a thing (noun) that acts or is acted upon (verb), and are the building blocks of human understanding. So both an infant's first word—a noun with a verb implied—and the most convoluted novel share something in common: both tell a story.

The patterning of ideas is what gives a story its power to communicate truth. Simple truth is communicated when the arrangement is linear: A + B = C. Most traditional education, whether it occurs in grammar school, Sunday School, or medical school, expects its students to memorize facts arranged in this pattern, or in no pattern at all. However, the most profound truth—that is, truth that affects our hearts while achieving a change in our memories (an engram)—is usually conveyed in a story where the ideas are arranged in nonlinear logic.

Well-crafted stories capture our attention, ambush our hearts, and then dazzle us with beauty and resolution. They are more than just a series of logical ideas or a grammatically correct arrangement of words. In fact, sometimes stories don't involve words at all. For example, recall with me Rembrandt's painting of the Crucifixion in which the artist placed himself at the foot of the cross. Without words, Rembrandt made a powerful statement about the state of his own heart—and a subtle statement about what the state of viewers' hearts should be. Were the artist standing in a corner of the painting, his back mostly turned to the cross, we would come away with an entirely different impression. Without doubt, this particular masterpiece—indeed every true masterpiece, whether a book, movie, opera, painting, photograph, poem, play, sculpture, symphony, or song—tells a story.

Almost without exception, the power of a masterpiece arises from relationships. It may be the relationship of notes, movements, or various instruments in a symphony. In a painting it may be the relationship of characters, colors, objects, and background. In opera, plays, movies, books, poetry, and song, the best works focus on relationships. When I look through our family album, the pictures can bring laughter or tears. And one of my colleagues—an agnostic—wept when he first saw Michelangelo's *David*. At that moment his soul and the soul of the artist met, transcending time and connecting my colleague with the eternal creative Spirit of God.

By contrast, modern art is notorious for not telling a story, other than the "story" that there is no story. The fragmented, sometimes chaotic, nature of this type of art presents the idea of a Story-less universe. In the same way, music without a coherent melody or chord resolution is Story-less. These trends, among many others, reflect the basic secular mindset of our times—that we are here as a result of chance, that life is going nowhere and, therefore, is fundamentally without meaning. This type of art not only has no meaning, but no one cares that it has no meaning.

In his book *On Stories,* C. S. Lewis said:

> I thought I saw how stories…could steal past a certain inhibition, which had paralyzed much of my own religion in childhood. Why did one find it so hard to feel as one was told one ought to feel about God or about the sufferings of Christ? I thought the chief reason was that one was told one ought to. An obligation to feel can freeze feelings. And reverence itself did harm. The whole subject was associated with lowered voices; almost as if it were something medical. But supposing that by casting all these things into an imaginary world, stripping them of their stained-glass and Sunday School associations, one could make them for the first time appear in their real potency? Could one not thus steal past those watchful dragons? I thought one could.[42]

Chuck Bolte, who was the executive producer of the popular *Odyssey* radio stories, told me that his mission was to produce good stories that in themselves carried God's truth to the listener, by way of the "theater of the mind." He had a strong faith in the power of story as a ministry tool, and believed that stories built around sermonettes do not reach the heart. Instead, he operated on this premise: "Truth emanates out of story, and not the reverse." He and his colleagues used stories to "steal past the dragons," allowing children to hear the truth, not because someone said they ought to listen, but because they wanted to listen.

For parents, this means that stories teach to the heart, and moralizing, sermonizing, and twaddle talk do not. We often assume that children cannot understand the message in a story, so we explain and paraphrase. Coddling children in this way for the purpose of persuasion disrespects their intelligence and impedes the power of the story.

Since I became a Christian, I've probably sat through more than two thousand sermons—most of them preached in three-point Greek logic, imparting information I can't recall. I regretfully admit that, on occasion, I have nearly dozed off prior to the preacher's final point. My wakeup call came when I realized that my entire family was having the same problem. Surely I did not want my children inoculated against faith. I wanted them inspired to discover faith's meaning in their own lives.

These days in church I often find myself wishing the message would never end, a sentiment shared by my family. As we drive home we animatedly discuss the truth the message carried. I am confident that if I bring unbelieving friends to the service they will be dazzled by God's truth. The difference—our pastor preaches in "story." I'm not speaking of a few illustrations, stories, or jokes designed to keep the audience awake. He's not an entertainer. He's a storyteller. He often teaches in a "story hermeneutic"—crafting his entire message around a story. The powerful truth carried to our hearts each Sunday on the vehicle of story breaks spiritual dams, flooding our lives with the inspiring, motivating, and convicting meaning of the "living and active" Word of God, that "judges the thoughts and attitudes of the heart."[43]

Jesus delivered His message largely through stories. He used parables to communicate divine truth directly to the human heart by starting with what His hearers knew—a barren fig tree, a fine pearl, a great banquet, hidden treasure—then nudging them toward what, or more accurately, *Whom*, He wanted them to know better. Those whose hearts were open to His message understood and believed. The key here is that He first called people to be His disciples through His personal impact on them, and then He taught them about Himself within that relationship.

By contrast, the religious leaders of Jesus' day, with their strict orthodoxy and onerous rules and regulations, often did not or could not—because of their preconceptions, prejudice, and hardness of heart—understand His meaning when He spoke of God or faith. They lived in a different paradigm, in which they preferred to remain. Sometimes, of course, they realized that He was describing them, which fueled their anger and desire to be rid of Him. Imagine being confident in your righteousness, only to hear Jesus compare you, publicly, to a whitewashed tomb, full of rotting flesh.

My perception is that the greater part of the Christian church today defines faith—and therefore many Christian parents are accustomed to thinking of faith—in cognitive, intellectual terms, rules, and regulations, which can produce dead orthodoxy, legalism, pride, and self-righteousness. Disputes and divisions are fueled by such attitudes, and relationships suffer—and surely the children of the families involved cannot understand how former friends who still attend their former church have suddenly become enemies. Many Christians are deeply concerned with teaching their children about God, the Bible, and doctrine, while the God Who inspired the Bible wants to win their hearts—which is surely not so much related to knowing *about* Him as to knowing Him, personally.

Theological disputation was prevalent in Jesus' day, but He didn't try to settle the various esoteric debates, even when they were brought to Him. Surely He would have addressed these issues, had He thought them important enough to resolve. Instead, He took His hearers back to the basics of knowing, and being known by, their heavenly Father.

Kirk Webb wrote:

Studying God's truths as if they were a blueprint or outline that hangs together at every point of tension is to miss God. Unquestionably, God is a God of order. One need only look at the structure of a molecule or the stars at night to come to that conclusion. However, to assume that understanding the order is equivalent to knowing God is to compromise one's own life. Each person lives in narrative form, thus representing the person of God—and to assume God can be known otherwise is to miss the possibility of knowing the core realities of who God is.[44]

Stories are our primary method for romancing our child's heart, first to ourselves, and then to God. Great writers, philosophers, artists, musicians, theologians, pastors, prophets, scientists, producers, playwrights, and other communication experts have imitated God and His Son, Jesus, by deliberately choosing to convey truth to the human heart through stories.

But my favorite stories have not been written down. They've been told or sung—sometimes for the umpteenth time—around the campfire, on front porches, during a walk through the woods with a friend, or around the dinner table. This kind of story is completely original, revealing the narrator's soul, which then connects with mine.

My kids share the same perspective. While Karey and I probably told or read a thousand tales to our kids as they grew up, they don't remember all those individual stories. They remember the table, and the company, and what they learned—the truth the stories carried to their hearts.

When Travis shared a few treasures from those days in writing his political science final exam at college, the professor asked him, in a tone that implied that he must have cheated or plagiarized, "Where did you obtain the ideas you used in writing this exam?"

He replied, "From discussions around the family dining room table as I grew up."

How do we learn to tell stories? Here are some ideas:

- invite interesting people for dinner and ask them questions (and let our children ask, too)
- read some of the stories listed or discussed in this chapter

- listen to audio tapes with our children, like the *Odyssey* series from Focus on the Family
- read aloud biographies of great people, or historical fiction
- watch and discuss quality videos and great films
- write and act out Scripture-based dramas or plays
- establish family traditions that revolve around storytelling.

Everyone has a story. We all live *in a story* in one way or another. And all our stories are part of the larger Story—whether we're speaking of campfire stories, or fairytales read to a child—and all are connected at the heart.

The only thing we can do wrong is not try. Our worst efforts will still be better than none at all. Children are not as much concerned about perfection as authenticity. The fact that we are *trying* to connect shows our love and draws us into the larger Story. This, in the end, is what they will remember, when all the dust has settled, and all the books are closed.

PART II:

THE WINNING OF A HEART

You called, You cried, You shattered my deafness.
You sparkled, You blazed, You drove away my blindness.
You shed your fragrance, and I drew in my breath, and panted for You.
I tasted and I now hunger and thirst.
You touched me, and I now burn with a longing for Your peace.

- Saint Augustine

5

ANOTHER SUITOR

Kneeling by my children's bedside
In the light of the moon,
I know Heaven is watchin'
And there's angels in this room.

B ack when I was an undergraduate studying geology, I saw a
picture on the cover of a *National Geographic* magazine
showing a panoramic view of the North Cascade Mountains of
Washington State. The picture dazzled me, haunting my imagination
for months. The following summer I landed a job on the crest of
the North Cascades—exactly where the photo had been taken. Our
helicopter-supported camp was sixteen miles from the nearest road,
with a spectacular view of the snow-capped volcanic mountain
named Glacier Peak.

My assistant was an experienced technical rock climber and mountaineer—so, naturally, on our days off from climbing mountains for work, we climbed mountains for fun. Peaks surrounded our camp that had been carved by God's own fingers, with names like White Chuck, Bonanza, Ripsaw Ridge, Spiral Point, and Fourth-of-July.

I'll never forget the first technical climb we did up the north face of Fortress Mountain. Days before the climb, we stared across the deep cirque just south of our camp, at the mountain's foreboding face, as we planned our route. During the climb I could not get over how cautious my assistant was. For the sake of safety, climbers sometimes connect themselves together with a rope. He wanted us to rope up almost all the time. It seemed like such a bother. The truth is that, in my ignorance and incompetence, I was a blind fool. I did not respect that mountain enough—though I did fear falling when I thought about it.

I soon learned that the most competent rock climbers are also the most cautious. They survive the dangers and make it to the top because they are prepared. Physically they are conditioned and strong. They wear special protective boots and a helmet. They carry heavy packs loaded with survival gear, food, first aid kits, sleeping bags, bivouac tents, ropes, carabiners, ice axes—everything they might possibly need. They are skilled, knowledgeable, and experienced in climbing. They predict the weather. They read the ice and the rock. They map out their route, concentrate, sweat, get bruised, scraped, tired, and hungry, but they reach the summit. They are not only competent, they are alert and careful, because mountains may be beautiful but they can also be deadly.

In much the same way as I did not take "roping up" seriously, we as parents can adopt too casual an attitude while raising our children. We fall into a foolish pattern of thinking: *Everything will turn out fine. I see no "famine, war, or pestilence" on the horizon. Our children attend a "safe" school, our neighborhood is secure, and our friends are Christians—all is well. There's nothing to worry about.*

Arnie Burron says that Ephesians 6:12 "ought to make us as alert as we would be if we heard a news report that a psychotic child killer were stalking our neighborhood, looking for his next victim!"[45] Here's what that text says: "For we do not wrestle against flesh and blood, but against principalities, against powers, against the rulers of the darkness of this age, against spiritual hosts of wickedness in the heavenly places."

My parents did an end run around the power of peer pressure.

We are not the only ones who want to win our children's hearts. We have a rival, a suitor with sinister designs—the villain of our fairytale. His name is Satan. Normally, we don't think of Satan as a "suitor." He is the enemy, described as a "roaring lion seeking whom he may devour."[46] Thus, we usually think of this struggle in terms of open warfare, frontal attacks, and vicious assaults—spiritual warfare in which we must fight the devil for all we're worth. Commonly, these battles also have a very real physical dimension— as our nation experienced on September 11, 2001.

The apostle Paul exhorts Christians to "put on the whole armor of God, that you may stand against the wiles of the devil."[47] Satan's wiles are tricks or stratagems intended to ensnare or deceive. The word implies skill in outwitting through trickery or guile. This word, attributed by God to history's ultimate beguiler, perfectly describes his designs on our children and his methods of trying to win them. While we focus on fighting obvious "battles of faith" on one front or another, Satan lurks in the shadows, waiting for just the right moment—when we are too preoccupied, distracted, or exhausted to be alert to the danger—to draw away our children's hearts, if he can.

The biblical view of Satan is far removed from the all-pervasive caricature of cloven hoofs, horns, and a tail, wearing a red suit and carrying a pitchfork. The very persistence of this image is strong evidence of this powerful creature's ability to deceive. He wants everyone to think that he is not real, or that if he does exist, he is relatively harmless—the butt of costume-party humor.

Satan was once a high angelic being, cast from heaven for rebelling against the Most High God. He can still manifest himself as an angel of light. He can speak with eloquence and seem stunning in appearance. He is brilliant, knowledgeable, and powerful, and he has a firm hold on our culture.

This complicates our efforts to romance our children's hearts to God. Yes, we can and should fight evil on all its fronts, as do many Christian parents and the organizations they support. For some people, their involvement in the fray seems like a modern holy crusade—with meetings, strategies, and other actions aimed at stemming the tide of evil and/or advancing the cause of truth, justice, and the Christian way. However, these well-meaning parents may never have considered that when they expend all their emotional, spiritual, and financial resources in righteous causes they are, in effect, playing into Satan's hands. For he knows that as long as he can keep them focused on *any* cause to the point of exhaustion, they will have little left with which to romance their children's hearts to God.

Don't get me wrong. The spiritual battle must be fought—even though we know that the war itself has already been won, and what we're seeing are the skirmishes and ambushes of a desperate, defeated foe. What I'm trying to point out is this: Our wily adversary does not war by the rules. Instead, he conducts covert guerrilla warfare, the main objective of which is to pick off his current and potential opponents one by one, by stealth, deception, trickery, and seduction.

At some point, each of our children is going to be tempted by or subjected to ungodly influences, some of which we overlook, take for granted, perhaps even feel safe about—as I foolishly felt safe while climbing the face of that mountain. When we feel most secure, our children may be most at risk.

The other suitor lures our children away through unsupervised television, videos, mindless computer games, unsupervised access to the Internet, some rock music and music videos, and questionable books and magazines. When our children spend time with friends, neighbors, and relatives we have not checked out, Satan is there, lurking in the shadows. During those many hours when they participate in extracurricular activities after school, he waits. Sometimes even activities of church youth groups and Sunday School classes are not exempt. He has the advantage anywhere our children may hear: "Your parents are just trying to keep you from having fun. Here, try this."

When this happens, each child will face a choice: the way of wisdom or the way of folly. I am confident that no set of rules, good habits, or orthodox beliefs, not even the fear of eternal punishment, will compel a child to choose wisely. These factors operate from the outside in, usually originating in adults who tell children what they should believe and how they should, or should not, act. If our children's faith is an "outside in" thing, they will almost surely fall into the snare of the devil because whoever, or whatever, was outside before and in control, is not there now.

In almost every case, the devil's snare is a counterfeit of something God has already created. God created man and woman to be one flesh in the beauty of passionate marital union. The devil perverts this into lust and promiscuity. God provides for our physical needs, giving us all things "richly to enjoy." Satan perverts this into gluttony and materialism. God instilled in us His creative image, to bring us happiness and joy as we create. Satan monopolizes art and music in the name of fame and fortune.

The path of life is paved with counterfeits of all kinds. Each of them beckons from the shadows, like the temptresses in Proverbs, to come here or there and find what we've been missing. We cannot completely protect our children from this seduction. But we can out-romance the competition so our children will make the response that will keep their hearts in the day of testing, allowing them to

assert, "I haven't been missing *anything*. I have all I need and more."
If we have won their hearts, their moral choices will come from the
inside out, and making the right choice will be as natural as taking
the next step on a path that leads toward God, not away from Him.

OUT-ROMANCING THE COMPETITION

My parents' strategy was a kind of end run around the power of
peer pressure. In my early teens, my artistic side was expressed in a
passion for clothes. I loved to dress in a unique—some might even
have said outrageous—way, including stunningly colorful Hawaiian
shirts. (Every time a girl passed by she would hum "Aloha" to me. I
loved it.) Mom drew the line at black leather jackets, but I knew she
was my kindred spirit in this artistic activity. She took me to stores
in downtown Milwaukee—far away from where we lived—where I
could find my "cool threads." Instead of fighting me tooth and nail
about every item of clothing—which most of my friends' mothers
were doing—Mom fought for my heart, and won hands down. I
think she viewed this part of the contest for my heart as a costume
party. Come to think of it, I always did take first place at costume
parties, whenever she handmade my costume.

Despite being a fashion-setter of sorts, I struggled desperately
with the youth subculture in junior high and high school. I didn't
know how to be accepted and at the same time avoid the constant
temptations and negative influences—dirty jokes on the school bus,
miniskirts everywhere I turned, the petty politics of fitting into the
in-crowd, and physical threats by young hoods.

My father knew that idle time could be dangerous for teenagers,
so from when I was fifteen he arranged for me to work with his crew
as a carpenter's helper. While all my friends did odd jobs, or more
commonly could not find work during the summer, I was working
hard with men, learning lifelong skills and developing a work ethic.
I listened with them to their adult music—polkas, classical, and big

band—and learned much about respecting authority. The low point—or perhaps the high point—was when the crew stapled me to the oak layout table—clothes, shoes, and all. My dad watched, but did not intervene. He let them tutor me in the sociology of his workplace. Beyond that, this experience introduced me to his philosophy of management.

My dad beat out the competition for my affection by setting before me a man-size challenge, believing I could do it, and mentoring me in the craft he knew best. He couldn't have given me a better gift.

Basketball entered my life during junior high. By high school, when I wasn't playing or practicing, I was thinking about playing. I trained with weights on my ankles, and slept with a basketball. I made it my goal to receive a basketball scholarship for college, to save my parents money as a way of saying "thank you" for all they had invested in me. They were supportive of this positive activity, which certainly helped me cope with the peer pressure. By the time I was finished playing high school ball, I held most of the school records, and I had qualified for a college scholarship.

The sport became more than a game to me. It was my primary arena of creative expression, and a platform from which to speak out for a more conservative approach to certain things that were already capturing the hearts, minds, and bodies of my peers. The most dramatic illustration of this came when I was elected "king" of the Senior Prom.

The standards of the beer-drinking, Saturday-night-dancing culture of Milwaukee did not mesh at all with the fundamentalist values my parents espoused. When I was elected prom king, I was torn between wanting to be accepted by my peers and wanting to please my parents, who made it clear that I would have to make up my own mind about what to do.

In the end, I turned down the honor because I didn't feel comfortable dancing any more. The decision may have been different in another time and another culture, but it was right for me then. By that time, I knew by intuition and experience that the way of my parents—which had become my own way, even when it was difficult—was superior to anything or anyone else that might whisper my name. Interestingly, though I had feared rejection by my peers, I found I had more friends after I made my decision known.

Although my parents had clear boundaries for us, they had few rules. Their boundaries were walls that did not move, but we had freedom within them. I had no curfew, and I was given the responsibility to make my own moral choices. I was also burdened with the consequences; I knew that, although they would still love me, they would not rescue me from any wrong choices.

My brothers and I usually chose to do what Mom and Dad wanted. None of us ever rebelled. I believe that our parents so completely out-romanced the competition that we were bound by an uncommon love that wooed and won our hearts. To violate their love in word or deed, in public or in private, would have been the same as raping our own souls.

THE BEAUTY CONTEST

In reality, the romance of a child's heart is more like a beauty contest than open warfare. Some Christians have a difficult time fitting beauty into their theology, because the culture we live in worships it. This is where Satan blindsides us, taking advantage of our negligence. Beauty is central to human-centered "theology"— even in cultures without the high standard of living we enjoy. Edith Schaeffer wrote:

> There were some Africans who were with us a couple of years ago, who sat in our bedroom talking to my husband and me. Each of them had been in some sort of a mission school and now were in European universities on scholarships. Each of them

at some time or another had come into the homes of missionaries and had observed various things during their boyhood. They each made a similar comment which impressed me deeply. Each of them said that the thing which had turned them away from Christianity was the lack of beauty in the missionaries' homes—and they were speaking of physical beauty. The God of the universe they saw created a beautiful world, but they did not see this beauty radiating from these Christians' homes.[48]

You can imagine how these Africans, who lived close to God's creation, had been confused when they heard truth but saw little beauty. The God they had seen in nature was obviously a passionate Creator—an artist. An evangelistic message without a connection to the creation confused them.

Beauty is profoundly part of God. He is the Creator and source of beauty. In Scripture, God's beauty and glory can only be indirectly described because it is so great. His divine presence is overwhelming—for God dwells "in unapproachable light."[49]

My mother is an artist, and her skill and creativity are evident in her homemaking. The beauty she brought to my life drew me to God. She made it clear that He was the Author of all creativity. She decorated our home with several original paintings, because she wanted us to learn to appreciate the nuances of texture and color that could not be detected in reproductions. More, she believes that we can only understand the soul of the artist through an original.

Two of these paintings now hang in my home. One was painted for my grandmother by a lumberjack. It is an oil rendition of a bull elk standing in a lake at the foot of a mountain, with tall spruce, willows, and granite rocks edging the water. Mom loved it because of her fascination with the Rocky Mountains—something she passed on to me. (In fact, she named me "Monte" because it means "man from the mountains.")

The picture is framed in rustic hand-carved cedar. Through the years I have lived this painted scenario many times as I pursued elk through the Rockies. I'm sure that a painting encountered in youth can instill a vision in a child's heart that will last a lifetime.

My mother painted the other when she was in college. The simple pine frame, made by my grandfather, enhances the romantic image of two whitetail deer bounding down a snow-covered glacial hill. A lone white pine stands in memory of the great Wisconsin virgin forest, and several white birches stand in stark relief against the snow. The little boy who hugged the pine stump comes alive in me every time I look at that picture, for it connects me with my heritage—the brush strokes are my mother's, and the setting is God's creation.

My own passion for science is primarily motivated by my sense of wonder as I see God's beauty reflected in creation. Every human being has an innate drive to create beauty, for we are created in the image of the Creator. We find happiness as we create order out of chaos and as we make things of beauty—from poetry to potholders.

Mom's artistry extends from oil paintings to pie making. I can almost smell and taste her rhubarb pie as I write. Her pies belong in art galleries—though of course they have all ended up in our stomachs. Mom acquired her pie-making skills while working in her parents' hotel, in a small northern Wisconsin town in the late 1930s. Those post-Depression days were filled with hard work, and Mom baked four or five pies every morning, before she left for school, in the hotel's monstrous wood-burning ovens. She could judge the oven temperature just by the feel of the hot air on her face, and fed the fireboxes with split hard maple in between rolling out and filling the pies. People came to the hotel from miles around just for her pies—especially lemon meringue and butterscotch.

We are all drawn to what looks good, whether or not it is good for us. If given the option, a child will always choose ice cream over a dish of limp, overcooked spinach. Similarly, in choices of the heart, a child will naturally be drawn to the most beautiful, deliciously wonderful option. It is how we are created. Thomas Aquinas said, "No man can live without delight." And Frederick Buechner called beauty as essential to the spirit as food is to the body. We are empty without it.

Satan's objective for every soul is disintegration on every level.

Satan's objective is to deceive, entrap, and enslave the human heart—the younger the better. His ultimate goal for every soul is disintegration on every level, resulting in alienation from self, God, and others, which leads to pain and aloneness forevermore. To accomplish this, Satan romances hearts and spins his web of deception primarily in three realms—empirical, rational, and spiritual.

THE EMPIRICAL REALM

The empirical realm is the concrete world: time, space, and matter—things that can be observed, measured, and experienced. Satan's strategy is to occupy parents with these things to the point of saturation, so that they seldom have the energy to compete with him. Even when they do compete, he claims this world as his own and is successful, not only in counterfeiting, but also in monopolizing for his own evil purposes the beauty, wonder, and mystery of the things God has made. One of his favorite strategies today is to so fill our lives with seemingly good options and opportunities that many families find it hard to spend even a few minutes together each day—or week—because there is always somewhere else to go and something else to do.

Our society's affluence has allowed these opportunities to grow exponentially both in quality and quantity. When I went to high school in the late sixties, I knew only one teenage friend who owned his own car and drove it to school. He had to park in the teachers' lot, because there wasn't another parking area. Today, one of our local high schools has three parking lots reserved just for the students.

Even my younger son's shoes demonstrate this point. Dawson has shoes for children's chorale, backpacking, running, mountain biking, church, ice skating, rollerblading, bowhunting, cross-country skiing, telemark skiing, canoeing, fishing, winter hiking, skin diving, fly fishing, horseback riding, and more. The only reason he doesn't have a pair for tae kwon do—where he reached the black belt level at age twelve—is because he works out barefoot. Interestingly, he usually goes barefoot around the house and outside—even occasionally in the winter. Could he be making an unintentional philosophical statement with his feet? These shoes, which overflow from his closet, reflect his life—filled to the brim with wonderful opportunities (and he does not even participate in competitive team sports).

Myriad world-class recreational and other opportunities—educational, social, and artistic—compete for our children's time, in the end threatening to possess them as basketball possessed me for seven years. With all the positive aspects of that involvement, I sometimes wonder what I missed by investing so much time, energy and passion into playing with that round ball. It's a dilemma, because we can usually find at least some good in each opportunity.

Besides the financial strain imposed by participation in competitive sports—including specialized equipment and training with experts—the other aspects, like transportation to and from, and attendance at, events, require time. Usually mothers end up carrying the heaviest load, becoming by default nearly fulltime chauffeurs—that cultural phenomenon we call "soccer (hockey-baseball-etc.) moms."

Recently, Karey and I spoke at a conference and shared this challenge. Several days later a mother wrote to us describing a miracle that had taken place in her family. Her husband had returned home realizing that he needed to turn off the TV and do productive things like Bible study with the kids. Even more miraculously, he decided that their son would only do one sport next year. She said that her husband had a vision during the conference, involving being with his family so they could make maple syrup, plant gardens, and go fishing. The husband said, "It's hard to get a project going when you have a game in three hours." Their son revealed what was in his heart when he said, "Now we won't have to rush so much and we can just be at home and do stuff."

"He is extremely athletic and loves sports," the mother added, to explain the significance of that comment. She also said that it brought tears to her eyes, standing at the window watching her husband at home on a day off, tapping maple trees with the kids, playing with the chickens in the yard, throwing a ball to the dog, pushing one of the girls on the swing, while they had a fire going outside and were loving it all. Her husband came in thrilled with this day, and looking forward to more like it, though he is still struggling internally with not being involved in so many sports. He knows he wants one thing, but it's hard to give up the other. The mother finished her letter by asking Karey and me to pray for them as parents, and for their family.

The value judgments we are forced to make today are not easy. When we try to preserve our families, we see opportunities slipping away. When we seize the opportunities, we see our families slipping away. Satan finds enthusiastic support from our culture's childhood "experts" who contend that children need all these opportunities—therefore, parents who withhold any of them are somehow negligent.

Allowing children to participate in everything may produce young people who are highly accomplished in several areas, without possessing a framework for understanding the world that calls them "accomplished." They are accustomed to material abundance and are easily irritated if things don't go their way. As Larry Crabb once said in a Sunday School class, "Blessings can be dangerous."

THE RATIONAL REALM

The rational realm is the immaterial world—its structure, form, and pattern as understood by our minds—including categories, ideas, logic, and our perception of knowledge, truth, and reality. It is the "glasses" through which we view the world. Satan's strategy is to convince our children to be philosophical skeptics—cynical rationalists. To accomplish this, he overwhelms them with secular ideas and deceptive logic, using the youth subculture to pressure them to conform. He also applies pressure from the adult world by exposing them, as early as possible, to a variety of moral dilemmas beyond their capacity to understand. There is much we can do to physically shield them from this exposure, but often their only protection is prayer.

One day in the late summer, our church decided to pray for and commission the college students of our congregation as they returned to their campuses. Words like "sending soldiers to war" and "they are warriors returning to a battle that is a life-and-death struggle" were said with sincere, heartfelt emotion. These precious sons and daughters were in the process of flying the nest. The reality of moral dilemmas, temptation, and the clashing of worldviews flavored our supplications to God. As the prayers became more and more passionate, we adults examined our own hearts and our place in the spiritual battle. Empathizing with our young comrades, we felt a yearning to be with them on the frontlines—standing alongside them, shoulder to shoulder in the fray, dressing their wounds and guarding their flank. We feared for their minds, knowing that rationalistic professors would attempt to browbeat them for their faith. We covenanted together to uphold them in prayer throughout the school year.

As the prayer time was drawing to a close, someone spoke up: "What about our high school students? They are going into an intellectual and spiritual battle as well. Let's commission and pray for them, too." This was a little awkward—to think about sending teenagers to war. Since the tragedy at Columbine High School, which some of our students attended, the concept had taken on a very real physical dimension. But we prayed for them and it felt right.

Then someone said, "What about our junior high students?" The next logical thought was, "What about our grade school children…and we can't leave out our preschoolers."

At that moment everyone got the point—a lightning flash of truth straight from heaven striking our hearts. We were sending children to war! There was an awkward, guilty silence, and finally someone said "amen" and, to everyone's relief, the normal part of the service began again. We wouldn't dream of sending children to war in the physical realm. But in the intellectual and spiritual realms, where so much more is at stake, we do this without a second thought.

THE SPIRITUAL REALM

The spiritual realm includes our personality, which is our spiritual fingerprint, the essence of our being. Secularists try frantically to explain away this realm by describing our consciousness in terms of biochemical electrical reactions. Obviously, there is more to it.

Humans express who they are through communication, relationship, and fellowship, and building healthy relationships takes time. But even when we set aside time for nurturing our relationship with our children, Satan can sneak in and distract us. He contaminates the fellowship, sometimes by manipulating our agenda until it is at odds with our child's.

When Dawson was nine, I took him fishing along a beautiful little mountain stream near our home. I wanted to spend quality and quantity time with him—a whole day fishing, just the two of us. For me, this stretch of stream held special memories. I had taken Travis and Heather fishing there—in sunshine, in rain, through thick mosquitoes, sometimes carrying them on my back for miles. But we always caught fish and returned home with ravenous appetites and satisfied souls.

Dawson and I left home early that day. We hiked about a mile and a half from the trailhead on the main trail, and then hiked another half mile on a little-known path to a secret spot of mine. My goal was to fish our way up to a special pool my brother had described, where he had once lost a huge cutthroat trout. The pool lay at the base of a tumbling waterfall where a beaver had built a high dam. Because of its remoteness, it had grown larger in my imagination, almost to the point of enchantment.

The day was beautiful and we were having a wonderful time. But gradually this changed. The passion for competition gripped me—not a contest with Dawson, but some nebulous fishing contest in my imagination that I now was intent on winning *through* my son. It became my mission to reach that special pool, so I hurried Dawson along from one pool to the next as we moved upstream. When he managed to catch trout along the way, I hardly acknowledged them as he held them up for me to see. I even made him skip some pools. He was catching fish, but I didn't care. I was on a mission—for him (so I thought) to catch the biggest fish in the stream.

Instead of relating to Dawson—which was why I had taken him fishing in the first place!—I was having a relationship with a mission. And he felt it in his boyish heart. We should have been two kindred spirits out enjoying God's creation and each other's company. Instead, slowly but surely, I was eroding and squandering the riches of my relationship with him, and destroying the key to romancing his heart that day. At first, Dawson's wonderful whimsical spirit resisted my prodding, but he soon gave in. It brings tears to my eyes now as I think about how I dragged him up that stream, sacrificing his sense of wonder on the altar of my mission.

By the time we reached my precious pool, I had managed nearly to extinguish his spirit. But he was resilient and, in spite of me, he tried his best to act excited. Ironically, the waters from the spring runoff had washed away the beaver dam and the pool was gone— poetic justice for a father who had lost track of why he and his son were together in the first place.

Dawson seemed quieter than normal just before we headed back. It was late, so I decided to bushwhack it to the main trail to save some time. But that almost turned into a disaster as we ran into an old forest-fire burn where recently sprouted aspen trees had grown up so thick I could hardly squeeze through. Threading our fishing rods between those aspen trees was a tedious challenge. In addition, there were huge spruce logs that we had to maneuver over, under, and around, and boulders everywhere. It was tough going, and almost overwhelming, for about a half mile. Dawson kept falling behind, and I was afraid that we might get separated, so I had to stop often to wait for him. This was not normal—he is usually in the lead. Even when we broke out of the trees and began hiking down the main trail, he quietly shuffled along behind me while I carried his pack and fishing pole. I felt impatient and irritated.

We ate trout cooked over an open fire—a moment of pure romance this father and son will never forget.

That night at home we discovered that he had come down with chicken pox. He had been sick and feverish all day. I had been so preoccupied with my fishing contest that I hadn't even noticed.

How easy it is to fail in romancing our children's hearts, even when we have the best intentions and plans. During that day of fishing, the other suitor had neutralized the positive effect I'd hoped for by tempting me with a seemingly noble obsession. But all was not lost. The larger Story of our relationship told Dawson that this was just a small detour in our journey together.

A few weeks later, we went fishing again. This time I did the following, letting my little "Tom Sawyer" set the agenda and lead the way. We lingered for a long time at some holes, and managed a fine catch of trout. At the end of the day we ate crispy golden-brown pan-fried cutthroat trout, cooked over an open fire in a lush meadow of lilac-purple fireweed under a clear blue Colorado sky— a moment of pure romance this father and son will never forget.

Perhaps, when Dawson is wooed by the other suitor, he will even think of this experience, and others like it that we've shared over the years—in which case he'll be able to say, "No thank you," when Satan comes knocking. "There's nothing you could offer me that I don't already have."

Perfection isn't the issue in romancing our child's heart. In the context of what I've shared, *distraction* is Satan's most common strategy, and one he uses effectively. As parents, just showing up for the contest is half the battle. And it's never too early—or too late—to begin. Children are so understanding and forgiving and, like Dawson, reluctant to remember it very long when we make a mistake. They are quick to see the good in us and to embrace it with uninhibited passion. How sweet life would be if this were as true of adults.

6

THE WATERSHED

There's a way of wisdom
And a way of fools;
And the way of wisdom
Is straight and true.

We live near the Continental Divide—the Rocky Mountain backbone of North America. When you stand on the Divide above the timberline at Loveland Pass (11,992 feet above sea level) and look east or west, peak after peak stretches out before you in a complex pattern of deeply carved glacial canyons.

In the late spring I've stood on a snowfield at the divide watching one rivulet of water flow east and another from the same snowfield flow west. The eastern rivulet will be captured by Clear Creek, which rushes straight down the Front Range, picking up and dropping gold along the way, until the creek joins the Platte River and from there flows into the Missouri and Mississippi Rivers. Finally, it reaches the Gulf of Mexico, from which it will be carried north by the Gulf

Stream, as a river of fresh water in the salty Atlantic Ocean, until it finally mixes into the North Atlantic Ocean somewhere west of Scandinavia.

The rivulet flowing westward will tumble down the North Fork of the Snake River into Dillon Reservoir, where it will become part of the beautiful Blue River. Then it will join the Colorado River, which winds its way through Lake Powell, Lake Mead, and the Grand Canyon, until it is diverted into Central Arizona Project's aqueduct to serve the land and people needs of the water-starved desert of Arizona—never reaching the Gulf of California and the Pacific Ocean.

This is how two droplets of water, once part of the same snow pack, can end up thousands of miles apart, in different worlds. The dividing line, in this case the Continental Divide, is called a watershed.

A crucial dividing line, factor, or turning point in a person's life is also called a watershed. The "rain" of life—life's experiences, including adversity and temptations—falls on the just and the unjust, as Jesus said. Sometimes this rain (or snow) has destructive results. Sometimes it simply waters the ground. But regardless of whether the "rain" is gentle or harsh, the direction the water follows after it hits is determined by a person's "watershed"—the "set" or established attitude of their heart.

The word "set" occurs in the Bible hundreds of times, often in relation to choices faced: the set of the mind (mindset), the set of the will, of the body, and of the heart. I'd like to make up a new word: "heartset." The set of the heart in every child and adult determines how they will respond to the inevitable testings and temptations of life.

One of my favorite Scripture passages describes how Jesus "steadfastly set His face to go to Jerusalem."[50] Why? To endure the cross, despising its shame, for the joy set before Him, which was the redemption of all who would trust in Him for their salvation. Jesus' face was set to take His body to Jerusalem, because His will was set, because His heart was set. His mind could not be changed, even when people like Peter tried to, for Jesus' purpose in life was to be lifted up on the cross to draw all men to Himself.

Up until a certain point in life, a child's thoughts and actions are more or less dependent on parental values and control. Parents stand like a buffer, protecting their children from life-impacting choices, offering guidance, and correction when necessary.

As children near adulthood, they begin to think more independently, choosing the way of wisdom, or the way of folly. This watershed choice will have dramatic consequences, with the potential for life destinations that are worlds apart.

Even a child of godly parents may go through periods of rebellion that leave the parents few options but to live by hope and faith, all the time praying for God's grace and wisdom. One of my friends, a minister, recalls how, once he got away from home and into a Christian college, he wrote his parents (his father was also a minister) that he no longer wanted to have anything to do with their God. Their response—beyond expressing their shock, concern, and dismay—was to let their son know that they loved him and to acknowledge that this, indeed, was his choice alone and they would not interfere. They showed respect for him as a person, instead of trying to manipulate him toward the choice they desired for his life.

Allowing this much freedom is difficult, especially for parents who have maintained close control for most of their child's life. In most cases, the greater the pressure put on a child to decide, the greater the chance the choice will not be made for God. But when God and His way of wisdom is an uncoerced choice, it will withstand temptation, and stand up to the tests of life.

Parents have the time from their child's birth to when they leave their protection to train and discipline them in God's laws, and most significantly to create a thirst for God in their hearts, so that, like the psalmist, they will cry: "As the deer pants for the water brooks, so pants my soul for You, O God."[51]

UNDERSTANDING A KEY PASSAGE

A verse in Proverbs tells us: "Train up a child in the way he should go, and when he is old he will not depart from it."[52] This verse is not only the key to this watershed event—its meaning is central to understanding the idea of Romance. Many Bible teachers interpret this passage to mean that the challenge to parents is to know their child well in order to train them according to their own "bents"—talents, abilities, spiritual gifts, and other unique God-given capabilities. I remember vividly how my parents worked hard applying this principle as they raised my brothers and me. They never hesitated to go out of their way in searching for and finding each of their son's individual bents, and praising us equally in our different accomplishments.

It is the parents' responsibility, not only to encourage the positive bents, but also to deal with the negative bents. Every archer knows that straightening a bent aluminum arrow takes time and patience. If you press too hard and too quickly on the bend you will break the arrow. If you do not press hard enough, you will not straighten the bend. In order to be successful, you must give the straightening process your undivided attention, with just the right amount of pressure for as long as it takes.

Looking at this verse from a larger biblical perspective, we see that training a child includes the idea of starting a child along a particular way.[53] The word "way" is one of the most common biblical words used to describe the walk of faith. In fact, the "Way" was the first name applied to the new movement that eventually was called "Christianity."[54] Even non-believers recognized that embracing Christ meant to adopt a new "way" of living. I have already described this way as the way of wisdom, and pointed out that this is a dynamic process—a treasure hunt for God's truth and its application to our lives.

In the book *You and Your Child*, Charles Swindoll explains that the original root of "train up" is the term for "the palate, the roof of the mouth, the gums." In the days of Solomon, this term described the action of the midwife. After a child was delivered, the midwife would dip her finger into chewed or crushed dates, and touch and massage the gums and palate of the infant with the juice, to stimulate the sense of taste and the sensation of sucking. The baby would then be placed in the mother's arms to begin breastfeeding. So the

> *While a child may be forced to comply, no one can be forced to love.*

expression "train up" also means to "develop or create a thirst."[55] Thus, the words "Train up a child in the way he should go" literally means to "develop or create a thirst in the child so the child will start walking in the way he should go"—in the way of wisdom.

There are two ways to create a thirst. The most common approach is behavioristic training, which causes a child to acquire a thirst for something he does not naturally desire. The goal of romance, by contrast, is that the child will develop a thirst based on desire. A balanced combination of these two approaches, especially in light of the child's age, is the proper biblical approach.

Starting a child along the way is theologically pivotal to romancing his heart. It comes after the thirst is created. We cannot simply place a child along the way as we would place him on a path to start walking. To be "along the way" means we are moving—it is a process, and process involves choosing which way to go.

During the time a child breastfeeds, bonding occurs, and eventually mother and child know each other through this intimate experience. Security and serenity are reflected in the child's eyes as he gazes on his mother's face. Trust is established between parent and child.

Once trust is gained, a child allows himself to be carried along the way on the shoulders of his parent's faith—a simple but important early training in choosing well. Their journey together introduces the larger Story, which is filled with delight, challenge, excitement, mystery and beauty, revealing the character of Christ in the parents' heart through the good times as well as in times of trial. Ultimately, this leads to a personal encounter with the Story's almighty Author—God Himself.

Until I was seven, I thought that my father was God. Once I discovered that this wasn't true, I began to look for the real God. A year later, I asked the Lord into my life during an Awana meeting. As far as I was concerned, this decision was only natural, because my father had projected the image of God so accurately, genuinely, and positively that I wanted to know Him personally.

Our first desire as parents is that our children will receive Jesus Christ as their personal Savior. To me, the phrase "when he is old he will not depart from it [the way of wisdom]" implies that a child who has started along the way will, on reaching adulthood, have climbed down from their parents' shoulders of faith and have chosen to continue walking along the way of wisdom. But it is important to remember that this thought is expressed in a proverb, not in a promise. It represents a general principle or axiom—not an absolute guarantee from God. In any event, this particular mature or adult decision is a watershed event, which normally establishes and reveals the heartset of the person and thus the probable trajectory of their whole life.

The crucial issue for us as parents is not what we know (although this is important) or how skilled we are at walking (although this is also important) *but whether or not we are actually walking in the way of wisdom ourselves*. Only then can we hope to start a child along this way. I'm not saying we must be perfect, for God's grace covers our humanness. The result is not determined by our performance, but by our dependence on His Spirit to work through us, and in our child, as this watershed event approaches.

Parents may try, sometimes desperately, to make their children conform to the way of wisdom. But, while a child may be forced to comply, no one can be forced to love. George Strait sings a song that expresses this truth:

You can't make a heart love somebody,
You can tell it what to do,
But it won't listen at all.
You can't make a heart love somebody,
You can lead it to love,
But you can't make it fall.[56]

We find our temporal and eternal identity, purpose, meaning, and fulfillment in the context of relationship—with God and with others. It is the web of meaning that connects all the components of our lives, making it possible for us to be whole physically and spiritually, and is not necessarily related to the amount of biblical doctrine that has been crammed into the child's head, or to how well the child's behavior and habits have been controlled by the parents. These efforts will be of little value without the child's willing heart. Navigators' founder Dawson Trotman said, "Discipline imposed from the outside eventually defeats when it is not matched by desire from within."[57]

This inward desire, capable of producing personal discipline from the inside out, can only come from love. We were made by Love, and for love. We do not love God because we must, but because "He first loved us."[58] We love God because He has romanced our hearts to Himself—through others, through creation, and through the cross.

THE ORIGINS OF ROMANCE

The word "romance" first appeared in southern France in the twelfth century, as the vernacular Latin word *romaz*. Later, usage spread to Italy and Spain. The verb "romance" described the process of wooing, drawing, or attracting for the purpose of winning the heart.

The noun "romance" described an extravagant story about the winning of a heart, usually characterized by great action, extraordinary adventure, chivalry, beauty, sacrifice, unconditional love, and the passions of wonder and curiosity. This type of story vaulted beyond the natural to the supernatural, soaring above the limits of empirical facts to ultimate truth as it dealt with the deepest matters of the heart. Romances were often sophisticated and psychologically insightful, with happy endings—as the heart that was romanced was won. Descriptive details were lavish as these love stories usually contained exotic, remote, and miraculous adventure. Often, a romance emphasized drama and human character, and the longsuffering of the romancer. Medieval authors (A.D. 1100-1400) wrote some of the greatest romances, including such classics as *King Arthur and the Knights of the Round Table*.

The Romantic Movement developed between 1700 and 1800. Romanticism emphasized passion rather than reason, and imagination and emotion rather than logic. It elevated all that is natural, promoting a pantheistic worship of nature. E. D. Hirsch Jr. implies in his article "Romancing Your Child" that romances not derived from a theistic worldview drip with disappointment and failure.[59]

Romanticism developed as a revolt against restrictive social conventions and unjust political rule. The gothic romances were written from this perspective. Romances by Sir Walter Scott and James Fennimore Cooper are famous examples. Although this type of romance literature was not usually about the winning of a heart, some works preserved this feature; for example, the powerful *Les Miserables* by Victor Hugo—a great story about grace versus justice.

Our current culture's concept of romance has grown largely out of a naturalistic worldview, in which there is no Creator—therefore no Author, no Hero, and no larger Story. We are a product of time, chance, and matter—biochemical entities alone in a universe ruled by chaos. Romance in the spiritual sense, therefore, cannot exist. Consequently, in our culture's eyes, the biblical romance is a simpleminded, naïve fairytale, and its Hero just a fool on the hill.

Another important factor in our culture is relativism—where no truth is absolute, and reality is what we wish it to be. We all have the right to make up our own truth, or create our own reality, as long as we don't force anyone else to accept it. This philosophical anarchy leads adherents into the lair of the great liar, Satan.

Toleration is the law where relativism reigns, except that the following claims are not tolerated: truth really does exist; some things are really real; some things are truly good (therefore, some are evil); God really does exist; and it is a good thing to teach these things to one's own children. We who long to romance our children to God and His way of wisdom are guilty, in our culture's eyes, of brainwashing our own children—tantamount to child abuse. We are arrogant "cultists" whose families are at risk to a degree that warrants government intervention.

Relativism is the antithesis and enemy of romance. Our culture stereotypes romance negatively, writing off any movie as "just a chick flick" if the main theme is human romance or relationship.

Although romance may appear to be an elastic word with many historical nuances, the genuine article is easy to recognize. A romantic person's soul is genuine and true, demonstrating such qualities as beauty, order, humor, peace, unconditional love, compassion, hope, enthusiasm, happiness, enchantment, and respect. A romantic person is a kindred spirit. "Big Story" romantics know that heaven is their destination, and so they cannot help but be full of smiles and joy.

My friend Jodi is an expert on the subject of romancing children, starting with her own, and a living example of how to win their hearts. She did her master's thesis on the essence of children—their hearts, and education—and now is the director of alternative education for a large city school district. During one of our long conversations over the years, when I had been researching and developing the material for this book, she asked me why romancing a child's heart is such a remote concept. I pondered this for months until I realized that "romance" is not a concrete term. It concerns relational truth more than propositional truth. We look for a formula, but romance is an abstract concept—the "smile of the heart."

Romance emanates from personality. This implies that it is not a passive trait, but a quality that flows out of a person. People have told me that when Jodi enters a room, she glows. Her whole being warms hearts and enlivens spirits.

By contrast, unromantic people are characterized by confusion, despair, dullness, fear, tension, boredom, skepticism, and cynicism—an inner deadness that sucks the life out of people around them. If there is a story in their lives, it is a tragedy from start to finish. Their hearts are hidden, held close and protected from the risk of relationship. They are strangers even to themselves. Most of their knowledge is theoretical and secondhand. They live from day to day without hope, and they seldom smile.

Most of us live somewhere between these extremes, swinging toward one or the other. For our children's sake, and our own, we need to spend as much time as we can at the romantic end. But we cannot put on romantic characteristics like a garment—they must come from the inside. If we want to romance our children's hearts, the truly pivotal watershed decision is our own. Do we yearn for a relationship with God that is characterized by firsthand knowledge and passionate love? Or are we content to know God in a theoretical, secondhand way?

Even as adults, we can be romanced to God. We can allow His love to penetrate our hearts like an arrow—not from the bow of Cupid, but from Christ.

THE ORIGINAL ROMANCER

The passion and longings of our Creator for us resound from Genesis to Revelation. In *The Sacred Romance*, Brent Curtis and

John Eldredge propose that our relationship with God is actually a love affair—a grand eternal Story or Romance, the pilgrimage or journey of a person's heart. Surely the result of such a journey will be far more than the so-called relationship with God so many Christians today seem to have because they "made a decision" or they "walked the aisle" or perhaps prayed a prayer they found at the end of an evangelistic booklet. The kind of relationship God wants with His own is not primarily intellectual in nature, or the believer's primary relationship would be with ideas, doctrines, theology, dogma, and "righteous" fulfillment of all the rules.

The relationship God desires with you and me is an affair of the heart—an eternally passionate Romance written before time began. God's intense emotional love pulsates through the voices of the Old Testament prophets: "For your Maker is your husband— …Though the mountains be shaken and the hills be removed, yet my unfailing love for you will not be shaken…."[60] Isaiah says that God experiences the same kind of joy over us as a bridegroom has for his bride.

God is a jealous God. In Him, jealousy is a positive virtue. In Scripture, it is presented in the metaphorical context of marriage where the husband is resolved to guard the marriage against attack. He is zealous about it—"a man of one mind." He will take action against anyone who violates it. He is grievously offended if His lover is inclined toward a rival. He burns with hottest jealousy, saying: "For I, the Lord your God, am a jealous God….for the Lord, whose name is Jealous, is a jealous God…."[61]

Jeremiah paints a picture of the passionately emotional nature of God's love: "I have loved you with an everlasting love…."[62] This love is depicted as consuming and fiery. He calls us His bride, pursues us as we run away from Him, and even agonizes over our rejection of Him. He says of His unfaithful people: "Therefore, behold, I will allure her, will bring her into the wilderness and speak comfort to her."[63]

The apostle Paul told us that, of faith, hope and love, "the greatest of these is love."[64] Philosopher Peter Kreeft says that, besides being greatest in value, love is also the greatest in size—that love is the meaning of the whole. He uses the imagery of the Song of Songs to paint a clear picture of the reality of the larger Story:

> We are all notes in God's symphony. When we listen only to our own note or to the few notes around us, it does not look like music or like love, but when we step back and look at the whole everything falls into place as great music….If you think you are making only meaningless noise, you are in Ecclesiastes' "vanity." If you think you are making music, you are in love. That is why Job is so dramatic: Job's question is ultimately: "Am I only making noise, or am I making music? Am I in vanity, or am I in love?"[65]

The primary value I see in the Song of Songs is that it elegantly legitimizes romance, placing this wonderful and dangerous realm into the spiritual context of the other dimensions of God's love that the Bible as a whole reveals. Other than in passing, explaining this is seldom even attempted from the pulpit. Perhaps this is another reason why the idea of romancing a child's heart may at first seem to be such a remote concept—to us, but thankfully not to God, since He thought of it.

Romantic human love, as depicted in the Song of Songs with all its longing, sadness, beauty, and joy, illumines the relationship of love between God and human beings. It also gives a high view of human romantic, sexual love and companionship, describing it in terms of beauty and wonder—even using the language of romantic fantasy. The author uses phrases that may seem, to the practical, rational Christian, almost embarrassingly passionate, intimate, and emotional, as he describes the relationship between lover and beloved.

The Song of Songs suggests that human love provides a way of understanding God's love. Three qualities of love are highlighted:

self-giving, desire, and commitment. We see through the highly sensual, rich imagery of the book that, just as with human love in the marital relationship, God delights in us, gives Himself to us, desires us wholly for Himself, and feels deeply both the pain and pleasure of relationship with us.

> *God's love for us is passionate, intimate, and emotional—in a word, romantic.*

God desires lovers, not guilt-driven moralists or Pharisees. He has held back nothing and has gone to extravagant lengths to win our hearts. This is clearly seen in the Scriptures. It is also seen in creation, a gift God made to dazzle us. As we smell a wildflower in the springtime, watch a blazing sunset over the desert, or witness a thunderstorm on a sultry summer afternoon, beauty and drama capture our hearts. Is the wonder we feel the response He hoped for as He created these things?

As a student of creation, I am confident that creation reveals another aspect of romance in God's heart. He is the first Quilter of prairies, the prime Painter of autumn colors, the archetypical Sculptor of mountains, the master Composer of the whippoorwill's song, and the original Poet of grace and truth. And He has imprinted His creative image in human hearts. This is why we have an innate desire, ability, and need to create. Our creativity—a reflection of Him—gives meaning to our lives. Burning curiosity, wonder at mystery, and delight at finding a solution that makes order visible—all these accompany creativity, giving us our fullest happiness and deepest satisfaction on earth.

Are the five senses He created in us specially intended for experiencing His creation—an extravagant gift of the Lover to His beloved? Why does Almighty God approach us so subtly, so gently, but so sumptuously? Could even time have been created in order to show us the heart of a longsuffering, patient Lover—Who gives us chance after chance after chance as He longs for us to come home?

One last word, which Philip Yancey has described as "the last best word," incarnates romance. No other word captures the essence of God's romance with us better than the word "grace." Grace is nearly synonymous with romance. It is at the center of the Sacred Romance. It demands nothing from us but that we shall await it. Yancey says, "Grace [comes] as it always [comes] free of charge, no strings attached, on the house. [Grace is] a gift that cost everything for the giver and nothing for the recipient."[66]

NOT JUST ANY RELATIONSHIP

If we will joyfully embrace God and His gracious, romantic love, knowing that this love cost Jesus everything and us nothing, we will be drawn into a love deeper than any human ever imagined— the perfect love experienced within the Trinity.

Jesus spoke of this love as it relates to us when He prayed "that they all may be one, as You, Father, are in Me, and I in You; that they also may be one in Us...."[67] It appears that God created us to share in the joy of His love. There is something here so basic to reality, so much a part of us, that we may tend to overlook it. God is interested in not just any relationship. He is interested in the kind of relationship found within the Trinity, and God apparently created marriage as a physical symbol of this spiritual reality that Paul refers to as "a great mystery."[68] Jesus prayed: "Holy Father, keep through Your name those whom You have given Me, that they may be one as We are."[69]

We may not be able to fathom what "one as We are" really means, but it certainly implies the greatest intimacy in relationship. Such intimacy can only be known within the context of unconditional love. Through being loved by God, and loving Him, we discover answers to life's most perplexing questions, including: "How did I come to exist?" "What is my purpose for being here?" "Where is everything heading?" and "What's it all about, anyway?"

It's all about love, which is the greatest—of faith, hope, and love—because it contains all the rest. God *is* love. And, because this is His essential nature, He created humanity to share this with Him.

Before the world existed, the Father, Son and Holy Spirit enjoyed unbroken loving relationship. Jesus said, in His prayer to the Father, "You loved Me before the foundation of the world."[70] We get a small glimpse of this indescribable fellowship when we sit around a dinner table or a campfire with close Christian friends and family. As we experience this fellowship, time stands still and we are immersed in the present—which is the only way to touch eternity, since God exists in the eternal present as the great *I Am*—the source of all being, in Whom we live and move and have our being. Such experiences are among the highest forms of pleasure and joy we can know on earth, as our souls mysteriously connect and we commune with each other and with God.

According to atheism, there is only human monologue, because there is no God and we are alone. According to pantheism there is only divine monologue, for all is God. It is only with theism that there is dialogue between God and us, and communion both horizontally and vertically. As Peter Kreeft points out, it is no accident that poetry and love songs, the product of romance, are written mainly in theistic cultures.

All of creation flows from the Triune fellowship—all of life, all of history. We are created with the potential to share this perfect intimacy and relationship, and God has placed within each human heart a longing for it. St. Augustine described it as a God-shaped vacuum—an innate knowledge that we were made for something more. The central, underlying principle of the universe is not about survival, chaos or chance, but about intimate relationship—with our Creator, Who loves us more than words can say, and has been wooing us to Himself since before the beginning of time.

When this divine Romance of our hearts becomes real for us, when its passion penetrates past our minds to our souls and we allow it to move us, emotionally, then we are ready to romance our children's hearts to this same loving God. This process will not be difficult, for, as I said about my friend Jodi (and as you have seen in others like her) it will flow from your inner self, like a stream of refreshing, life-changing water, to everyone with whom you have a relationship—including your children.

HEART-TO-HEART REALITY

Many Christians have looked to a particular passage in Deuteronomy as a blueprint for parenting: "And these words which I [God] command you today shall be in your heart. You shall teach them diligently to your children, and shall talk of them when you sit in your house, when you walk by the way, when you lie down, and when you rise up. You shall bind them as a sign on your hand, and they shall be as frontlets between your eyes. You shall write them on the doorposts of your house and on your gates."[71] We gravitate towards these things to "do" because they define a clear, straightforward list. In biblical times the Jews took this passage literally, and actually tied little boxes containing these verses on their arms and foreheads, and fastened them on their doorposts. This approach simplified their life, by compartmentalizing these truths.

Instructing our children in disciplines and imparting knowledge to them throughout the day seems to be the most obvious way to apply these verses to parenting. But the key to successful teaching of God's truth is the state of our hearts, which must be so permeated with the truth that what we teach is an overflowing of our relationship with God—not merely a repetition of correct ideas about God. This passage says "these words shall be in your heart"; a parallel passage says "lay up these words in your hearts."[72] Effective parental *doing* flows from *being*.

As fallen beings, we are naturally drawn to legalism. Relationship with a living person is less comfortable than relationship with a formula or a "to do" list. Legalism makes primary matters secondary and secondary matters primary. The Pharisees thought that by following the law impeccably they were closest to God, worthy of His love. The legalistic conscience is haunted by a vague uneasiness about ever being in a right relationship with God—which is why the Pharisees invented ever more convoluted ways in

Long before children can read words, they can read hearts.

which to fulfill the law of God. Legalists want to feel safe with God, but the closer they approach Him, the less safe He appears.

It is our personal relationship with God—knowing Him, not just knowing about Him—that makes us legitimate and believable to our children. Without this firsthand relationship with Jesus Christ, our overture will not be on pitch, and our words will sound hollow to a child's sensitive ears. We can romance a child without having a relationship with God, but in that case we will be romancing him to such things as materialism, legalism, agnosticism—effectively releasing him into the grip of the other suitor—Satan.

Romancing our child's heart requires heart-to-heart contact. Both hearts must be open and receptive. What a child reads in his parent's heart is the key that will unlock the door either to a heavenly romance or an earthly tragedy.

In the words of my friend Tia, "I wish I could always come from my time with the Lord so full of fresh insight, some delightful truth, some tender encouragement…that the Spirit of God overflows into my children, who then know how real and alive my Lover is. But when I neglect my time with Him, there is no supernatural overflow for them."

The Hebrews in the wilderness collected their manna every day. They were not allowed to store it up because God wanted them to learn that they were dependent on their relationship with Him for their daily needs. He wanted them to learn to live in the present. The proof of our genuine relationship with the living God is found in our daily gathering of His sweetness, His Story, and His beauty in a world that can be bitter, cold, and tragic. Like Israel in the wilderness, we must learn to live in the present—in moment-by-moment relationship with the One Who lives in the eternal present. In the present we touch eternity through our relationship with Christ. This is what enables us as parents to give, not only to our children, but also to anyone else He brings into our lives. And the giving does not diminish us, for the refreshment others receive is from the stream of His living water welling up from within our souls.

A mother I know said, "I thought of all the elements that you talked about in the delightful task of romancing our children's hearts, and the various tools the Lord has given us to do that. I read a bit from C. S. Lewis where he was mentioning our eagerness to simplify everything, even religion, and how God is actually wonderfully complex. Can you simplify the use of all of these things into one encounter? I feel that this is such a living and vital and constant part of my parenting, like a flowing river that has bends and rapids and calm pools. Romancing means meeting each [child] with the skill and life that the challenge pulls out of us. It's interactive, dependent on the need of the moment, and the needs of the children. All I know, as a mother daily living this, is that if I try to oversimplify something, I get frustrated. If I reach for a handle that can apply to everything, it can make me lazy about being responsive and alert to what the Spirit is saying."

My friend is describing the reality of a true relationship with God lived in the present, as she listens and responds to what the Spirit *is* saying. I think what makes one mother successful and the other not, even though they may "do" the same things, is whether they are having—at any given moment—a firsthand relationship with God. Their child will sense this more than anything, because long before children can read words they can read hearts. And romance happens because it comes through the mother from the Spirit of God.

People who *know* God impact us greatly. Someone who comes to my mind is a worship leader who was living in our community while looking for a new church in which to continue his ministry. Our small church had no worship leader at the time, so we asked him if he would lead worship for us on an interim basis. In a gracious, humble spirit, he agreed. I will never forget the first service. We all shuffled in, expecting the usual hymn singing. But something electric was in the air. The focus of that Sunday morning service was worship—not in theory, but in reality. He didn't bring in new songs or organize a contemporary worship band of professional quality. He relied on something else. I will never forget the spontaneous comments of the congregation in answer to the question, "What is so different?" The consensus was: "He must meet with God."

The good news is that anyone who wants to can meet with God. For Jesus said that the Father is seeking those who will worship Him in spirit and in truth. You can do this. It's not a matter of where you worship or how long your prayer times are or whether or not you have regular personal or family "devotions." It's a matter of the heart. And it's a matter of what you want. Jesus is waiting outside the heart's door to come in and have fellowship with whoever will open that door to Him: "Behold, I stand at the door and knock. If anyone hears My voice and opens the door, I will come in to him and dine with him, and he with Me."[73]

Will you open that door to Him? His invitation is always open. This is not so much a passage about how to be saved as how to have true fellowship with Him. I love the context—sitting around a table sharing a meal and sharing life. I trust this is what we all want for ourselves, and our children. I'd like to end this chapter with a prayer:

> Lord, You know my heart, and the heart of the parent reading these words. We long to know You and Your love more personally and passionately, a love that heals all wounds, forgives all failures, and lifts every burden, filling each heart with joy and a peace that passes all understanding. May this day-to-day experience of Your love become a continual wellspring of love for others, especially the children You have placed within our care. Draw them to Yourself, through us, and may we always help and never hinder this result. Amen.

7

PREREQUISITES TO ROMANCE

'Cause children's hearts are tender,
That's just the way they're made,
They're sent to us from heaven,
They stay a few short days.

Our daughter, Heather, was adventurous and outgoing as a little girl, providing unsolicited advice to adult strangers in the grocery store, capturing the lead role in musical dramas, and dreaming of becoming, of all things, a race-car driver when she grew up. She was a fearless skier—she always stood up when she shushed down a hill, while Travis, who is now an expert downhill skier, always sat down on his skis.

As with most children, the line between her imaginative fantasy and rational reality was blurred, with the result that her unhindered creativity took her on many adventures. Several times she ventured out alone on wilderness treks and got lost. One that I will never forget occurred during a new moon on a warm summer's night in the desert mountains west of Tucson, Arizona. That night you could not see your hand in front of your face. We had some guests over for dinner, and while we were distracted Heather disappeared into the night, wearing flip-flops and shorts.

The Sonoran desert is alive on summer nights—mountain lions, scorpions, rattlesnakes, javelina, Gila monsters, and a host of other creatures are out looking for a meal. Even now I cringe when I think of Heather walking through that jungle of cactus and over the sharp volcanic rocks that surrounded our house. It was hard enough to navigate there in daylight without being stuck, stabbed, poked, punctured, or pricked. I had no idea in which direction she had gone, and when we called for her there was no answer. How I found her an hour later I don't really know, but without doubt our confident, determined little Heather had a very special—and very busy—guardian angel.

So when, at about age ten, Heather became shy and timid, and her physical growth seemed to be slowing down, we took her to a growth specialist to determine whether these changes had a medical cause. The specialist did many tests and concluded that nothing was wrong, except that Heather's developmental pattern did not match the norm of the bell curve. Her development was normal *for her*, but she would be a late bloomer—about three years late, based on an x-ray of Heather's hand—and we should expect her cognitive and emotional development to follow a similar course. The specialist added, "You should try to enjoy Heather's extra-long childhood. Kids grow up too fast these days anyway. One day they're little; the next day they're in college."

We also took Heather to an educational specialist, who shared with us a simple but powerful metaphor. She told us that Heather was like a rosebud. If we pulled the petals apart before they were ready to open, we would bruise and damage the rose. But if we waited patiently, the flower would open according to its own timing and become the sweet and beautiful rose God had planned it to be. We followed the advice and her prediction came true—Heather has blossomed into a special, sweet, beautiful adult.

As Heather's age-mates moved quickly on in life, she continued to live at home. She attended a community college and eventually graduated from a culinary arts school. Since then she has worked on numerous dude ranches and is happy living out the romantic dreams most young women only wish for. She also drives a classic 1977 Ford 250 pickup truck with a roll bar—a vehicle that most young men would love to own. I am glad that her race-car-driving passion landed in such a safe place. Recently she attended a Bible college in Wyoming, and now she feels that God is leading her into geriatrics, so she found a job at a life-care center and then began to study for certification as a nurse's assistant. Children and old folks love her childlike spirit and her loving and generous heart.

I'll never forget the day that Heather laid aside her dog-eared Berenstein Bears storybook to pick up a historical novel. Just as the doctor had predicted, she moved from one stage to the next almost overnight. Had we forced the issue earlier just because Heather was "too old" for her bear books, we would have only frustrated her, quenching her spirit and wounding her heart— bruising and damaging the flower. Knowing her timetable enabled us to protect her heart—giving it time to develop and ultimately giving us access to it.

A child's heart isn't a container into which you pour romance at your convenience. A child's heart is more like a garden. The soil needs to be cultivated, and the timing must be right. Fertile soil takes time to develop—to be ready to receive seed. And then, as love takes root, it must be protected and nurtured.

Too often we rush in, caught up in the busyness and complexity of life, expecting our children to follow the timetable of our particular romance agenda. It is like planting seeds out of season in soil that is untilled and not fertile. Whether we like it or not, there is a window of opportunity for romance that is open for a specific time—and then it closes.

Eric and Leslie Ludy, in their book *When God Writes Your Love Story*, make the point that a young man is in essence defrauding a girl if he romances her before he has earned the privilege through the ability to support her financially or to provide a home. Similarly, parents need to earn the privilege to romance their children. Certain prerequisites are required if parents are to gain the privilege and right of courting—and ultimately winning—their child's heart.

BECOME A STUDENT OF YOUR CHILD

It is virtually impossible to romance the heart of a person we do not know. We need to begin preparing for the romance by becoming students of our children. We must really come to know them. This kind of knowing requires ongoing research, observation, and data gathering, since children are continually growing and changing, developing and maturing. Whether our children are early or late bloomers, our task remains the same.

Our culture's concept of parenting is out of sync with children—in fact, our culture's concept of *children* is out of sync with children. I heard a radio newscaster launch a report with the statement: "Children are our most valuable commodity." Children are not commodities. They are individuals, worthy of respect. David Elkind, in his bestseller about the "hurried child" syndrome, wrote, "We are going through one of those periods in history, such as the early decades of the Industrial Revolution, when children are the unwilling victims of societal upheaval and change."[74] Charles Dickens built many of his greatest works around this type of child abuse.

Ironically, many of today's politicians pretend that everything is "for the children," while in fact children are just pawns, not only for professional politicians, but for business and entertainment companies, some of which would say: "Children are our most valuable *customers*."

In many homes, one or both parents work long hours, returning home exhausted and stressed over ever-mounting debt, while convincing themselves that they are doing it "for the children"—so that their children can have the latest gadget, gizmo, game, trinket, or toy. The children are left to raise themselves. Or rather, to be raised by things—television, videotapes, videogames, MTV, the Internet. Elkind says that this assault on children has produced crippled, hurried, and stressed "latchkey kids," who "mimic adult sophistication while secretly yearning for innocence...." This trend has "fourth graders dieting to fit into designer jeans and children of divorce asked to be the confidants of their troubled parents." Elkind suggests that forcing young children to make adult decisions and value judgments is developmental hurrying, which occurs "whenever we ask children to understand beyond their capacity to make decisions or to act willfully before they have the will to act." In a phrase, "they're all dressed up, with no place to go."

Elkind further states that research, clinical experience, and expert opinion have documented these childhood development patterns, which clearly indicate that it is incorrect and unhealthy to ignore them.[75]

Childhood development can be divided into three stages. During the first stage, the child is primarily an emotional being. The senses, coordination, and cognitive ability are developing and coming together, but they are not in balance. The child is not ready to assimilate a heavy diet of facts, or to face serious moral dilemmas. Often, simple things such as low blood sugar just before a meal will profoundly affect their personality. Peer pressure and highly structured academics are likely to damage a child who has not progressed beyond this stage. If this first developmental hurdle is ignored, a child's wonder, creativity, and curiosity can be starved, stifled, and possibly crushed before they reach third grade. The childlike nature may become adultish, defensive, and cynical. Children hurried in this way lose their fluidity of mind, and their spirits shrink, pull inside, and close. For example, children forced to read before they are developmentally ready commonly have lifelong reading problems.

CHILD DEVELOPMENT CHART

CHILD	ADOLESCENT	ADULT

Cognitive Being

Emotional Being

Adolescent Crisis
Puberty

LEVEL OF DEVELOPMENT

PROTECTION

PREPARATION

STAGE 1   STAGE 2   STAGE 3

Integration of senses. Coordination Cognition

Balancing of Right-left Brain Lobes

Kinesthetic - Auditory - Visual Balance
Corpus Collosum Sheathing
Growth Completed

CHILDHOOD
fantasy-reality continuum
strong creativity / curiosity and
sense of wonder

ADULTHOOD
able to handle: winning / losing
goal setting
moral dilemmas

GRAMMAR   LOGIC   RHETORIC

AGE   5   10   15   20   25   30

The second stage begins when the child's senses and coordination come together. Typically, this correlates with being ready to read, to handle some academic structure and limited peer pressure. The child continues to be an emotional creature, and has a difficult time understanding such things as winning, losing, and goal setting. The line between fantasy and reality is often blurred, and the imagination soars high and free. Broad exposure to nature and life through actual physical experience and good books is strongly recommended. This is the stage in which our daughter remained several years longer than her age-mates.

In the third stage, the child makes the transition from an emotional to a cognitive being. The balancing of the two lobes of the brain and the development of the corpus callosum—the nerve connection between the brain's two lobes—usually occurs between ages eleven and thirteen, and is often accompanied by what is referred to as an "adolescent crisis." New studies show that this maturation is occurring later—sometimes not until between the ages of nineteen and thirty. Stress is thought to delay this development—the body's ultimate balancing act. Until this process is complete, intense focusing on goals, competition, and moral dilemmas (some within families, though many come from movies and TV), is confusing and detrimental to the child's development.

Ignoring the importance of this developmental transition can cripple a child's spirit and cause chronic low-grade stress that may become a lifelong pattern. Experiments on animals have suggested that the thickness of the nerve sheathing around the corpus callosum—which correlates with the brain's ability to think cognitively—is affected by environment. The experiments concluded that natural environments—as opposed to high-stimulation or sterile environments—contributed to maximum physical brain development. This implies that a safe, secure home, unstructured play, and exploration of nature will help give your child the maximum possible physical brain development.

In 1997 the national media reported that research concerning the effects of television on children's brains had shown that it is not the content but the nature of television that is most detrimental to children. TV negatively affects their brain function and impedes their development by mesmerizing them into a paradoxical hyperactive, yet passive state. Television patterns permeate children's brains, leaving little room for active, creative, and critical thinking.

Jean Healy tells us "the deprivation of appropriate stimuli can dramatically—and perhaps irrevocably—limit the brain's potential, regardless of genetic inheritance." She also calls the tube "public enemy number one" because [I summarize] it artificially manipulates the brain into paying attention by violating its natural defense mechanisms with frequent visual and auditory changes; it induces neural passivity and reduces "stick-to-it-ive-ness"; it may have a hypnotic and possibly neurologically addictive effect on the brain by changing the frequency of its electrical impulses in ways that block normal mental processing; it has all but displaced reading as a leisure activity; and its "Sesame Street" type of educational programming is a total sensual assault on children's brains. (Sesame Street "alumni" find reading boring.)[76]

One moonlit summer night years ago, I went for a walk through a neighborhood in Tucson, Arizona. The perfume of blooming cacti and mesquite was in the air. All was peaceful and quiet. But something was wrong. The front porches were empty, and from every window came an eerie blue glow—light from color television sets. The situation inspired these lyrics: "Empty porches asked me, 'Where have all the children gone?' And from windows, unholy lights told of good deeds left undone." These words captured my sadness over television's impact on children when their parents are, as the song goes on to say, "In a daze."

Other factors contribute to childhood development. These include temperament, learning style, birth order, and personality type. *The Way They Learn: How to Discover and Teach to Your Child's Strengths* by Cynthia Tobias (Focus on the Family Publishing, 1994) offers excellent insights on this subject. But we must be careful not to use any of this information in a purely deterministic way. Children tend to embrace labels and stereotyping, and live according to those expectations—even using them as an excuse for wrong behavior.

A final developmental factor—one that profoundly affected my own development and that of one of my sons—concerns vision. Verbal development, auditory-verbal match, sensory-motor skills, health, nutrition, emotional state, and heredity are important, but visual development is by far the most important—for it connects and relates all these together.

When one of our sons began to endure many headaches, we took him to the local pediatrician who said that the cause was probably diet or eyestrain. We then took him to an optometrist who just happened to have a special interest in childhood development. He discovered that our son's eyes converged objects closer than the actual distance of the objects he was focusing on, and so he was tending to see double. This caused him to do more neurological work than normal, as his brain tried to bring the double image together. It tired him out, and eventually caused headaches. He now has reading glasses with prism lenses that allow his eyes to relax as he reads. He says the page is clearer and he doesn't get sleepy any more. He is also doing visual perception developmental exercises, which strengthen the eyes to solve the convergent problem so in the future he will not need glasses.

If our timing is off, and we ignore the rhythm of relationship, we may miss the music and pass right by their heart.

Not discovering this one thing could have had profound implications for our son's education—and his life. Improper convergence causes a whole array of symptoms, such as daydreaming, short attention span, and headaches, and it forces a child to waste energy by compensating with the other senses. Fortunately, because of my own experience as a child, I was able to recognize that our son had this problem before damage occurred.

BE SENSITIVE

Genuinely sensitive parents will naturally know their child—for they listen, they watch, and they touch. They are capable of sensing minute changes because all their senses are tuned in to their child's physical, emotional, sociological, and spiritual status. They are aware of the child's needs and interests, joy or pain.

Sometimes, however, even normally sensitive parents can act insensitively.

One summer, we decided to take a two-week whirlwind tour of Wyoming, Montana, Utah, and Colorado. Our vision was to give our two oldest children in particular an overview of all the national parks and monuments of the region, so the trip involved many short stops with long periods of driving in between.

We set out confidently, and everything seemed to be going well, although stopping at nearly every road cut to let our nine-year-old son Dawson out to collect rocks, wood, and bones was slowing us down and turning our vehicle into a traveling museum. This did fit in with our strategy of using creation to romance his heart to God, but eventually we had to curtail his explorations to save time—so that we could accomplish our objective.

Soon after we made that decision, we noticed that Dawson seemed to be struggling with something. I watched him in the rearview mirror as we drove—his face contorted and his body straining to get loose from the seat belt. We tried to reason with him, but it didn't help much. His brain did not seem to be connected with his heart. It reminded me of the difficulty I had experienced sitting at a desk in a grade school classroom, hour after hour, year after year. Dawson's struggle came and went in waves. Soon he lost his desire to look out the window, and even refused to look at the sights we pointed out. He began giving his older brother and sister trouble. Such behavior was not normal for him.

When we did stop, Dawson hit the ground running, and took off toward the horizon. We will never forget watching him climbing barefoot up a red and pink sandstone mountainside until he was just a tiny dot in the distance. We wondered what drew him up there. When he came down, he was carrying three different-colored sandstone specimens, and his pockets were full of sand he had collected for his "museum" at home.

At the end of a very long drive, we stopped at the North Rim of the Grand Canyon. But Dawson didn't even want to look over the edge, and we had a difficult time keeping him on the trail. At Lake Powell, after another long drive, he disobeyed us as we let him out for a couple of minutes to look over the rim of the canyon at the water a thousand feet below. He took off running and would not stop when we called. This was blatant defiance and I knew it was time to discipline him. But I felt terrible because I suspected that we were causing the problem.

Ironically, we had stopped during the trip to speak at a conference in Utah, where we had presented our ideas about romancing your child's heart. We had urged the parents there to be sensitive to their children. We had described teaching from the inside out instead of from the outside in. As we reflected on the conference, a novel thought occurred to me: *Why not practice what you teach?*

At the conference, we had used Dawson as an example of a hands-on learner who loves to explore and experience nature. For days we had been touring the beautiful Rocky Mountains—a trip that Dawson had anticipated intensely as we planned it together. With his kinesthetic learning style and adventuresome spirit, Dawson longed to touch, taste, smell, and hear what the rest of us were content to see mostly through the car window as we whirled on by. Dawson needed to experience God's creation as much as he needed to eat. He was hungry for it, and frustrated because our trip thus far had been like taking a tour of a cafeteria, only pausing from time to time for a few tiny bites of the tantalizing food.

Soon after I realized the dynamics of all this, I spied a mountainside of layered sedimentary rocks. Dawson and I took on that mountain with rock hammers in hand and empty packs on our backs, while the rest of the family sat in the vehicle reading and watching the naturalists explore. The naturalists, meanwhile, were discovering that each layer was filled with fossils and rocks with fascinating color and texture. Dawson was transformed in those few minutes into a serious young scientist—a mature adult in miniature. I was in awe of my little boy. His enthusiasm was contagious, and made the experience wonderful. Coming down with packs, pockets, and arms full of rocks, Dawson began hypothesizing and sharing the geologic history of the mountain with us all. His older brother and sister just smiled; the real Dawson had returned. He was satisfied for a long time after that. And whenever we sensed that he was "hungry" again, we stopped and let him "feast" upon creation.

In order to become more sensitive, parents must pay attention—make it a daily priority to concentrate consciously on each child. The other component is time—both quality and quantity time. Quantity time is probably the most difficult for a parent to spend today in our fast-paced lives. But sometimes a child may need an entire day with us before they will share what is really on their heart. If your experience is like mine, this tends to happen during the last few minutes of the drive home together. Why do they wait so long? This is the rhythm of relationship. If our timing is off and we ignore the rhythm, we miss the music, repudiate the relationship, and pass right by their heart.

Is a whole day with them too high a price to pay for a few minutes of heart-to-heart conversation? Not on your life. Nothing substitutes for a large quantity of quality time. Sensitivity requires patience, patience requires time, and time together is the stuff of which relationships are made.

SHOW UP

My father was consistently strong, compassionate, and positive. He put relationships first, beginning with his love and respect for my mother. I cannot recall that he ever lost his temper.

Despite working long hours, sometimes to the point of exhaustion, Dad spent time with his sons. He attended every basketball game I played (as well as all my brothers' games—nearly five hundred in all). He took my brothers and me on trips from coast to coast, so we could experience America firsthand. He made us a baseball diamond with a huge backstop fashioned from telephone poles he split by hand. He built shelves in our bedrooms, and drawers to hold the things we were always collecting. And, as we grew older, he allowed us to help with certain projects, sometimes stepping back to let us work things out ourselves.

Are we responding to their behavior, or to their hearts?

My mother's sensitive, loving heart set the atmosphere of our home. Despite a tragic automobile accident that cast a dark shadow over her close-knit family when I was three, Mom found sunshine where she could. She protected my time, giving me freedom to run uninhibited in my explorations and creative projects. My Saturdays were not crowded with chores, because she knew that I needed a respite from the many hours and pressures of school. She was always there for us with soothing words and actions, protecting me in so many ways.

In order to achieve heart-to-heart intimacy with a child, we must be there with our whole being, not just physically while our mind is distracted by concerns of yesterday or tomorrow. The greatest challenge for some parents in the romance of their child's heart is simply to show up for the romance. Fathers in particular have this problem because they tend to have a narrow focus. They are wired this way and for good reason—because their traditional roles include protector and provider for the family. But when they are overly focused and miss important moments and opportunities to be with their child, this strength becomes a weakness. Just try to have a conversation with a man who is watching television. Chances are he will not even notice you are there. The culture has picked up on this tendency and stereotyped and ridiculed men with jokes and stories. (Of course, this applies to some women nearly as much as to men.)

I have often wondered why it is so enjoyable to sit around a dining room table or a campfire with some people, while with others it is uncomfortable, even stressful, laborious, and irritating. I can almost hear the sucking sound as they drain my emotional tank. Often I feel that they have an agenda for me—I am just an object slotted into their schedule, or they want to use our friendship to make money in some pyramid scheme. What has always confused me is that it does not seem to matter how many things we have in common, how "Christian" they are, whether they are related to me or not, or even if they have unquestionable integrity.

I think the primary reason for the difference has to do with who or what they are relating to at the time we are together. People I enjoy being with have a relationship with *me*. They are here in the present with me. They are respecting and honoring me by being with me, and it feels good. People I don't feel good about being with live in the past or the future, and are relating to something or someone there—a mission, morality, good deeds, a goal, a person—any number of things. But it is clear that their heart is somewhere else, implying that whatever has their attention is more important than spending time with me. I might as well be alone. In fact, I'd rather be alone.

A close friend and mentor of mine, Gene Swanson, once said, "All our major family decisions were made around a campfire." Gene had a well-used fire pit encircled with stones near his home. It was also rigged with traditional cast iron utensils that have been used to cook many wonderful meals. We caught this vision from Gene and have built our own fire pit, cradled in a natural amphitheater just below our house. I staked logs into the concave hillside for seating. Two aspen trees serve as sentinels and the evening thermals always flow down hill, carrying the wood smoke away from where we sit.

A campfire almost demands narration and response from those sitting around it. Everyone has a story, as the circle of light and warmth draws us in out of the darkness. We feel far from the distractions of our urgent world. We are also not on a stage—expected to perform. We are just here, now, together. Campfires magically create a sense of camaraderie and community in the people encircling the fire, from children to adults, providing a setting where the deepest communication can occur, not merely through words, but intuitively, through feelings—the connector of human hearts.

COMMUNICATE—HEART TO HEART

Children need more than to *know* they are loved unconditionally. They need to *feel* it. They need to touch our love, hold it in their hands, and feel that it is theirs. This gives them emotional wholeness. Children are sensitive and emotional beings—not cognitive adults. Their fund of knowledge is small and they communicate primarily through their feelings. The eyes of the heart determine how they perceive family members, their home, their friends, and the world.

Ross Campbell says that children's emotional need for love and affection is paramount in their lives. How these emotional needs are met determines what they feel and how they behave—both the state of their hearts and their outward response. Children have emotional "tanks" that need to be filled. A child with an empty tank may be angry, depressed, disobedient, whiny, and withdrawn. This child has nothing to give—is empty, a flat tire. But a child with a full tank is joyful, obedient, content, and playful—filled with creative energy.[77]

Children use behavior to communicate their feelings, and they recognize our feelings by our behavior. They are more skillful at this than adults, because they are less distracted. We think that our words have power in themselves to communicate our feelings to our children, because we underestimate our children's ability to "listen" to the way we behave. They read between the lines and they are watching us all the time.

Children are naturally generous. They freely give when their tanks are full. Only then can they be expected to be moved by our romance. There is rarely an exception to this, for children by their nature are responsive even to the feeblest adult attention. But if we don't fill their tanks, they will eventually get them filled somewhere else, and possibly respond to another—a false—romance.

Gary Chapman in his book on the love languages shares five ways that parents can fill their children's emotional tanks: words of affirmation, quality time, giving gifts, acts of service, and physical touch.[78] In order to keep our children's emotional tanks fill-able, we must avoid poking holes in them by overreacting to childish behavior that may on the surface appear to be defiance. As long ago as 1978, Dr. James Dobson wrote, "Our objective [as parents] is not only to shape the will of the child…but to do so without breaking his spirit."[79] Nothing breaks the spirit of a child faster than punishing him for just acting like a child.

When Dawson was four years old, he built a fort out of pillows in our parlor. At the end of the day Karey went to help him put the pillows back in their proper places. She reached down to pick up the first pillow and it would not move. She tried another—and then another. They were all nailed through the carpet into the sub-floor! She just stood there in amazement—and then laughed and even praised Dawson for his creativity (of course making sure that he understood this was not at all good for the pillows or the carpet). He has never done it again. She often shudders as she imagines how she would have reacted had this happened when our older children were young, when she was less experienced and knowledgeable about a child's creativity, spirit, defiance, and will.

Our older children, Heather and Travis, would probably never have thought of doing anything like that. They are simply wired differently from Dawson. I suspect that, had they done the same thing, it would have been an act of defiance. There are some difficult judgments a parent must make, but I would rather err on the side of grace, by interpreting such actions as childishness. I would rather overprotect than under-protect their spirits.

Punishing a child for anything apart from purposeful disobedience is risky. In fact, how we respond to offensive behavior or misbehavior in our children reflects on us, and judges us. Are we responding to their behavior, or to their hearts?

As a boy, I always knew that there were certain "lines in the sand" my parents drew that I had better not cross. Once, when I was twelve, after some neighbor girls complained about my BB gun, Mom and Dad told me to be more careful. Later, I was down by a neighbor's pond with some friends and my BB gun. For a while I was content shooting at various inanimate objects in the water. But, egged on by one of the other boys, I rolled five BBs into the barrel of the gun, and then shot them all at once, like a shotgun, at a duck.

One BB hit the water about thirty feet out—and fifty feet short of the duck. Another hit the water at twenty feet, another at fifteen, another at thirteen, and the last one plopped into the pond at ten feet. I thought it was an intriguing experiment in kinetic energy.

My mother disagreed. When I came home, she met me halfway up our driveway, yanked the gun from my hands, and wrapped it around the trunk of the nearest black cherry tree. She ordered me to turn my bike around and head for the florist, to pick up flowers for the lady who owned the pond. I was to deliver them in person, and apologize for killing her duck.

Now, it was the boy who had egged me on who killed the duck. I hadn't come anywhere near to hitting it. But, in my mother's eyes, I was guilty by association and by action. I was speechless before her passion for justice.

Delivering the flowers and apologizing for something I hadn't done was both awkward and humiliating, but it taught me never to cross a line my parents drew. Although Mom later said she had a strong feeling of compassion for me, and that she felt bad about trashing the gun, she never regretted doing it. I got the point, and didn't make that mistake again. The line I crossed that day was like a solid wall that did not move. It gave me a very real sense of security that I wouldn't have had if my parents were more lenient.

SHELTER AND PROTECT

Sometimes people have asked me: "Aren't you overprotecting your children?" To me, this question is illogical and fundamentally flawed. Of course I am overprotecting my children! I would never think of under-protecting them. As John Neider wrote: "When young children are morally assaulted they suffer from confusion which produces deep-seated anxieties and profound insecurities. Their young minds cannot comprehend information presented by an increasingly sick adult world."[80]

Our culture under-protects our children in the name of "preparation." This idea, too, is fundamentally flawed. In their book *Saving Childhood*, the Medveds say that preparation should mean learning such life skills as homemaking and family headship. By contrast, our secular society believes that children should be prepared to live in a world permeated by violence, sex, and drugs. Children are exposed to these things at younger and younger ages so that they may become "moral-dilemma literate." The world may believe that this is necessary preparation for adulthood, but in reality all it is doing is shredding them and their innocence. Before puberty, children need to be children. Early destruction of innocence does them long-term damage, and can cripple them with chronic psychological and spiritual problems as adults.[81] This perspective closely follows the childhood development stages I have already described. Protection decreases, and preparation increases, at appropriate age and developmental levels.

The challenge for us as Christian parents is how to protect them and shield them from this assault. Our children are entrusted to us and we are responsible to God for their welfare. For some, this will mean closely monitoring their children's friends and extracurricular activities, or even philosophically examining family vacation plans. Limiting Internet access and eliminating unwholesome videogames is an obvious action. For a few it may require a radical step, such as moving to a new community, simplifying their lifestyle, or considering educational alternatives such as homeschooling. For others it may simply mean controlling or throwing away the television, and closely screening and limiting home videos.

The amount of profanity—and particularly the taking of the Lord's name in vain—in home videos is much greater than most

Christians realize. Many movies built around a great story, with positive characters and quality production, have questionable or even blasphemous language strategically sprinkled throughout, as though we were being subtly conditioned to accept it. We would never tolerate this from other sources. As we watch, an objectionable word flashes by, but we continue to sit there, in the grip of the story. This sends a message to our children. We may rationalize this away by thinking that they will have to face this someday, so why not let them face it in the safety of our home? But surely this is counter to biblical thinking: "Finally, brethren, whatever things are true, whatever things are noble, whatever things are just, whatever things are pure, whatever things are lovely, whatever things are of good report, if there is any virtue and if there is anything praiseworthy— meditate on these things."[82]

One simple, practical way to stop the barrage of crude words, profanity, and filth flowing from our video monitors is to purchase an electronic filter for the VCR or cable TV, which can be programmed for specific words. A typical PG-rated movie will commonly contain at least fifty words to which Christian parents would never expose their children in other settings. This technological marvel screens them out as you watch. It is available from "Curse Free TV" (call toll free 1-877-662-8773 or check the web site www.1cursefreetv.com).

When Dawson was eight, we once asked him to describe his favorite night. He gave us heaven-sent insight and wisdom when he said that his favorite night is when we are all home and we read and do crafts together as a family. No videos, no Internet, no friends over, no television, no entertainment, no special treats—just family, stories, and creativity. The song "Once Upon A Time" by Michael Martin Murphy echoes this sentiment:

So turn the TV off,
Put the video games away,
Come sit down beside me,

ROMANCING YOUR CHILD'S HEART

Tell me what you did today.
And I'll sit you down and
I'll take you around to a
World of fantasy, where
Anything you dream tonight
Waits there for you and me.[83]

How many nights like this do we experience? How many adults comprehend that this is what children desire, deep down in their hearts? Obviously this will not be very palatable for children who have already been captured by the competition. "Boring" would be the first word out of their mouths at the suggestion of the night Dawson described. But, to him, a night like that, together, is great, because it is focused on our relationship as a family.

DEMONSTRATE ONENESS

For most of my childhood, I lived in a one-story house that my dad built. Every workday morning, throughout my childhood, I heard my mother get up at a quarter to four. I remember the aroma of coffee drifting into the bedroom I shared with my brother. Mom packed my dad's lunch box while breakfast was cooking. At four, she woke him, and they talked together as they ate. Dad left for work in the predawn darkness, many times returning home after sundown, having worked ten or twelve hours through stifling heat and humidity, or sub-zero cold. I often lay awake in bed between the time Dad left and the time we were supposed to get up, wondering at my parents' strength to do this day after day. Their commitment, dedication, and willingness to sacrifice for their children—whatever it took—gave me a genuine sense of security.

My parents were a team, pressing on together toward the common goal of raising their sons. I believe it was their unconditional love, more than anything else, that won our hearts then, and that still binds us to them as adults.

Jay Kesler, former president of Youth for Christ, observed that, after many years of counseling young people, the only common thread he found among successfully raised children was that their parents hugged each other. Parents who are not intimate friends, sharing the same goals for their family, do not ordinarily hug very much.

The only common thread he found among successfully raised children was that their parents hugged each other.

They also do not ordinarily pray together, which is one of the keys to developing and maintaining the intimacy in marriage that will draw children to Christ. Once when I was addressing a hundred Christian men I asked, "How many of you regularly pray with your wife?" Three hands went up. It turned out that one man did not understand the question and another was kind of hedging. Only one out of a hundred did actually pray regularly with his wife.

Why? Some men have told me that they find it difficult to move to an intimate relational level with their wife. It is emotionally awkward and hard work, so they avoid it. Beyond this, once a man has forced himself to do it and he is over the initial awkward embarrassing feeling, it is even harder for him to make it a daily discipline because of modern schedules and logistics.

One father told me that the reason he avoids praying with his wife is because he is afraid the prayer will become a ritual and a moralistic platform for preaching to her. I suppose this may be a danger, but I think it is worth the risk. After all, we take the risk of colliding with another vehicle every time we drive, but we still get behind the wheel.

A husband needs to catch the eternal vision and perspective of the larger Story—the Sacred Romance—if he is to begin praying with his wife. Otherwise, it will be just a performance anyway. Sometimes, it requires a shock to his life, such as being told that his wife is terminally ill. Every man I have known who has been in this situation began earnestly praying both with and for his wife.

Perhaps the main reason most men avoid this issue is that they don't really know what praying is. Once we get the idea, we realize that life is one long prayer. I think the apostle Paul meant this when he said "pray without ceasing."[84] The external act of prayer is not really praying, but getting ready to pray, as our "living" now is but a preparation for real life. Real prayer begins when we get up off our knees. The "getting ready" part sweeps away the distractions and sets our mind on God's plan for the day. When we invite God's company on the day's journey, we will have ceaseless communion, perpetual dialogue with Him. Prayer isn't something we do as a means to an end. It is an attitude, part of who we are, a practical way to know God and be known by Him—in the present, where He constantly dwells.

As we parents walk the way of wisdom, inviting our children to walk with us, the most important thing is that we walk together, always aware that we have a divine companion walking with us and living in us. This is why prayer infuses the power of God into any relationship, especially marriage.

Several years ago, our friend Vicky Goodchild asked me to write a song about relationship. Her idea had a counter-intuitive twist to it, which provided a great hook for the song. She said, "Monte, the most important love we can give our children is not the love we give them directly through our relationship with them, but the love we give them indirectly through the love we have for our spouse."

This is oneness demonstrated. A husband and wife loving each other provide security to their children, and paint a living picture of Jesus Christ and His bride, the church. The chorus for the song goes like this:

And they'll know that we love them
By the way that you love me,

And the way that I love you
Is what they want to see.
You can't buy it with silver
And words will never do
All that really matters is
You lovin' me; me lovin' you.[85]

This does not mean that single parents cannot successfully romance their child's heart. God's grace and power can overcome the challenge of providing a sound foundation for the home without the husband/wife relationship. A single parent can communicate the spiritual truth that underlies a marital relationship if he or she is in relational oneness with Christ. And God has promised that He is "father of the fatherless, a defender of widows."[86] His special sustaining grace is extended to those who lack the equivalent human relationship.

Mentoring is a crucial ministry that the church can extend to single parent families. A friend who is a single parent described it to me this way: "A father and mother together see with two eyes—dimensionally, in stereo—while a single parent sees with only one eye." Depth of perception is more difficult, so it is important for a single parent to find godly mentors who can help bring a three-dimensional perspective into the life of their child. Two-parent families that open their homes to single-parent families give children without a father or a mother the opportunity to see and feel the oneness of a husband/wife relationship, which provides them with a framework on which to hang their developing understanding of God's relationship with His children.

Oneness is foundational to the prerequisites to romance. Parents living in true oneness, entering their child's world together, give authenticity to the message that they love their child with a true and good heart—as God does, Who even stepped down from heaven to walk among us in sacrificial love. Entering our child's world in the way Christ entered ours prepares the soil—and the soul—for the romance. This parental incarnation is central to the romance of a child's heart.

8

PARENTAL INCARNATION

So we traveled on back in my memories,
We got lost in boyhood dreams:
Baggy pants and a fishin' pole,
And carefree sunny days—
The child in me and my little boy
Became the best of friends.

When our friend Ray comes home from work, his priority is to enter the small world of each of his children. The second he walks in the door, he lays aside his adult power and positions himself on his kids' level—first on his knees, eventually lying on the floor with the kids climbing all over him. Then, even if there is only five minutes of daylight left, he will often grab a ball and take his kids outside to play because he knows that now, not later sometime, is really the only time he has available for his children. He has played many games of basketball with them on his knees.

In order to envision this, you need to know that Ray holds the record for tackles as a linebacker for that college football powerhouse, the former national champion Colorado Buffaloes. Yet this big man has a passion for small things, from miniature cars to shadow boxes. His fingers are the biggest in the house, but he can untie the tiniest knot on his kids' sneakers.

As Ray engages in physical activity with his children, wrestling or playing catch, he continually shares with them facts and information he learns at work or in his reading. His older children are following his lead, sharing what they learn with the younger ones just as their dad does with them. As Ray and the kids watch a football game on television, they constantly discuss the finer points of the game—offense, defense, the game plan and various strategies, refereeing, replays. In this way, he redeems even the time spent watching an athletic event.

Ray told me once, "It's like giving up being an adult for a little while. And it's not easy. I didn't have any role models, growing up in a dysfunctional non-Christian family. One reason I do this with my kids now is because I wish somebody had done it with me. But the biggest reason is that I want to have a close relationship with them—as close as possible—in order to win their hearts for Christ."

C. S. Lewis's Narnian logic would say that entering a child's world as an adult is hard because our adult world is actually the smaller world, constricted by adultish logic, limits, and concerns. The world of children is infinitely larger—its boundaries stretch to the limits of the imagination. It is filled with wonder, mystery, and adventure. Hope and optimism rule.

"And," says Ray, "when I'm in their world, the cares of mine go away for a while."

When Ray enters the world of his children he is following the example of Jesus, Who entered our world in order to deliver God's message of love and to fulfill His plan of redemption—in person. "And the Word became flesh and dwelt among us....No one has seen God at any time. The only begotten Son, Who is in the bosom of the Father, He has declared Him."[87]

IF JESUS WERE A PARENT

Theologians call Jesus' taking on flesh "incarnation," from the Latin words meaning "in flesh." The apostle Paul's celebration of Christ's choice reads like a hymn—which it is in the original Greek:

> Let this mind be in you which was also in Christ Jesus, who, being in the form of God, did not consider it robbery to be equal with God, but made Himself of no reputation, taking the form of a bondservant, and coming in the likeness of men. And being found in appearance as a man, He humbled Himself and became obedient to the point of death, even the death of the cross.[88]

When parents lay aside their adult status and power to enter their child's world, they *incarnate* the mind, or attitude, of the Lord Jesus—our Servant-Savior, Who romanced us to Himself by demonstrating God's character. He said, "'He who has seen Me has seen the Father....'"[89] A primary purpose of Jesus' life was to show us what God is like.

Our task as parents is similar—to so fully incarnate the character of God that our children will desire to follow Him and His way of wisdom. And His character is expressed in us through the fruit of His Spirit: "love, joy, peace, longsuffering, kindness, goodness, faithfulness, gentleness, self-control."[90] We cannot produce this spiritual fruit by trying harder. It comes only by allowing the Spirit of God to live in and through us.

The apostle Paul exhorts us: "Therefore be imitators of God as dear children. And walk in love, as Christ also has loved us and given Himself for us....See then that you walk circumspectly, not as fools but as wise, redeeming the time, because the days are evil...understand what the will of the Lord is....be filled with the

Spirit…submitting to one another in the fear of God. Wives, submit to your own husbands, as to the Lord….Husbands, love your wives, just as Christ also loved the church and gave Himself for her….Children, obey your parents in the Lord, for this is right. And you, fathers, do not provoke your children to wrath, but bring them up in the training and admonition of the Lord."[91]

I could have quoted only the last part, since it seems to be the only portion relevant to our topic. But this passage must be understood in its context if we are going to apply it properly to parenting. The context is godly relationships as one journeys on the way of wisdom, and the basic attitude required is the humility of a servant.

"Be imitators of God" is a clear command to parents. What did God do that we are to imitate? He, Jesus, accomplished our redemption by setting aside His divine rights and power to become a human baby, born in a stable, worshiped and adored by shepherds, wise men, a mother and an adoptive father, all of whom He, the Lord of the universe, had created. Even in that manger, Jesus was God incarnate. As He grew in stature and wisdom, and in favor with God and men He remained God incarnate…still humbling Himself by remaining under the authority of Mary and Joseph, even though He, at the age of twelve, had been found in the temple, sitting in the midst of the teachers, listening and asking them questions.[92]

He was tempted, in every way that we are tempted, but He did not sin. He had an itinerant ministry for about three years, healing, teaching and discipling His chosen few until, unjustly condemned, He died a criminal's death on a Roman cross, demonstrating for time and eternity that God's omnipotent love conquers evil in all its forms.

I've heard a lot of men say they would gladly lay down their lives for their children. That's a laudable sentiment, but it's not often what their child perceives as reality. Let's look at a child's side of the relationship:

One afternoon, as a father is editing the manuscript of his book on parenting, he hears the footsteps of his young son approaching his office door. He sighs. *Another interruption. I'll never finish this book!*

Seconds later, still concentrating on his computer screen, he hears, "Dad, what is your consulting rate?"

The father says, "I'll tell you later. Can't you see I'm working?"

> *Children need our time now, not when we think we'll be able to spare it.*

The son gets the message and obediently walks away.

Later that day the father is walking out the door for his daily run when his son asks, "Dad, how much money do you make?"

"I'll discuss it with you later," he says. "I've got to exercise while it's still light."

"Okay," his son says, and goes off as he has so many times before.

That evening after dinner, the father has just settled into the parlor couch with a book he needs to read as background material for his manuscript when his son approaches him again and asks, "Dad, how much do you charge your clients?"

This time the father is annoyed. He has put in a long day. He's tired, and ready to relax with his book before going to bed. Besides, he's about to read the chapter on how to be a better father—so this is a legitimate activity. He says, "Give me a few minutes and I'll come up to your room and discuss it with you."

An hour and a half later, the father walks into his son's dark room. His child's even breathing tells him the boy is sound asleep. In the dim light the father can see that on the table next to his bed is an overturned piggy bank. All his son's money has been sorted into piles. On a piece of paper in columns his boy has added up pennies, nickels, dimes, and quarters. Written at the bottom of the paper, next to the sum, are the words, "I hope this will be enough to buy an hour with Dad."

Although this story is fictitious, I can be as guilty as other Christian fathers of wasting opportunities to be with my son when he simply expresses an interest, needs my companionship, and desires to share his heart and be my friend. To squander these moments is a loss that, someday, when the footsteps are no longer heard at our office doors, will grieve and break our hearts. The challenge is to seize every moment, every day. This is what the apostle Paul means when he says that wise people redeem, or make the most of, their time.

The key to understanding and applying the core message of Ephesians 5 and 6 to parenting is the phrase "the training [nurture] and admonition [instruction] of the Lord." In other words, we can only be successful as parents as we learn to emulate the sacrificial love of Jesus Christ in our relationship with our children.

We romance our children by walking humbly before them and with them. When they see and experience the superiority of the way of wisdom, it dazzles them, woos them, and draws them, captivating them like the best story they have ever heard or the greatest film they have ever seen.

Jesus became one of us so He could communicate with us, know us, identify with us—with our joys and sorrows, our testings, tears, and pain, even the pain of death and separation, for a time, from those He loved. If we are to imitate Him successfully, and win the hearts of our children to Him, we must realize that gaining or exercising power is not the central issue.

We cannot control our children's watershed choice by controlling what they eat or wear, their choice of music or hairstyle, what sports or hobbies they pursue, their friendships or other exposure to the youth subculture. Although it is necessary and appropriate to protect our children during childhood, parental power of this type is asthenic compared to the power of love. Compliance is not the goal of Christlike parenting. "Perfect" behavior—whatever that is—can be enforced through childhood, perhaps a little longer, but eventually every child will emerge from the parents' control.

Children whose spirits have been beaten down for years through this forced compliance in the name of Christianity often bear the fruit of rebellion—against parents, and against the God in Whose name this misguided discipline was administered. The parents have, through their overzealous control, exasperated their children, provoking them to wrath and so producing the opposite result to what they had hoped for.

Force may accomplish certain short-term goals, including making the parents look good in the eyes of their peers. But force will never win a heart. Only sacrificial love can do that. Power may control—even seem to change—conduct for a time, but only romance can produce sincere love, because at the core of romance is our credibility as fellow pilgrims with our children on the journey we call life. We're either on this journey together, or we're on it separately, and they know this—at first intuitively as young children, and then by observation as they mature.

Just as Jesus stepped down from His throne to share our journey, we must step down from the self-importance of our adult world in order to communicate and connect with our children. We must view their decisions and behavior in the context of their lives, not ours. Jesus was still God when He walked among us, and we will still be adults when we enter our children's world. But both incarnations have the same goal—connecting on the level of the heart for the purpose of redemption.

Our pastor once shared the story of how, when he was seven, he and some friends found a copy of *Playboy* in a field. The future pastor knew that pornography was something his Christian father hated, both for what it represented and for what it might do to his son. But the temptation proved too powerful that day, and he and his friends amazed themselves with what they saw in the magazine— a beautiful thing twisted and corrupted by the other suitor.

The boy had planned to keep the incident secret, but within hours of returning home he could no longer keep it to himself. He called his father into his room where, through a flood of tears, shaking and sobbing, he confessed his sin. Instead of receiving the belt, he received from his father a hug, and the assurance: "Peter, I forgive you." And then, because the father saw that the punishment his son was inflicting on himself was worse than a thousand spankings, he gently inquired, as he left the room: "Are you going to be okay?"

The key to this interchange was not just what happened in those few minutes, but what had taken place during the previous seven years. All the boy's life, his father had not only disciplined and discipled him—he had shepherded him, too. As a result, the son's worst fear was not that he might merit a spanking, but that he might hear the words, "You have disappointed me." The father's love had earned a higher place of authority in the son's heart than any paddle could occupy.

This parallels the Christian's deepest concern—that they might grieve the Holy Spirit. Through the years, in the words of our pastor, his father had not just told him what keys to punch on the piano of life, but he had let the boy hear the music of his parents' incarnational love.

Parental love like this always takes sacrifice. There is no other way. I painfully recall an incident involving our son Travis, which occurred when he was five years old. I can still see Travis standing on the porch outside our sliding glass door that spring day, as Karey described his misbehavior—the nature of which none of us can remember now. But we all remember what happened next. It was my duty to administer the proper justice. But when I looked at our little boy, so sorry and scared and obviously willing to accept any punishment I decreed, the traditional discipline just did not seem right. The next thing that happened surprised even me. "Travis," I said, "I'll take the spanking for you."

Karey administered it with surprising severity, as Travis watched in horror. Through the creativity that only God's Spirit could have provided at that moment, God used me and a paddle as His means to incarnate for Travis the meaning of grace and the sacrificial love of Jesus, Who took the punishment for our sins upon Himself at Calvary. It so impressed him that he never again needed a spanking. In fact, the lesson was so powerful that I can't recall him ever being defiant or rebellious since that day.

There is a place for spankings or groundings, suspension of privileges or whatever methods of discipline may work best with each of our children. But whatever temporary force we apply or power we wield should always serve the larger goal of romance—with a view toward winning a lifelong place of authority and influence in our child's heart.

For the sake of love, Jesus became like us. He sent the Holy Spirit to live in all believers so that we *can* become like Him. Where the Spirit of the Lord is, there is liberty—not license and not fear, but freedom to be and to become all that He has called us to be and become. If we become like our children, they will want to become like us. And the romance we offer will free and empower them to do so.

Such servant love is sacrificial, exhausting, and sometimes messy, for the child controls the time and energy required. It is humbling, sometimes humiliating, for example, when we have to say, "I'm sorry." It is courageous—for it takes great courage to lay aside parental power, knowing we cannot control the outcome, which may be that we will be hurt when the child makes mistakes.

By contrast, grasping parental power and refusing to take the risks seems safer. We may feel more secure when we keep our children dependent upon us, emotionally and financially, imposing our will through bribery or threats. It seems to reduce our vulnerability when we always rescue them, instead of giving them the freedom to fail. Control and dignity seem more assured if we hold tight to the reins.

The problem is that it is possible to reform behavior without changing the heart. Children can pretend just as well as, and sometimes better than, adults. Compliance without heart is deadly to the development of authentic faith. The parent may seem to win in the short term, but the coerced child, apart from God's grace, is most likely to become a rebel or a Pharisee, whose soul will eventually shrivel up and die. George McDonald put it bluntly:

> But the more familiar one becomes with any religious system while yet the conscience and will [the heart] are unawakened and obedience has not begun, the harder is it to enter into the kingdom of heaven. Such familiarity is a soul-killing experience, and great will be the excuse for some of those sons of religious parents who have gone further towards hell than may be born and bred thieves and sinners.[93]

Sinful behavior obviously originates in a sinful heart, but doctrinally correct behavior can also originate in a sinful heart. All of us have sinful hearts, because of our sin nature, but through Christ our hearts can be made new. Is our child's relationship with Him dynamic and growing, or is it stale and stagnant? Is it a relationship of deep, romantic love or a relationship with ideas, concepts, words, and works? If the latter, the child will almost surely fall, for the other suitor of the soul will find a way to convince them that sinning, just this once, is not such a big deal. But if the child's relationship with Christ is deep and strong, the Savior will whisper, "I am yours, and you are mine. We'll stand against this trickery together."

SEEING GOD IN STEREO

I believe it is most important that the father be the romance leader in the home. Remember the apostle's exhortation to fathers, not to exasperate their children, but to bring them up in the training and instruction of the Lord.

One summer I mentored an eighteen-year-old boy. It was a transitional time for "Joe." He had been depressed for several years, partly as a result of his parents' divorce. During the school year he had been living in a semi-lockdown Christian boarding school—a place for youth who had not gotten into trouble but were beyond the help of their parents. I thought that if Joe lived with us for the summer, I might be able to reach past the hurt to his heart.

One thing I had neglected to factor in was how Karey's pattern of relating to Joe might differ from mine. I was so focused on the goal of winning his heart that I sometimes looked past his behavior—though I drew the line at anything I felt might negatively affect our family. Karey was so focused on his behavior that she found it impossible to form a personal relationship with Joe. Looking back, I think that this unresolved tension taught both Karey and me a lesson—we gravitated to two different approaches. In spite of our differences, we did win his heart, though he continued to struggle with his behavior. Bad habits, addictions, and lack of self-control are much harder to change once a child is grown.

I suspect that the pattern of attitudes—and conflict—Karey and I experienced during that summer may be common. Mothers and fathers have differing roles in the romance. I believe that the most common pattern is for the husband to focus on principles—the big picture or the goal—while the wife tends to focus on down-to-earth, practical details.

Once Karey spent two weeks in the hospital, and I was the homemaker. As most men know, the job is impossible—for us. Women really do seem to have eyes in the backs of their heads. They are aware of who's playing where, who's fighting, what glass is breaking, what cabinet is opening, what stuff is being flushed down the toilet, and who is swallowing what. At the same time, they are putting a meal on the table.

Women typically have forty percent more connection than men between the left and right lobes of the brain. While a male baby is in the womb, sex-related hormones and chemicals destroy some of the connecting nerve fibers (corpus callosum) between the two lobes. Girls enter the world with more two-sided thinking than boys. Messages and electrical impulses travel faster between the two lobes. This in a sense specializes the brains of men and women into two different ways of thinking.

The left brain houses more of the logical, analytical, factual, and aggressive centers of thought, while the right lobe houses feelings, relationship, language, and communication skills. It is said that women comprehend more information than men do as they walk into a room. This is because a man tends to focus on the destination, which in this case may be a person in the room, whereas women are more conscious of the details along the way, while still being able to take in the person in the room.

This difference is often reflected in the way a mother and father romance their child's heart. Although romance may be more important to women, men are traditionally the initiators—knights in shining armor, with more of a proactive role.

Often it is hard to judge, in the raising of a child, which spouse has better balance in focusing on behavior or romance, especially as the child's needs change according to age and personality. Perhaps the husband and wife together create the ideal balance. We at least are wise to acknowledge that such differences exist, thus avoiding confusion and conflict that can only hinder our achievement of the ultimate goal.

A story told by our pastor illustrates this well:

> Tom and Jane have a three-year-old son, Brandon. One day Tom comes home from work, too exhausted to do anything but sit on the loveseat in front of the TV, his arm around Jane. Brandon, on the other hand, has lots of energy. He runs into the dining room, grabs a chair, and drags it to the kitchen—scratching the floor along the way. He climbs onto the counter and opens the cupboard where the cups are kept. As he takes one out, several fall to the floor. On his way back down, Brandon grabs a bag of chocolate chip cookies, but the bag snags and rips, scattering cookies everywhere. Jane is about to intervene, but Tom gently restrains her because he wants to see what their mini-cyclone will do next.
>
> Brandon is already at the refrigerator. He pulls out a full gallon jug of milk, but it is too heavy for him and he drops it. The lid pops off, and suddenly the kitchen floor is swimming in a cookie milkshake.
>
> Next, just as Tom is about to exert his authority to protect his home, Brandon picks a cup out of the mess, pours in some milk, scrapes up some cookie remains from the floor onto a plate, and runs toward his father, saying, "Daddy, I made it for you!"

Unfortunately, the little boy's foot catches on the edge of the carpet right in front of his parents. Brandon does a face plant in Daddy's lap at just about the same time as the cookies and milk arrive.

What do the parents see? Jane sees an awful mess and a child who needs training. Tom sees a son who loves him enough to bring him cookies and milk when he's tired.

Yes, they will clean up the floor, together. Yes, they will work on Brandon's kitchen skills. But first they will enjoy this rare moment together. Having a clean kitchen is nowhere near as important as reinforcing the compassionate love that made it dirty. In this, Tom and Jane are incarnating the love of God for Brandon—and for them—a love that ignores the pervasive messiness of our lives in favor of the beauty of a heart in love with Him. Such a heart is produced, not by power, but by romance, a process focused not so much on the small details as on the big picture of what is happening in a child's heart.

THE KEYSTONE OF A CHILD'S HEART

Traditionally, the words "training," "discipling," and "mentoring" have been used to describe various approaches to winning a child's heart. More recently, the word "shepherding" has come into use through a book by Ted Tripp. These words actually describe different kinds of relationships common between parents and children. They seem to overlap in practice, but there are significant differences.

Training is essentially the development of habits. The key concept in terms of parenting is molding the will without breaking the spirit. This goal is especially important for young children, not only for their character development but also for their safety and well being. Training also instills in them skills and behavior essential for living in society. An untrained child like Joe will usually have difficulty controlling his behavior even after his heart has been won.

Discipling is teaching spiritual truths and/or academic knowledge. The goal is the personal mastery of spiritual disciplines and acquisition of knowledge by the disciple through a course of study that lasts for a limited time. Discipling is driven by the discipler's agenda; respect for the discipler is required. A person may disciple hundreds of individuals during his or her lifetime. Today it is common for the discipler to follow a manual written by a more experienced and mature discipler. It is typically administrated through a local church program, or a discipling-focused para-church organization.

Unfortunately, because many such organizations specialize in discipling, many Christian parents abdicate their discipling responsibility, which is part of the Great Commission to "make disciples of all the nations."[94]

Mentoring is caring for, helping and supporting a person toward maturity—in essence, it is the development of a person. It is practical exposure to all relevant areas of life, and is more relationship-focused than content-focused. It concerns the protégé's goals and agenda. It is usually a long-term commitment and process that does not require a specific curriculum. Respect, and a natural compatibility or attraction, are necessary. Mentoring is done most naturally between a parent and a child, but other relationships are also common and effective. A person may mentor many individuals during a lifetime. Jesus Christ mentored twelve.

A century ago, mentoring happened everywhere, especially on front porches or around dining room tables. It was a normal part of life—assumed, expected, and essentially unnoticed. But television, entertainment centers and the Internet have replaced front porches. Family time and conversation around the dining table have been replaced by fast food and microwave relationships. Thus mentoring, which should be a prime activity in human relationships, is rare even though the word is currently enjoying a renaissance in our culture.

Shepherding is the blending of discipling and mentoring in the context of parenting. It balances behavior training with heart training, showing a child how to know God and the true nature of reality. It infects children with a worldview that is focused on glorifying God and enjoying Him forever. Shepherding leads a child on a path of discovery, discernment, and wisdom.

In summary, training deals with the development of proper behavior and good habits, discipling emphasizes knowledge and disciplines, mentoring emphasizes the application of these to life, while shepherding includes them all with a focus on changing the heart, not just the behavior.

These approaches are foundational to the winning of a child's heart, but they are of little value if the child does not develop a heart after God. This happens through romance, the keystone in the spiritual structure of a child. Without the keystone, an arch will

THE SPIRITUAL STRUCTURE OF A CHILD

collapse, for the wedge-shaped keystone locks the other pieces in place, making a strong and stable structure. Of course, without the other pieces in place, there is no place in which to set the keystone. A heart that is won without a proper foundation of training, discipline, biblical knowledge and wisdom will flounder. It will be carried away, irresponsible and foolish, in the currents of culture.

While I was writing this chapter, Dawson spent two full days designing and building with Lego. He was an engineer, architect, and sculptor. The whole dining room table was covered with his creations—Native American villages, forts, cities, skyscrapers, animals. The third morning, as I was researching arches, vaults, and keystones, I heard Dawson waking up. Before he came downstairs, I ran over to his creations, got down on my knees and started playing with them. As he came into the room I didn't even have to see the smile on his face as he walked up behind me—I could feel it. I had demonstrated how I valued his work, his art. He saw the child alive in me. This deepened our relationship as I shared in his passion and accomplishment. He knew where my affections lay, because I had taken the time and invested the energy to enter and share his world with him. Parental incarnation really isn't that hard, after all.

PART III:
ROMANCING YOUR CHILD

I long most of all to be like the story
of a man I read about,
who shunned ivory palaces
to cook a meal on the beach with his buddies.
I can see him more clearly than ever before
in my mind's eye:
my squatting, smiling, fish-frying friend
who serves up his food on paper plates,
like the kingly feast that it is.
Our supper is very plain, yes.
We eat the bread of wonder.

- Joy Sawyer
(Give Us This Day Our Wonder Bread)

9

CHARACTERISTICS OF A ROMANCER

I've heard that they are angels in disguise,
If you want to find a treasure, just look into their eyes.
And the touch of tiny fingers will make the foolish wise,
So watch for these angels in disguise.

We were created to be in relationship—with God, and with each other. Yet in our modern world we have misplaced, perhaps even lost, the art of relationship—the basics, the etiquette, the tools. This overview of the characteristics of a romancer is intended as a springboard from which we can leap into a richer relationship with our children as we romance them to the heart of Christ.

A CHILDLIKE HEART

A local church we attended hosts a costume party called Family Fun Night as an alternative to Halloween. Several years ago, three nights before the event, Heather and Travis reminded me that they needed costumes. The theme that year was biblical characters. Impulsively, I suggested Jonah and the whale. Karey looked at me with question marks in her eyes, so I said, "Heather will be the whale. Travis will be Jonah. And I will be the designer and builder—the creator."

We spent the next three days sculpting the whale from cardboard, papier-mâché, and wood, and then painted it blue. It was thirteen feet long, five feet tall—and three feet wide, so that we could still squeeze it through our front door. (I hesitate to think how big it might have become had we no horizontal limits.) Our whale had a hinged tail that moved back and forth, with a stick inside to control the movement. The front half had no bottom, so Heather and Travis could propel it by holding onto a horizontal waist-high pole inside the whale and walking. When Heather lifted the pole, the whale's head rose and the mouth opened wide—I had hinged it so that the lower jaw would rest on the floor by gravity. Big white teeth lined the opening.

We had read somewhere that one of the reasons Jonah got the attention of the people of Nineveh was because he was bleached white by the stomach acids of the whale. So we bleached Travis's clothes and painted him white. We attached a lobster and some seaweed to his shoulder. When he stepped out of the whale's mouth, he, like the original Jonah, caught the attention of everyone. As I recall, they did not even take a vote in the contest—our costume was, fins down, the best by far. But that didn't matter. What mattered was that Travis and Heather had been on a three-day-long wild ride with Mr. Dad, whose childlike imagination had been unleashed.

C. S. Lewis said, "When I became a man I put away childish things, including the fear of childishness and the desire to be very grown up."[95] But wait! Isn't that an oxymoron—a mature man with a childlike heart? A childlike heart produces what may appear to be irresponsible, frivolous behavior. A child's nonverbal vocabulary includes skipping, hopping, dancing, jumping, running, laughter, peek-a-boos and winks.

Can a parent—particularly a father—afford the luxury of a childlike heart? A better question is, can we afford not to be childlike, if we want to romance our children's hearts?

I once heard of a father who planned a wonderful vacation for his family. He was always dependable, and put his family first, but this time, at the last minute, he told them something had come up at the office and he wouldn't be able to go. He assured them that they would have a great time without him—and everything had already been paid for. So the mother and kids packed their suitcases and drove off.

The father was all too aware of their heavy hearts. He flew to a city he knew they would be driving through, and the next time they saw him, he was standing at a prominent exit along the interstate, with his thumb out! Imagine the scene as the children saw their father there, hitchhiking. Extravagant? Perhaps. But our children are gifts from God Himself. No price is too great to pay when we are trying to win their hearts.

Teddy Roosevelt was my grandfather's hero, so I've heard many stories about this great man. In reading his biographies, I've always been struck by the descriptions of his relationship with his children. Tender, true, and winsome, he was their playmate, whether racing or roughhousing. He put as much energy into an obstacle race on the White House lawn as he did into a presidential campaign. He was both champion, and champion of, his family, helping them to grow in courage, strength, and compassion, inspiring them to ever-richer adventure and higher service—with him leading the way.

Once, the president was entertaining visiting statesmen when he exclaimed, "I must ask you to excuse me. We'll finish this talk some other time. I promised the boys I'd go shooting with them at four o'clock, *and I never keep boys waiting.* It's a hard trial for a boy to wait." This man knew how to romance his children's hearts.

Roosevelt also gave his heart to his children—through his actions, and through his pen. He wrote thousands of letters to them. I suspect that many fathers today have not written even one letter to their children.

I know that when I receive a letter or package, the handwritten part always captures my attention first. My sister-in-law Linda believes there is something special about handwritten letters—they communicate the heart in a way that emails or telephone conversations cannot. She loves to write notes to her children, and they save them—even hang them on their walls. But she also sends nonverbal "notes" in the best of an endearing and hilarious childlike spirit. Her children shared with me how, besides enclosing little jokes and notes in their lunches, she often takes a bite out of each of their sandwiches—just to remind them how much she loves them. When they open their lunch boxes they all say, "Oh, Mom!" because there, for their friends to see, is her "love bite."

Jesus said that, in order to enter God's kingdom, we must receive it as a little child. We must take it simply as a gift—coming to us not because we deserve it, but by grace. He gave His disciples a classic lesson when they were arguing about who should be the greatest in the kingdom. Jesus set a little child before them, to show them the true nature of the kingdom—since they obviously did not understand it. He told them that they could not enter into the kingdom except by becoming like little children—by humbling themselves.[96] This is an infinitely deep truth because it provides insight into the fundamental nature of God.

When children throw themselves creatively, imaginatively and wholeheartedly into whatever they are doing, they are "unselfconscious" in the most basic sense—forgetting about themselves. The Greek word for ultimate *self*-consciousness is *hubris*, which means "pride"—putting oneself at the center of the universe. The "child-likeness" Jesus spoke of is the opposite. It is to be hopelessly enthralled, responsive, and open to the possibility that fairytales are true after all—that there really is a "place beyond time"—a "Brigadoon." Childlikeness resurrects in our hearts visions of our true home and of our loving heavenly Father.

We need to find a way to nurture and nourish the child within us before we can hope to romance the hearts of our children. There is no formula or checklist, no "ten steps to recovery" program. We must simply set the inner child free again. We must remember how to play.

One of the feature articles in *Time* magazine's April 30, 2001 issue was entitled "Whatever Happened to Play?" Based on the recent book *The Over-Scheduled Child: Avoiding the Hyper-Parenting Trap*, the article stated that, thanks to videogames, the home computer, the disappearance of vacant lots, and an encroaching fear of danger in public parks, "play in our society has become a four-letter word....the enemies of play must begin with adults, who make the rules. If play is endangered, it's parents who have endangered it...."

If we will become playmates to our children, we will be half the way back home.

SIMPLE FAITH

My father, eighty years old as I write this, is still a hero in my eyes. The image of the fatherhood of God flows out of his life, just as it did when I was seven years old. It is not created out of sophisticated theology or great religious works. It is his genuine trust and relationship with God that has always impressed me.

Our family never missed church. There was no question about going or not. One Sunday, my dad drove us there through a blinding blizzard. In Wisconsin, that means something you might expect just south of the North Pole—snow falling horizontally at sixty miles an hour, wind howling through tightly shut doors and windows. You know that if you get stuck on the road, they'll find your frozen body in the spring, after the drifts made by the plows have receded to twelve feet high. Experiencing one of those blizzards is enough to make anybody "get religion."

We could barely see the hood of the car. Ice was so thick on the windshield wipers that they looked like white PVC pipes. Not even suicidal snowmobilers were out. How we made it I'll never understand, but we did—to discover that we were the only people at church. The preacher hadn't even made it—and the parsonage was next door to the church! The fact that we got there—and back—left an indelible impression on my mind.

Another thing that impacted me permanently was watching my father sit down at the dining room table, a few minutes before we left for church, to write the family's weekly tithe check. Even as a youth, I perceived this to be a serious, hallowed moment, both because of the sacrifice required and the spiritual reality of this act of faith. It told me in no uncertain terms where my parents' treasures were.

Dad gave freely, sacrificially, of everything he had. And he simply loved me with no strings attached—my agenda was his.

When I began building my first home, he was there laying out the construction, sawing, and pounding nails. Many times now, when I call home, Mom will say, "Dad is out in the pole barn," and then she describes his passionate reaction to some challenging problem and how through creativity and resourcefulness he has come up with a solution. You can tell that she loves him and is in awe of the energetic optimism bubbling out of his boyish heart.

Recently I found in our attic a cedar box that Dad built years ago, just so he could send a "Big Wheel" to Travis as a Christmas gift. In my eyes, the box reflected his resourcefulness, since he used what he had at the time to accomplish his goal. I've kept it through the years because it represented this part of my dad. One year, for Heather's birthday, I rebuilt that box by lining it with aromatic cedar, and adding brass hardware. I left the distressed look on the outside. Now it is a beautiful chest that Heather will have as a keepsake to remind her of her grandfather.

Dad had trouble swallowing in the fall of 2000, and was soon diagnosed with an aggressive form of esophageal cancer. With no previous symptoms or lifestyle risk factors, this development took our family completely by surprise. Fortunately, Mom and Dad live near a world-class medical center specializing in research, so he was soon assigned to a team of top-notch physicians.

There is a yearning in all of us—especially in our children —for a real Superman.

The doctors did all the tests and decided to make Dad a research project. They said that, first of all, he had the body of a forty year old, which made him a great candidate for aggressive treatment. But most importantly, they were stunned by his simple, strong, childlike faith. Why did "simple" and "childlike" impress these highly educated physicians? Because God's Spirit was obviously present. In fact, these doctors refused to give a formal prognosis because of this factor. They could not quantify his chances. This of course left us all up in the air—right where we should have been, anyway, resting in God. Medical science's wonder at Dad's faith caused my childhood hero—the one who first communicated to me the character of God—to loom large once more in my eyes.

Dad began radiation and chemotherapy immediately, and he did well, just as the doctors had predicted. However, there was one tense moment, when at the height of the treatment he decided to go deer hunting. It was November in northern Wisconsin—in other words, cold. He parked his four-wheeler and walked a short distance to his tree stand, but was too weak to climb the tree, so he sat at its base until dark. Then he returned to the four-wheeler, but it would not start, and he was too weak even to begin walking down the logging road back home. He was faced with the reality of freezing to death.

That's when a guardian angel in the form of a neighbor walked out of the woods and helped him home. Apparently he had been watching over Dad the whole time. The primary care doctor said, when the story was told to him, "It is important during treatment to continue your normal routine—although this is beyond what I would call normal."

The radiation and chemo killed the cancer. Dad had the affected part of his esophagus removed through major surgery, and he returned to normal. During one of his last check-ups, my mother thanked the physician in charge, and remarked how wonderful the clinic was—the personnel, the choice of treatment, and of course the fact that many people were praying. The doctor looked her in the eye and said, "Ma'am, I would reverse the order if I were you."

My mother recovered quickly from the horrible shock of the initial diagnosis. Through the long ordeal, she courageously supported Dad—never losing hope. Getting up twice a night for months, cleaning and filling his feeding tube, was physically difficult for her. Yet she never wavered, because she knew she was a key to his recovery. She told me that God is the only explanation for the strength she found. Watching her face this overwhelming challenge inspired all of us, and drew us closer to God.

Travis once played a song for me, by a band with the curious name "Crash Test Dummies." The message has haunted me ever since. The chorus goes like this:

Superman never made any money
For savin' the world from Solomon Grundy
And sometimes I despair the world will never see
Another man like him.[97]

The message of the song is elusive and subtle. When I asked Travis what he thought it might be, he said he was not sure but it gave him an overwhelming feeling of nostalgic sadness. I believe that the last two lines sum up the point of the song. There is a yearning in all of us—especially in our children—for a real Superman. The longing ripples through our dreams. We have experienced it through the fact that many of the truly tragic figures in history were deprived of this image.[98]

Parents are heroes and heroines, larger than life, in their children's eyes. These natural and important roles give children a vision of what they wish to be. When children have this view of their parents, they have hope and strength to dream. They have goals and a high purpose for their lives, as their gaze is lifted from the ground toward the stars, toward God rather than man.

Mothers and fathers complement each other in these roles, as they each communicate different attributes of God's character. A father may portray the brave-hearted image of God the Father, protecting us and taking us on great adventures; a mother may represent the tender, kind-hearted mercy of Christ, Who reached out and touched us with unconditional sacrificial love. These images emanate not so much from the actions as from the hearts of mothers and fathers, and color forever their children's perceptions of God.

A COURAGEOUS SPIRIT

Surely He [God] shall deliver you from the snare of the fowler and from the perilous pestilence. He shall cover you with His feathers, and under His wings you shall take refuge; His truth shall be your shield and buckler. You will not be afraid of the terror by night, nor of the arrow that flies by day....[99]

There are tragic chapters in each of our lives that seem antithetic to, but really are part of, the larger Story. The tension of these trials lifts the possibility of romance to higher and more dazzling heights, in proportion to what is at stake. Without God's grace, the trauma would surely destroy us. Tension demands resolution and produces a climax. Suspense, surprise, hope, courage, heroism, and joy are all connected to our stories. The heroic courageous suffering of Christ on the cross is the most essential ingredient in the original love Story. It has an infinite capacity to inspire, as history proves, and to "draw all men" to Him. To the extent that we reflect Christ as we face life's tribulations, we also play a role in moving our children's hearts.

Recently, I had a once-in-a-lifetime spiritual experience as I said goodbye to a great man, Colonel Dick Kail. He was a mentor and spiritual elder in my life for years. Even though he came from the military world, a place I have respected but never visited, we felt a deep camaraderie with each other. I knew this relationship was a treasure and I cherished it.

Dick had a powerful ministry to couples in the military. He had lived his own life well, from Vietnam to the Pentagon. The last time I visited with him, most of his household was in boxes, as he and his wife Brenda were moving back East to be near their sons. Dick was wearing a plastic body brace, because his backbone was crumbling. After a seven-year battle with cancer, it was clear that he was nearing the end of his earthly life.

This kind of visit can be heart wrenching and depressing, but Dick's courage and spirit were inspirational. The joy I experienced lifted me to a spiritual plane that took my breath away. As he sat on the lone couch left in the house, Dick encouraged me in a way that I have never been encouraged before. He gave me a fresh eternal perspective for life that brought the Sacred Romance into clear focus.

As always, Dick wanted to know what I had been doing. I told him about my investment of time and resources into the lives of families who sincerely desire to live biblically, and described the concept of romancing a child's heart. I mentioned this book and how I hoped it would help.

Dick then asked me if I had seen the movie *Saving Private Ryan*. I told him I thought it would be too graphic, and also that I felt I already had a deep appreciation for the horror of war, and the cost of placing one's body between the enemy and your family. My grandfather had fought in the First World War, and the stories he had told me were filled with passion and sacrifice. His whole being had been intent on reaching that one goal—victory. At the end of his life he was still fighting that enemy.

Dick's view was that people who are ignorant of what it cost to win their freedom would benefit by seeing *Saving Private Ryan*. "The movie is accurate—almost too accurate," he agreed, "with bodies of fallen soldiers everywhere on the D-Day beaches, body parts tossing in the surf, wounded soldiers limping and barely crawling while snipers systematically take them out.

"That depiction of real war," Dick continued, "is a realistic picture of spiritual warfare. Your ministry, in the same way, is a matter of life and death. In your neighborhood there are many mothers and fathers who have lost heart—whose souls are wounded. Many are captives in prisons of despair, addiction, and boredom. We were born into this war. It has been long and vicious and all around us parents are taking hits and collapsing.

"Monte," he said, and his eyes looked deep into mine, "I see things very clearly. The vision you just shared with me of winning children's hearts, of the biblical balance you seek between supporting your family, following your calling, and engaging in ministry, is right on track. Don't be distracted by other voices. Listen to your heart and to God's Spirit Who resides there. Live this script you shared with me, because God is obviously the Author of it. I feel it, sense it, and know it."

Then, with all the strength he could muster, he stood up, gave me a hug, and said, "I'll be seeing you in heaven."

The power in Dick's words was intensified by the heat of the crucible from which God was about to remove him. His own pain acted like a prism to focus, clarify, and beautify the "last words" of this great man. Later that day, I shared the experience with my son Travis, who was deeply moved because he knew Dick and sensed in my spirit the sacredness of this story.

William Gurnall said that hell is enraged by the image of God reflected in His children. It is against this, he added, that "demons hurl their mightiest weapons." Those moments I spent with Dick were a witness to the image of Christ in him, and the reality of the larger Story—more evidence for Travis that hope for a Christian extends beyond life on earth.

JOY

Our ability to experience joy in the midst of adversity is one of the surest signs that we are consciously living within a larger Story. We know that the chapter including our present suffering will be but a vague memory when the last page is turned. Children who see this in their parents will be drawn—romanced—to the Source of their parents' hope, as Travis and I were drawn to the source of Dick's hope. And they will be far more likely to adopt the same perspective when sorrow comes to them.

Our witness to our children as we share times of distress can either confuse them or connect them to Christ, Who has promised that someday there will be no more death or mourning or crying or pain, for the old order of things will have passed away.[100] There will be only joy in His new world. When we have this joy, now—especially in the face of great difficulty—it confirms to our children that we really do believe in something bigger, more beautiful, and more wonderful than life itself. Without doubt, this is real evidence of a firsthand relationship with Almighty God.

C. S. Lewis knew deep sorrow and jubilant joy. In his book *A Grief Observed* we find the "mad midnight moments" of a husband watching his wife, Joy, slowly die of cancer. In his early autobiographical book, *Surprised by Joy*, we find the musings and meanderings of a skeptic who flees the hound of heaven through the labyrinth of his own mind until he returns to the faith of his youth, only with a more mature perspective. He describes the Spirit's invitation to faith as "like distant music which you need not listen to unless you wish, like a delicious faint wind on your face which you can easily ignore....The odd thing is that something inside me suggested that it would be 'sensible' to refuse the invitation....Then I silenced the inward wiseacre. I accepted the invitation...and passed in a state, which can be described only as joy.[101]

By now, you will have realized that I love the words of C. S. Lewis. One of my favorite books is *The Screwtape Letters*, quoted earlier, in which Lewis plays a literal "devil's advocate" through the incisive and increasingly vitriolic letters of Screwtape to his understudy, Wormwood. As I read these letters, I can almost hear Lewis laughing heartily in the background. Such levity disgusts devils, according to Screwtape, because it suggests a larger reality—which the devils cannot comprehend—a deep happiness (joy) that comes from knowing that what we see with our physical eyes is passing away, but what is seen by the eyes of the heart is eternal.[102] Screwtape writes:

> Among adults some pretext in the way of jokes is usually provided, but the facility with which the smallest witticisms produce laughter at such a time shows that they are not the real cause. What the real cause is we do not know....Laughter of this kind does us no good and should always be discouraged. Besides, this phenomenon is of itself disgusting and a direct insult to the realism, dignity, and austerity of hell.[103]

Jesus promised His disciples that His joy would be in them and that their joy would be complete.[104] Joy-induced laughter makes perfect sense for a Christian, though many seem to be about as oriented to "realism, dignity, and austerity" as are the devils of hell. At the heart of Christianity is Joy. It is a gigantic secret that draws us, woos us, and romances us into the company of the cross, which Jesus endured "for the joy set before Him"[105] —our redemption. The journey for a pilgrim can be long, difficult, and exhausting, but when we least expect it, when our hope is nearly extinguished, a turn or a twist surprises us, producing a knowing smile and, soon, laughter. It is an inside joke between us and the One writing the script of the larger Story. It is the last mile along the maple tree-lined country road of my childhood before reaching Grandpa and Grandma's house for Thanksgiving dinner after a thousand-mile trip, when I've been away too long.

The reality of the Sacred Romance produces, in those willing to live in it, C. S. Lewis's nostalgic longing for heaven, "the feeling that you are coming back tho' to a place you have never yet reached...."[106] Lewis also said, "Our best havings are wantings."[107] Proverbs 25:26 reminds us: "Like cold water to a weary soul, so is good news from a distant land." The best news from a distant land is really a reminder—that we are just pilgrims now, on the way to an eternal destination, sometimes called heaven, but known today as Joy.

LAUGHTER

If you are like me, you are far more attracted to someone who can laugh than to someone who is as serious as death all the time. We are drawn to this type of Christian because they seem to have a special, personal, and intimate connection with God. One of my friends makes me laugh, but sometimes after the fact I can't recall what was so funny. On one occasion, for example, we were out to dinner and he kept us laughing for nearly two hours, until I started getting cheek cramps. The strange thing was, after we left the restaurant, I couldn't recall a single "joke." It was more a sense of lightheartedness, marked by wit with some wisdom thrown in besides, that made our night so enjoyable—plus the fact that this particular person has all the reason in the world to be bitter instead of funny. He can still smile and laugh even though the world around him has crumbled and Christian friends have deserted him, because he clings to the hope that the larger Story is true. This is why I consider him one of the most heroic men I know.

A joyous heart—especially in someone who could as easily be sad—is a testimony to the redeeming power of God, and an affront to Satan. We all have one reason or another to be sad. If you don't, then just wait a minute. Humor, a playful attitude, gladness, or joy, a childlike heart—these are "a direct insult to the realism, dignity, and austerity of hell" because the devil wants humans to believe that the sense of helplessness that can accompany sorrow renders everything, even life itself, futile.

> *One of a father's most endearing qualities is the ability to laugh at himself—in front of his children.*

Chuck Bolte once told me, "Fear and laughter are close bedfellows; which of the two will be experienced is determined by the direction the story twists or turns in the end. The pleasure we derive in laughing is an enjoyment of relief from a negative or perplexing expectation."

Bob Farewell and I were discussing this very point by phone as he watched hurricane Floyd barely miss their Florida home. "Humor," he said, with relief in his voice, "is the purging of tension."

The medical profession has recently rediscovered that humor is good medicine. In this, they echo Solomon, who wrote: "A merry heart does good, like medicine…" (Proverbs 17:22). Laughter has the power to disarm an adversary, open a closed spirit, relieve stress, and even stimulate a person's immune system.

It is common to overlook laughter in the romance of our children's hearts, because it seems so familiar, so ordinary—even earthy. It is easy to lose our ability to laugh as we work hard meeting the responsibilities of parenting. But if we are in relationship with God, our hearts will be sunny with gladness, ready to burgeon out with cheer at any moment.

Few children will trust a father who rarely laughs, for his heart is a mystery—an unknown entity. One of a father's most endearing qualities is the ability to laugh at himself—in front of his children.

Sometimes we have no choice. One day, I turned on our tap and filled a new dark-blue enamel cup with ice-cold mountain water from our well. (It's worth it living here in Colorado, just for the water!) I took a sip and thought it tasted kind of funny. Looking into the cup, I saw there was an oil slick on the surface of the water. I dumped it out and filled it again. Another sip, and there was the slick again, swirling with telltale rainbow colors.

Immediately, I alerted Karey, and instructed the family not to drink our water, because it was contaminated with oil. With our children watching, I, their heroic protector, launched my investigation.

This was right up my alley. I threw all my training, experience, and expertise in engineering and geology at the problem. I racked my brain trying to come up with possible sources for the oil. I called several friends who were water-system experts. I consulted well-water companies that I found in the phone book. I had long, passionate technical conversations. I felt like the Sherlock Holmes of home water pollution.

The only conclusion I could draw was that the pump deep in our well had begun to leak oil.

After several days of drinking bottled water, I examined the oil slicks with my geologic hand lens, and noticed tiny white particles floating in the oil. These, I suspected, were chemical precipitates. (Later, I concluded they were food particles.) I immediately reported this to my "expert" friends, who were even more mystified.

Then, quite by accident, I examined a glass of bottled water from which I had taken a drink. It, too, contained oil! This confused me. Then I filled a glass from our tap and examined it. No oil. At that point, it dawned on me that the oil slicks only appeared after I had taken a sip of the water. The "oil," it turned out, was from my own lip balm! We all wear lip protection in Colorado at dry times of the year. The reason I had never seen it before was that I had never drunk our well water from a dark-colored glass.

What a relief! But what an idiot I had been—taking up my friends' time, and even getting preliminary estimates for a new water pump.

However, I actually enjoyed going back to those I had consulted, informing them that the "great oil slick mystery" had been solved. Everyone—especially my children—thought it was absolutely hilarious.

I have found that humor opens up my children's hearts, as they see that as a father I do not take myself too seriously. It breaks down communication barriers and creates an atmosphere of openness. A warm smile from "big strong Daddy" immediately opens a child's spirit. As a father, I need to be full of laughter and surprises, jokes and joy. A heart in relationship with God bursts with gladness and cheer. Humor gives us hope, and hope brings life to the romance.

A "GLAD GAME" SPIRIT

We've already looked at the "glad game," which is the central theme of the book *Pollyanna*. This game is really quite simple. When something happens that doesn't line up with our wishes or expectations, we look for anything in it that we might be glad about. The more difficult it is to find the glad thing, the more exciting and challenging is the game. Kids play this game naturally, but it seems harder for adults.

On one occasion, I had to make a last-minute geology trip from Denver to Reno, Nevada. Searching the Internet for a decent plane fare, I settled on a redeye special with an awkward connection. When my family dropped me off at the airport, I was sulking and had few words to say as they drove away. I boarded the plane with a bad attitude. A silver lining in the clouds was the farthest thing from my mind.

I had the middle seat in an exit row, and figured I would end up claustrophobically squashed—big guys, both sides. It was even worse than I had imagined. The guys were huge, and they both wore black suits. I cringed as they made their way toward me.

To my embarrassed surprise, after they took their seats, one of them pulled out a Christian book and began to read. I couldn't resist remarking on the book, which he promptly handed to me with a friendly, "Feel free to read it." I soon learned that they were Christians returning home from ministering at a conference. One was the basketball legend Meadowlark Lemon, and the other was professional football star Earl Edwards.

Sheepishly, I admitted to myself that it was my honor to be in that middle seat. Our conversation continued as we disembarked—in fact, I almost missed my connection.

It was very late when I boarded the next plane. My mood had certainly improved, but I still didn't expect another positive segment. However, on this leg I ended up sitting next to a banker who became enthralled with my science. After an entire flight of stimulating conversation, he offered to help me find a motel, since I had not been able to book a reservation before I left. He found me a great place to stay, and even drove me there. I was speechless.

The two-segment flight, which I had expected to be an exhausting ordeal, had turned into one of the most memorable trips of my life. God had played the glad game on me. I felt so foolish having shut my eyes to the larger Story. And now I was going to have to face the embarrassment of explaining it to my family when I got home.

On another occasion, I was preparing for a presentation at a conference in my hometown. Everything seemed to be going fine—the text was solid and I knew the material well. I had even written a song that would drive the main point deeper into the hearts of the parents. Dawson was going to emphasize the message by shooting his bow on stage.

I wanted to do an especially good job, but I came down with a viral throat infection three days before the event, which left me barely able to speak, much less sing. Dark clouds gathered in my mind, obscuring my vision for what we were trying to do at the conference. I was on the verge of depression and anger.

Then I thought: *What would Pollyanna do?*

It occurred to me that I have a tendency to speak too loud, and with too much force. Sometimes I turn people off by coming on with too much passion. The weak voice I was stuck with might be just the ticket, especially in my own hometown. Although I knew it would be painful, the pain could help me to focus. It might even bring a better balance of humility and tenderness to my delivery. I would also have to rely more on God. I began to see something to be glad about.

Dawson was quietly watching my every move.

It turned out to be one of our best presentations ever. Dawson set the scene by nearly doing a "Robin Hood"—hitting the center gold of the target with his first arrow, and nearly splitting it with the second—in the tradition of Robin Hood's great feat at the archery contest in Nottingham. Then, as I spoke, he loved seeing me keep hanging in, as my voice got progressively weaker. There was a strong connected feeling between my material and the audience. I was focused on the message, and, as a result, less self-conscious than usual.

I had barely enough voice to finish the presentation. For the rest of the day I could only whisper a few words to the people with whom I interacted. Since I couldn't talk, I had to listen more. People became more friendly and open, and my compassion grew for them because, instead of half-listening to their words while preparing to share my "expert" advice, I heard what was in their hearts.

When we play the glad game, we look for evidence of the larger Story in what might otherwise be a difficult situation. I know of a large family in which this process is a private joke. The key phrase is, "Oh, wow!"

"Wow" backwards is still "wow" so, no matter what life throws our way, we can still find the WOW in it.

FINDING BEAUTY WITH THE EYES OF LOVE

My all-time favorite film is *Rigoletto*. Although it was never shown in movie theaters, it is available through the company Feature Films for Families. Critics might describe *Rigoletto* as low budget and unsophisticated, but what matters to me is its beautiful message and music, which so powerfully nourish my soul that I weep every time I watch it.

The main character, Bonnie, is a young girl who is able to see, with the eyes of her heart, past the superficial ugliness and meanness of Ribaldi, a stranger from a faraway place, to the beauty and goodness within him. At one point in the film, Bonnie acknowledges this paradox to her mother: "How could he do something so wonderful if he's supposed to be so bad?" In referring to Ribaldi's beautiful friend (the "princess" in this fairytale) she asks, "How could someone so beautiful love someone so ugly?"

Her mother answers, "I don't know. Then maybe there is something more to Mr. Ribaldi than meets the eye."

The storyline of this "fairytale" is filled with poetry and music—beautiful music and beautiful words that bear witness to the larger Story, of which it is an accurate reflection:

There is no curse or evil spell
That's worse than one we give ourselves;
There is no sorcerer as cruel
As the proud angry fool.
And yet we cry "Life isn't fair!"
Beneath our cries the truth is there—
The power that will break the spell
We know very well, is locked within ourselves.

There is a melody
Locked up inside of me
But now it's free

It found a place
Embraced by harmony...
Sweet harmony. [108]

The ability to perceive beauty, even in apparently ugly people or things, is a quality of God Himself, Who sees even in the vilest of sinners and the most horrendous of circumstances the potential for good. When we parents exhibit this redemptive quality, children are drawn to us as we are drawn to God.

I stated earlier that the romance is, in a sense, a beauty contest. This contest fuels the romance, kindling a stronger desire for God as it nourishes the heart in a unique way. But beauty can also cause us to be uncomfortable in its presence to the point of writing it off as earthly or simply trivial. We must not cede this God-created glory to the domain of the devil. Fyodor Dostoyevsky said, "Beauty is not only a terrible thing, it is also a mysterious thing. There, God and the Devil strive for mastery, and the battleground is the heart of man." [109]

TRUSTWORTHINESS

Once a friend of mine hired a Christian life coach to help her sort out the positive challenges, opportunities and visions she had for the future. The coach said, "You must put your 'big rocks' in your jar of life before the pebbles, sand, and water are poured in, or the big rocks—the important things—will not fit." During the process the coach gave her a personality test, which revealed a surprising pattern—her mercy and compassion score was essentially zero. The coach, who was also a licensed counselor, was surprised, although he knew that she had always been awkward at expressing sympathy. He eventually concluded that this was a coping mechanism that had probably developed early in her life. Since she was healthy and happy, he did not recommend therapy.

My friend, after reviewing her childhood memories, concluded that this was her way of coping with broken promises. On the surface her childhood had been happy. She lived in a beautiful house; she loved to travel, visit her grandparents, and go on adventures with her family. Her father was a pleasant man who was always talking about all the things they were going to do together—in between watching television. His greatest passion was for the country club culture and golf, so he designed most family vacations around this sport. Gradually, the number of promises he broke left all his words hollow and laced with lies. My friend learned to cope by learning never to anticipate or hope for anything, because her young heart could not bear to be disappointed again. If she expected nothing, then when something did come she would be surprised and happy. She understood and forgave her father, and had moved beyond those memories—but they left a scar.

Another friend of mine, Kathy, once said, "God doesn't tease. He's not like that." She wasn't referring to ordinary play, but to someone with power playing with someone vulnerable, as a cat plays with a mouse. Trust is incompatible with abusive teasing. Parents often get away with such behavior because children are resilient and responsive, and they forgive easily. But they have their limits, and eventually they do suffer damage—to their emotions, their spirits, their view of the world, and most importantly to their ability to trust God. A parent's trustworthiness will place either solid ground or quicksand under their child's feet.

Jesus made it clear how serious it is to deceive or lead a child astray. He said, "Whoever causes one of these little ones who believe in Me to sin, it would be better for him if a millstone were hung around his neck, and he were drowned in the depth of the sea."[110] Can't you sense God's anger toward anyone who abuses a child in this way? A child's faith is of great value to God.

A PASSION FOR TRUTH

I love the book *Meditations on Hunting,* by the Spanish philosopher Jose Ortegay Gasset, in which the author describes his attempts to "hunt down the hunt." He uses hunting as a metaphor for the search for truth by describing the hunter as the "alert man" who tries to see all at once in order to anticipate where or for how long his quarry will appear, and exactly what it will look like.

Plato used the hunting metaphor in the same way:

> The time has arrived, Glaucon, when like huntsmen, we [philosophers] should surround the cover, and look sharp that justice [truth] does not steal away, and pass out of sight and escape us; for beyond a doubt she is somewhere in this country: watch therefore and strive to catch sight of her, and if you see her first, let me know....Here is no path...the wood is dark and perplexing; still we must push on....Here I saw something: Halloo! I said, I begin to perceive a track, and I believe that the quarry will not escape.[111]

Karey and I experience excitement like this in our own search for God's truth. Karey wrote, "Isn't it in our passionate pursuit of Him [God] that we become ourselves? I long...to inspire and influence [our] children's hearts with the flame of [our] own zeal for life."[112] Proverbs compares the way of wisdom to a treasure hunt for God's truth and its application to life, the discovery of which brings great pleasure.

Journaling is a wonderful help in this "hunt" for truth. Though the word "journal" usually brings to mind a blank notebook filled day by day with thoughts, feelings, poetry, a record of what we've done or where we've gone, a journal need not be a formal book. Anything will serve—scraps of paper, serviettes at a restaurant, brown paper lunch or grocery bags. The only thing that matters is that we capture and preserves ideas and insights, which can later be integrated into our personal pursuit of truth.

Our home has nine libraries, and many filing cabinets filled with notes, data, and papers we have gathered over the years. Karey and I love the journey along the way to wisdom—taking anecdotal data, information, and knowledge to a philosophical level, and putting the puzzle together in the context of a Christian worldview. This is the way we've done our journaling. We collect truth, file it, save it, and synthesize it—like Sherlock Holmes and Watson on the trail of a mystery, or archeologists discussing the results of a dig. It is no small thing when our children witness this. I know our curiosity is contagious, for they all have begun their own search for truth.

Conversations around our dining room table are intense—a "downloading" of our research, our working hypotheses and theories. We love nothing better than to sit for hours discussing theology, science, culture, art—anything involving God's truth and how it applies to life.

There are many sources from which to gather clues in the search for God's truth—personal experience, nature, sermons—but books are among the richest. This should not surprise us, since God uses a Book as His primary mode of communicating truth. Karey and I drag books all over the house—from the bedroom to the bathroom—until we can't walk anywhere without tripping, and we have to return some to the shelves. We often wake up with fascinating ideas from our bedtime reading, carrying them to the breakfast table and beyond. Sometimes our kids raise their eyebrows at each other, wondering what in the world we are talking about. It's exciting to think of all there is to learn, observe, and contemplate for the rest of our lives.

Karey has always read aloud to our children. We let them have books in their cribs, and often peeked into their bedrooms to see them looking at their books when they woke up from their naps. They learned that books were precious, not to be ripped or marked up. To emphasize this, we never even tore pages from magazines in front of them. They have adopted our attitude in the high regard we place on the written word.

Clarence Cook, in a book on interior decorating written in 1878, wrote, "A house without books is no house at all." I readily agree. Don't you feel a warmth in a room with books? I am drawn to areas filled with books even while eating in restaurants. Charles Dickens spoke of a little room off his childhood home where his father kept a collection of books. He said they were a constant comfort to him, keeping alive his imagination and his hope in something beyond that particular place and time.

Our family's passion for books, which began when we lived on the road in that crammed Chevy Blazer, has never diminished. We searched out used book sales by calling libraries and women's auxiliary groups, plotting the dates on the calendar. We went with plastic bags and boxes in hand, trying to be near the front of the line when the doors opened. The kids and Karey ran for the children's and youth sections, while I scurried all over. Our plan was to grab all the books that looked old; then, one person was designated to guard our stash while the rest kept looking. This person, usually one of the kids, would soon be curled up next to our boxes, deeply engrossed in one of our finds.

At some sales, the checkout people gave us great deals once they knew we were not dealers or collectors, but just people who loved to read. All those book-buying excursions, with their rich conversations and shared emotions, knit us together as a family, and gave us so much to talk about. Today, when people tell me they don't know their children, or can't communicate with their teenagers, it wrenches my heart. Travis still calls us from college begging for more books. He reads, not because it is required of him, but because of his passion for truth. This desire has become part of his nature, and will no doubt have a central place in his vocation.

Parents can only expect to infect their children with godly character and virtue if they are themselves contagious. What our children "catch" from us will impact their hearts more than what they are taught in more direct ways. Our character—made up of characteristics like those described here—is the hammer that drives home the truth of what we say into the minds and hearts of our children. And what we do is a reflection of that character. Methods of romancing our children's hearts are as essential to our role in parenting as tools are to a craftsman.

10

METHODS FOR ROMANCERS

Draw them, woo them,
And touch them, too;
Love them and romance them,
'Til we win their hearts for You.

S axton Pope—one of the most famous archers in the tradition
of Robin Hood—wrote, "A bow, like a violin, is a work of
art….Every good bow is a work of love….A true archer must be a
craftsman." [113]

Using Pope's book as a guide, Dawson and I sculpted a longbow
from a seasoned stave of Missouri Osage that had once been a
fencepost. This golden-orange wood is considered the best for
making longbows, because of its straight, true grain and resilience.
Our challenge, as craftsmen, was to follow the grain God created
in the wood in order to release the bow that already existed within

the old fencepost. Our goal was to "romance" the bow out of the wood. This required vision, patience and skill, as well as special hand tools, including a drawknife, bench vise, spoke shave, jackplane, and calipers. The tools were essential in order for us to produce a bow with proper proportions, tiller, symmetry, and arc— one that would brilliantly cast an arrow along the right trajectory.

So it is with romancing a child's heart. The methods of romance are the tools. As in crafting a bow, the key is the skill with which we wield these tools.

YOU CAN BE YOUR CHILD'S HERO

It is Saturday morning and I am engaged in a household project. I discover that I need a few more screws from the hardware store. I don't really want to go because it disrupts the project. If I quietly slip away alone I could be back in twenty minutes. Like an efficient machine I head for the pickup truck.

As I back down the driveway, I notice my son watching through the living room window, his face squashed against the glass. I can see little round fog rings under his nose. Without doubt, he longs to go with me.

So why not take him? Sitting beside me on the front seat—if I don't turn on the radio—he'll have my undivided attention. He'll know, even if only intuitively, that I value him and enjoy his company.

After we reach the store, we don't go single-mindedly on a hunt for the screws. We do a little exploration. We stop a minute and smell the "3-in-1" oil, and the new tanned leather of the latest fancy tool pouch. I teach him about hardware and the geography of the store. I ask his opinion. I let him help me find the right screws.

On the way home, we stop at the local ice cream parlor and sit awhile, sharing a cone. I listen to him, look him in the eye, and let the boy in me become friends with my son.

Driving back up to our house, he feels like a prince. Even if he doesn't shout it to the world, he is saying in his heart, "I'm sitting next to my dad, and he's my hero!"

So, does it matter that my little errand took an hour instead of twenty minutes? When all is said and done, this small investment will return much bigger dividends than an efficient trip alone to the hardware store for screws could ever return. I might even believe that this need for screws was set up by the Author of the Story we are living, as an opportunity for me to romance my son's heart. It happens that way, minute by minute, day by day.

> *Storytelling is a kind of music with the storyteller as the instrument. And the melody romances the heart.*

For every little boy or girl in our world, there is a father or mother who is too often so focused on achieving life's little goals that he or she fails to see the opportunities to make their child prince or princess for an hour, or a day—and so do an eternal work in their hearts. Our noble missions—even legitimate ministry involvements—steal time that ought to be given to our children.

When our daughter Heather was a child, I was helping friends by mentoring a boy named Kevin. I really enjoyed our times together, as he reminded me of myself when I was a child. One Christmas morning, Kevin's whole family was at our house for breakfast. Karey had made our traditional Swedish potato sausage, aebleskivers, ostakaka, and fruit soup. After breakfast Kevin, his sister, Kim, and I took off on a long cross-country ski trip through the woods behind our house. We skied down some old logging roads and then headed into the black timber on a steep north slope where the snow was deep. When we circled back to the logging roads, I noticed some little footprints on top of our ski tracks, but I was too preoccupied with my ministry to pay them much attention.

When we got home, Karey asked if we had seen Heather. My heart sank. I immediately realized that the footprints I had seen were hers, following us. By then, the December light was fading. I set off like a skier possessed, straight down the hills, through the trees, searching for my lost little girl. I knew she was out there somewhere, up to her waist in snow, and at risk of hypothermia as the temperature dropped.

Heather wrote about the experience she had that day in a little book she called *The Mountain Girl Follows Papa*:

> Once upon a time there lived a mountain girl named Heather. She followed Papa, Kim, and Kevin. She tried to find Papa, Kim, and Kevin, but she didn't at first. She had her boots on and followed their ski tracks. She heard Papa's, Kim's, and Kevin's voices down in the spring and went through the barbed wire fence. She went to a cliff and found ribbon on a stick. She went to the end of Papa's tracks and stopped... [She] went up to the tree and started to cry.
>
> She went to the tracks again and followed the tracks all the way to another barbed wire fence. The snow made her shiver and cold and she was tired of walking and was too tired to step any further. The snow was past her knees.
>
> By a very large woods she stopped and listened and heard wild dogs. She broke a stick off with her hands because she wanted to hit the dogs with it. She was so scared. Then she heard Papa's voice and she whistled for Papa and Papa got her on his back and he walked up the hill with her on his back. Then Papa skied down the mountain with her on his back....
>
> Travis and Mommy said they had prayed for Heather and she was glad they did because what if wolves came or she was scratched by a panther, then Papa never would have his Heather back.

I had overlooked the opportunity to share an experience with Heather on Christmas morning, of all times, in order to try to minister to two other young people. However noble that other task might have been, it left my young daughter with an overwhelming longing that drove her to search me out, and left her both physically and emotionally vulnerable. You can imagine how I would have felt—how I would still feel today—if Heather's guardian angel hadn't led me to her that day, just before dark.

A minister friend of mine wasn't so fortunate. One day, he and his three-year-old son, Jonathan, were riding in their car, talking about this or that, when they passed a dead deer by the side of the road. All at once, their conversation took a different direction. "Daddy," Jonathan asked, "if I was killed, would you still be able to find me?"

It was a golden opportunity to talk about eternity and faith, and a whole range of related things, but my friend figured there would be another time for that, and he changed the subject. He didn't know that in less than three months Jonathan would no longer be with him, and he would be left forever wishing he had followed his son's questions wherever they led.

If we are wise, especially as parents, we will make the most of every opportunity, because the days are evil.[114] The evil one will steal away opportunities if we let him. Even interruptions can be opportunities. If they irritate us and we ignore them, we may be missing the best blessings in life, because they may have more to do with God's plans than with ours. We need room in our lives for relationships, or we miss the best part. Richard Swenson says, "Margin allows availability for the purposes of God. When God taps us on the shoulder and asks us to do something, He doesn't expect to get a busy signal."[115]

The same should be true for our children, when they tap us on the shoulder.

TELL STORIES

In the May 26, 1982 issue of the *Chicago Journal*, an article described children's answers to the question: "What would happen if there were no stories in the world?" One child said, "People would die of seriousness." Another said, "When you went to bed at night it would be boring, because your head would be blank."

Storytelling is an art form we all practice. It is a craft that is accessible to virtually everyone. The narrative world is dynamic, fluid, and by definition relational. Stories are nets that catch truth, and they are mirrors that show us truths about ourselves. Stories are both hygienic (healthy) and therapeutic (healing). Jay O'Callahan, a storyteller from Massachusetts, said, "Storytelling is a kind of music with the storyteller as the instrument."[116] And the melody romances the heart.

Norma Livo and Sandra Rietz describe "storying" as "a vehicle for transcending time, for binding people together with the future, the past, and one another, for extending commonality of experience, for ordering events to make existence more sensible and meaningful." In storytelling we bring "a higher level of comprehensibility to the things we do" because "we join with others emotionally and intellectually, and we generate a sense of 'rightness' and belonging."[117]

Storytellers are found everywhere. In Elko, Nevada there are cowboy poets. On the front porches of Tennessee there are grandfathers. In "Lake Woebegone" there is Garrison Keillor. In pulpits across America there are preachers. In the diners of North Dakota there are farmers. In Hollywood there is George Lucas. At "The Rendezvous" in Fairplay, Colorado, there are mountain men. There have always been storytellers.

In the early twentieth century, children performed recitations and monologues in schools and libraries. Storytellers traditionally were trained at home as the art was passed from generation to generation. "Oral" households were characterized by a family storytelling tradition featuring a story hour, usually at night around the woodstove. These times knitted families together, creating lifelong bonds, and romanced children's hearts to God's truth. But storytelling has suffered a serious decline since the advent of television. Our hearts, along with our hearths, have grown cold.

Most people, especially parents, are natural storytellers. Sitting around a dinner table, fireplace or campfire, sharing a cup of coffee with a friend, stories roll off our lips—about our families, our friendships, our lives. So we should have no difficulty telling stories to our children. Telling children our own stories puts us in a position of vulnerability, and so produces an intimate "from my heart to yours" feeling. It goes far in teaching character, in bonding and developing intimacy with our child. Writing a story down saves it, and is important, but telling it verbally brings it to life.

This does not, of course, mean we should pour out our whole past to our children—mistakes, failures and all. We do not want our children to desire, or feel they have the right, to follow in our wayward footsteps. Some parents seem to enjoy bragging about their youthful sins or, worse, use their children as therapists as they unload the garbage of their past. Discretion and common sense are in order.

I believe it is the father's responsibility to establish a storytelling tradition for his family. This may involve controlling, or even getting rid of, the television. I like the way this is expressed in the song "Once Upon A Time":

> Daddy was a family man and
> The only way he knew
> To entertain the children when
> Ole Man Winter blew
> Was to sit them down and gather them
> Around that great big fireplace,
> And say these words as he watched
> The firelight flicker on each face.[118]

We have only a finite number of days with our children. Once we grasp the importance of storytelling as a tool in the romancing of our child's heart, we will realize that we need to begin at once. Storytelling is an art, and every culture has had its master storytellers, but we can all be effective, especially if the stories are from the vast and deep store of our own experiences.

When Travis and Heather were young, I used to take them with me on the wings of story back into my memories. I told them stories in which they met me when I was a boy, about the same age as them. These fantasies created a charming paradox when I introduced them to my mother. They loved it, and they got to know me as a little boy. The stories were simple and homemade, but they hung on every word.

If our grandparents are still alive, they also have lifetimes of stories to tell. Just ask them. Their stories provide children with a sense of history and human identity, conveying truth, adventure, beauty, and drama, romancing their hearts to God. Grandparents who have lived without God also have valuable stories to tell. Often these stories point clearly to God, offering us a golden opportunity to share with our children in private about the way God leads or provides, even when the people involved may not recognize His care themselves. The relational linkage children can develop to their family roots through such stories provides them with a sense of security when the storms of life rage, and a sense of home no matter where they are. It gives them a more complete perspective, and therefore a more accurate picture, of the Sacred Romance—a God's-eye view of life.

In the past, such interchanges between generations took place regularly and naturally around the family dinner table. Today, complex family schedules have made the dining room table a nostalgic memory in many homes. This may be one of the most damaging blows the nuclear family has ever experienced. It is another reason for shutting off the television when we are together, so that the natural flow of conversation around the table will be stimulated toward, and flavored with, storytelling.

All we need to do is ask the right questions, direct the conversation, keep it uplifting and edifying, and make sure no one is left out. Start with questions such as, "How was your day?" or "What do you want to do this Saturday morning?" Follow these with specific questions concerning how the children feel about some event of the day. When a story begins, encourage the child to tell it in detail.

At the dining room table, children should be seen and heard.

Jane Healy said that an executive mind (in the good sense) is created through dialogue between a parent and child. An important time for this to happen is around the dining room table. The disappearance of the dining room table correlates with the appearance of what she terms "McLanguage." Verbal fast food, she says, consists mainly of inflection and gesture; for example, "Its like...(shrug). You know, like...." She adds, "Because the development of human language is the foundation for the development of human thought, this sloppy syntax is a symptom of a serious problem—kids don't think."[119]

When adults engage in passionate philosophical conversation, children are all ears, and when we ask them their opinion, the answers are often profound. They have a knack for speaking truth directly and clearly, when adults might tend to hedge. By including them in our conversations, we build important relational bonds. It lets them know that we respect their opinions. This is especially true in the presence of guests. The phrase "children should be seen and not heard" is so wrong. It depreciates children to something less than persons of worth. We need to welcome children into the conversation. In their childlike hearts they will think they are adults (people) among adults (people) doing adult (people) things. Before we know it, they actually will be adults, remembering those dining room discussions. At that time we will deeply desire their presence, and will harvest what we have sown.

When we have guests for dinner, there are obvious questions to ask, which will stimulate all kinds of stories: "How did you two meet?" "How did you get into that career?" "What is it like to live in Brazil?" "How did you come to know the Lord?" In this way, we also teach our children, indirectly, good conversation etiquette, by focusing the discussion around our guests rather than ourselves.

One of the greatest benefits of hospitality is that guests bring the world to our table through their stories. Our own children, as they grew, lingered longer and longer around the table. They would leave and then come back, and eventually they would stay. Many times we have been spellbound, or we laughed so hard we literally cried, as we listened to our guests' stories. Even dreams can be realized around the table. It can be a place of romance in more than one sense. Scott and Christine Dante express this truth well in the words of a song:

> *So we never got to Paris*
> *And found the café of our dreams*
> *But our table holds a whole world*
> *of memories.*
> *No, we never went to Venice*
> *And strolled the streets alone*
> *But we built our worlds together*
> *And we got the best of both.*[120]

Fathers, let's make storytelling a priority in our schedules. Plan, anticipate, and establish some goals. One way to begin is to tell our children our own life story, right from the beginning, a chapter a night. Our parents can help by filling in details we don't remember.

It takes creative and emotional energy to tell a good story. If we are running on empty in other areas of life, we need to pull back and simplify, so that we have something to offer from the recesses of our hearts.

ESTABLISH FAMILY TRADITIONS

Family traditions should be a central part of our curriculum of faith. We can use each holiday season as an opportunity to honor

God, instead of simply going through the motions and hoping that the commercialization doesn't infect our children.

The first five books of the Bible are called the Torah, which means "guidance," "direction," "instruction," and "information." The word "teach" in these books means to repeat God's truth by telling it to our children as we sit in the home, walk by the way, lie down, and rise up. Devout Jews actually began to take God's instructions literally, and wrote His words on the doorposts of their homes. Our aim as parents is to etch the truth on the doorposts of our children's hearts.

When our children see, hear, smell, taste, and feel the Word of God, it becomes part of them. As children participate through our traditions in the dramatization, they enter the Story. This is not some make-believe play—it is reality for a Christian, because it connects us to eternity past and brings God's mighty works throughout creation and history into our lives. We should be saturating the atmosphere of our homes with God's presence.

The word "remember" occurs over three hundred times in the Bible, indicating the importance of sharing and reminding our children of God's truth through the telling of His Story. Zakar is the Hebrew root word for "remember" and "memorial." Another meaning from this root is "one who remembers" or "remembering one," implying that we are the ones who carry on the story.

God instructed the Hebrews to use traditions, remembrances, and reminders as means to teach their children. As an old proverb says, "Put something where you can see it, so your eye will remind your heart." More recently, Danish philosopher and theologian Søren Kierkegaard said, "Repetition is the daily bread of life that satisfies with benediction."

Traditions build feelings of security in a child, and our relationship with our children grows as we experience things together. Traditions communicate to our children that we all belong to something bigger—something of deeper significance than stories about Santa Claus or the Easter Bunny. Our shared experiences will draw them in, captivating their affections, romancing them to God.

The word "holiday" is derived from "holy day"—a special day that was set apart for a spiritual purpose. The primary purpose of these times was to point to the larger Story through celebration and feasting—usually around the family table. Praise of God was the focus, and it was done not out of duty or obligation, but out of joy. Relationships grew as God's love, care, and will were communicated in a clear, dramatic style.

Celebrations like these write memories on our children's hearts. Children are visual, physical, emotional creatures. Specially dramatized and visualized "holy days" are highly effective in affirming their faith, as we communicate what we believe through reenacting historical events.

Even a good tradition can become routine, especially if parents shoehorn themselves and their children into it out of a sense of duty. Legalism and empty ritual are often the result. For this very reason, the Lord says, "I hate, I despise your feast days, and I do not savor your sacred assemblies."[121] We tend to fall into routines, forget about His Story and get carried away with the busyness of life. Our traditions soon focus on propositional truth, doctrine, and theology. If this happens, they become dry, oriented to formula instead of relationship, and lose their real meaning.

One way for families to combat this danger is to create their own traditions. The apostle Paul says, "Some think that Christians should observe the Jewish holidays as special days to worship God, but others say it is wrong and foolish to go to all that trouble, for every day alike belongs to God. On questions of this kind everyone must decide for himself. If you have special days for worshipping the Lord, you are trying to honor Him; you are doing a good thing."[122]

I inherited several family traditions from my childhood that Karey and I have observed with our own family. When I was a boy, my parents celebrated Christmas in the tradition of their Swedish

Christian parents and grandparents. Christmas Eve was a special and sacred family time, focused on Jesus. For days beforehand they prepared special foods that would set the day apart. This preparation heightened their anticipation of the celebration. And they made the most of what they had.

There was a shortage of meat in those days, so they mixed it with potatoes and made a special potato sausage. They took bones and the little meat remaining and simmered it all day on the wood-burning cook stove. During the mealtime, the family lined up and dipped bread in the broth. This dipping party, called *duppa i gryta*, communicated unconditional love and family unity. They had special rice pudding and fruit soup for dessert. Papa read the Christmas story from the family Bible, and the presents were opened that night.

My parents adapted these traditions to their unique family, and Karey and I have expanded them in ours. For example, the first present we open is the family Bible. Our latest addition is our "third day of Christmas" smorgasbord—a whole day dedicated to ethnic foods and fellowship—reflecting on our human heritage and contemplating how God has worked through it. We invite close friends of different heritages to share their histories. We exchange stories about God's hand in our lives. Times like these around our dining room table are times of authentic fellowship, offering a glimpse of heaven.

Another tradition we created for our family is the celebration of our children's spiritual birthdays—the anniversary date when each received Christ as personal Savior. The featured activity is a treasure hunt for our meal, which is either Colorado-style tacos, or curry. These dishes have many condiments, which can be hidden throughout the house with clues. The children go from clue to clue searching until all the food has been found. Children love the challenge of solving the puzzle by reading the clues, trying to find the pieces that fit. Having found one, they want to find another.

When the pieces are all found and put together, we have a complete meal.

For our older children, we have made the clues increasingly challenging. During the meal we recall past treasure hunts and remind them of their treasure in heaven, and the conversation is directed to sharing their testimonies.

Tom Strong and his family live north of Cheyenne, Wyoming, along the Platte River, a locale famous for its blizzards and arctic air. When Tom noticed how their Christmases had become too focused on the gift process, he decided to move the opening of gifts to a week after Christmas, so that the family could focus on the birth of Christ on Christmas Eve.

Tom also proposed that the family make a stable, and sleep in it on Christmas Eve. To his surprise, they bought the idea. They borrowed thirty or forty hay bales from their horses, and built an eight-by-eight foot shelter with a makeshift roof in their front yard. The family began Christmas Eve by walking to neighbors' homes and singing Christmas carols. Later, they piled into the cramped "stable" for the night. It was wall-to-wall people. At one in the morning, Mom went back to the house—her hay fever getting the best of her. Their daughter and her friend from college were in by two-thirty, joining Mom for some hot chocolate. But all three boys, including Tom, spent the whole night in the stable.

They woke to fresh snow. Tom had wanted to do some teaching out there, but in the end he realized that they had already learned through their senses what he might have tried to teach in words. The vivid experience had brought home to them all the real meaning of Christmas.

SHARE UNIQUE EXPERIENCES

Spending Christmas Eve outside in a hay-bale stable in Wyoming qualifies as a unique experience. Sharing unique experiences romances the hearts of everyone involved. We are connected to our friends and family, not only by facts or beliefs, but by experiences we have shared. Each experience is like a link in the chain that is the story of our lives. The more unique, unusual, and vivid the shared experiences, the greater the strength of the links. The most traumatic, challenging, exhausting, exciting, exhilarating, scary, mysterious, and costly experiences are the ones we remember best.

Why not design these unique experiences with your children? Shock them tonight by pitching a blanket tent in the living room. Then crawl in (you won't even have to ask your children to join you) and read a book to them by candlelight. The next step is actually to go camping. Camping is one of the greatest ways to bond as a family—just you against the elements.

One time, our family went camping together with Karey's cousin Terry, his wife, Joanne, and their children. We did a pack trip with horses up one of the northern canyons of Red Table Mountain in Colorado, to a secluded aspen grove. Terry and I had bowhunted there for elk, and we wanted to share the beauty of the area with our families.

We loaded two horses with all our gear and started up the mountain—horses, children, moms, dads, and a shaggy white dog named Partner. With about a half mile to go to the campsite, it began to rain hard just as we were crossing a steep bare clay slope. The horse I was leading started to lose its footing. The saddle and panniers, with about two hundred pounds of gear, began to slip off its back. I stepped below the horse to try to adjust the saddle, which slipped down over the horse's tail and back legs to the slimy ground. (Outfitters use chest harnesses on packhorses to prevent this problem, but we hadn't thought of it.) At the same time Terry's horse, a young spirited mare, began to buck and slide down the slope, dragging Terry along behind her. Since the horse I was leading only had one eye—on the uphill side—it fortunately could not see the disaster unfolding, and did not panic.

Holding the saddle with one hand, so it wouldn't roll down the mountainside, and with the other hand pushing on the horse so it wouldn't roll over me, left me in a dangerous position. One slip and a thousand pounds of horse would have planted me in the mud. As I looked up at the kids slipping and sliding, dressed in makeshift rain gear—black plastic garbage bags—and Karey and Joanne both trying to stand in place, I thought all was lost. But somehow, Terry calmed down the mare and came to the rescue. I have no idea how we ever got that saddle back on my horse—or I should say how Terry got it on, because it was all I could do to push on the horse to keep it from sliding down the hill.

After reaching a less slippery spot, we turned around to see the most incredible rainbow, arching across the narrow canyon below us. Above the rainbow the sky was a dark bluish black, and below it the sky was exploding with dazzling golden brightness. We were all speechless with wonder. It was a scene, and an experience, we will never forget.

On another occasion, Dawson and I spent a cold June night on a high lake in Utah. At midnight we were bowfishing for carp with a close friend who was a champion carp shooter—he had won Arizona's tournament a few years earlier. Dawson was only about nine, so this was a huge adventure for him.

We had not picked the best night. The water was murky and it was really cold—just at freezing—so cold that eventually I just huddled down out of the wind and gave up. But Dawson never quit. He stood the whole time on the shooting platform in the biting wind, armed and ready with his little bow. In reality there was about zero chance of him hitting a carp—the bow was too weak, the distance too far, and the carp too small.

Why was he so serious about bowfishing in these terrible conditions? Because my friend and I had invited him into our adult world, and Dawson was making the most of it. The fact that we were skunked was irrelevant to Dawson, because for those hours he was one of us. I'm sure he never wanted it to end.

Such experiences become primary links in a powerful chain of eternal moments—each lived in the present—that form the permanent memory collection we call life. This chain links us to those who will come after us, starting with our children, as well as to those who have gone before. And someday, I believe, we'll all look back in wonder at the way God included us, by His grace, as players in the drama of history called His Story.

ALLOW FREEDOM IN THE HOME

My mother met the challenge of keeping house for four very athletic sons with her usual artistic panache. She reasoned that we were programmed to be physical, and to fight or try to control this innate tendency would frustrate us, distract us from our schoolwork, and create unnecessary stress for everyone. So Mom and Dad boy-proofed the house, to relieve our stress and save Mom's valuable antiques. They bought two sturdy four-legged end tables, and metal lamps. They threaded the lamp cords through holes drilled in the tabletops, and bolted down the lamps. Of course, when we knocked a lamp the whole table fell over, but it was easy to set it up again. The most humorous part of the whole thing was that the first "boy" to overturn this ingenious device was Dad. When it happened, we all looked at Mom to see her reaction—first a smirk, then a smile, then laughter. She was, indeed, a kindred spirit with all her boys.

The floors were similarly durable: hardwood, linoleum, tile, and, in the living room, the toughest industrial-grade carpet obtainable.

Our boy-proofed house still had unmovable boundaries that our parents set for us. Grandmother's antique curved-glass china cabinet was symbolic of one of those boundaries. It was left in the house, filled with delicate dishes, vases, and bowls, many of them from Sweden. By God's grace, that cabinet was never touched, even when my youngest brother convinced Mom that it was essential for him to practice dribbling his basketball indoors. He had visions of helping his team win the high school conference championship as point guard, and simply had to hone his ball-handling skills through continuous practice on the hardwood floor.

Perhaps Mom was a bit weary after raising three boys already. Or perhaps she was still experimenting with parenting strategies. At any rate, she said, "As long as you don't bounce the ball off the walls." Believe it or not, no basketball or baseball ever touched that china, which still survives in my parents' house, despite the frequent visits of three generations of kids.

The bottom line in such matters depends upon our highest objective as parents. A mother once told me, as she reflected on raising several sons, "If I had it to do over again, I wouldn't spend as much time cleaning the stove. I would spend that time with my boys. The stove is long gone and nobody really cares anymore, including me, how clean it was."

Some of Karey's favorite sayings are: "dust is country"; "cobwebs can wait, but children's hearts cannot"; and "it's not clutter, it's creative activity." Her priority is family, relationship, and creativity. When we built the house we now live in, we designed it around food, music, and books. We built an informal bed and breakfast suite for guests. Hospitality is our priority. We have pushed this philosophy to the limits, but every time we do we end up with a little taste of heaven.

For four years, we hosted a family camp. Each time, sixty people stayed for a week. I had to build a bunkhouse for the girls. The boys slept anywhere they found themselves when they were ready to go to sleep, while the parents pitched tents and set up trailers. We rented portapotties. Karey still has dreams (nightmares?) about preparing food for that mob. We thought that hosting so many people for such a long time might put our house at risk, but it recovered. Most importantly, family, friendship and fellowship flourished during those weeks. Our children loved sharing their home—it seemed so natural and right. It gave them a sense of community that is rare these days.

Travis and Heather bring their friends home often—sometimes ten at a time—to sample Mom and Dad's cooking and the home atmosphere. It is important to them how Mom and Dad relate to their friends. They always ask, "Well, what did you think of Josh (or Shelly)?" And then we have a deep conversation. We always try to engage their friends in philosophical conversation, while asking them to tell us their stories. I also ask our kids, "What do your friends think about me?" Without fail they say, "You come across so intense and passionate they hardly know what to make of you, but they all want to come back."

> *As parents, we must part with our adult agendas, and embrace our children's dreams and plans.*

Recently, Dawson asked me if he could hang his sparring bag—an old canvas duffel bag he had stuffed with basketballs, volleyballs, and soccer balls—up in the house somewhere so he could practice his tae kwon do. He said, quoting me, that the only way to exercise consistently is if the equipment or the place is convenient. At first I was hesitant, but then I realized it could hang from a beam in our great room, away from the furniture. It worked fine, and he is able to practice his moves every time he walks by the bag. It has turned into a hit with visitors. Of course, it is not a permanent fixture, but I suspect that someday, when Dawson is grown up and has left home, we wouldn't mind seeing it swinging there, with another little boy kicking and punching it.

My sister-in-law Chris Swan, who has adopted a similar approach to atmosphere and freedom in the home, wrote this story:

> It was a typical morning in our house. I woke up, rolled out of bed, walked to the bathroom, looked in the mirror…and "they" were there. I quickly put my contacts in and went outside for some fresh air on the deck. As I opened the patio door, I gasped as I saw "them" again.
>
> I hurried back to the kitchen for a drink of water. I peered out the window at the fresh new day and again "their" presence greeted me. Without hesitation I bolted for the front door to see if I could escape, but as I was leaving "their" numbers seemed to multiply.

Opening the van door, I quietly slid inside, feeling certain I would escape "them" now. Closing my eyes, I sat paralyzed half in fear and half in hopeful relief. I lifted my head and, as the early morning sun shone through the window, I could see "their" shadows falling across my body. In a gesture of bold surrender, I looked around and, yes, "they" were there—before me, beside me, and behind me, on each and every window.

I hung my head as I realized that, for this mother of four boys, there is no escape from fingerprints.

What a picture of a home! Her boys inhabit every square inch of it and she loves it.

Once I was talking by phone to my cousin Bekki, who lives on a dairy farm in northern Wisconsin. I had just asked her something about parenting and family lifestyle when she began laughing. "What's so funny about that?" I demanded.

Bekki said, "Oh, it's not your question—it's the answer." And she painted a picture for me of her eighteen-month-old son, Moses, sitting on the linoleum floor pouring a gallon of maple syrup over his head, and then happily splashing, slapping, and trying to swim in it. Rather than getting upset, Bekki savored the sweet moment.

It's not that I'm recommending parents provide their children with jugs of maple syrup with which to experience sweet moments. However, Bekki's answer illustrates what comes to my mind when I think of a home atmosphere that contributes positively to romancing a child's heart. Children need a safe, secure home where they belong, where they are free to relax and be themselves—free to create, laugh, and cry. They need a warm-hearted, reasonably well-functioning, cheerful home—a healthy haven where they can let down their guard, take off their masks, and be nourished, fed, and rested. My uncle once said, while visiting the suburban foothills of Colorado, "These people build houses for other reasons than living in them." I think what he meant is that many of the people in question lead sterile, deprived lives in houses filled with material luxury—all the while longing for a real home.

CHOOSE TO BE A KINDRED SPIRIT

When Dawson was ten, I took him with me to have our bikes tuned up for his birthday party—a mountain bike trip in and around Moab, Utah. Several fathers and sons were going to join us, camping in the high desert, sharing a campfire, and then riding some of the best trails in the world. I am not much of a mountain biker, but I recognized Dawson's love for the sport, and his need for supervision. It was an easy choice to invest in mountain biking and in my son. Visiting the bike shop was a great experience for Dawson, but the main point was that his dad was excited about the same thing he was, and that we were doing it together.

Dawson had visited the shop with Travis when he was only four. I asked him to direct me there, making him more than just a passenger as we drove. He couldn't remember the exact location, but he helped me look for the sign. When we rolled our bikes in, I told the owners, "We're here to have you tune up our bikes and to get some instruction in shifting. I want to bike the backcountry with my son. The last time I rode a bike was ten years ago and I never got it out of high gear. I peddled up a mile-long hill, and was sore for a month." They laughed, and we all talked bikes for half an hour—Dawson, the bike shop owners, and me.

Then I noticed that they rented telemark skis and boots, so I asked, "If you had a ten-year-old son, would you start him out in telemark or downhill skiing?"

Telemark was the unanimous choice. We then had a great time dreaming and planning with Dawson concerning the best way for him to develop skills in this lifelong sport. The focus was on how Dawson and I could ski together. After discussing pros and cons, we decided we would stick with cross-country skiing for a couple more years before taking up telemark skiing.

I asked about avalanches, and Dawson heard stories of drama and danger—the stuff dreams (or nightmares) are made of. The men told Dawson that he needed to begin studying avalanches now if he planned on someday skiing steep chutes with deep powder in the backcountry.

As we drove home, Dawson was at peace with the world. The process of dreaming, preparation, anticipating adventure, and tangible action with his dad had brought genuine contentment to his boyish heart. You could see it in his countenance. This is the goal in relationship—journeying together, not simply arriving at the destination. I had shown up, and he had owned the adventure with me. I had shown him respect. He knew that the object of my affection was more than mountain biking or skiing or even him. It was our friendship, our camaraderie, our partnership. We were kindred spirits because our objective was sharing passion, hard work, and creativity. This fundamental principle is so easy to overlook, even when we have the best of intentions. It costs more—of our time, energy, and money—but is definitely worth it in the end.

As parents, we must part with our adult agendas, and embrace our child's dreams and plans, if we desire to be kindred spirits. When children share music, a book, or an idea, they are looking for our approval, support, and respect. We need to see things from their perspective—walk in their shoes, empathize with them.

My brother Scott has sons who excel in the all-American sports of basketball, football, and baseball, all of which he loves. However, when one son took a liking to soccer, which Scott never played, and for which he had little affinity, he said without hesitation, "If my son likes soccer, then I like soccer."

Scott is a creative father. He loves to fish, something that never attracted his older boys. However, they all love snorkeling, so Scott combined the two—they fish underwater. Although it is hard to cast, they have had incredible success. Recently I was riding with Scott in his minivan and asked him what the odd smell was. "Oh, it's just a frog," he said. "It escaped out of my pocket and we never could find it." I'll let your imagination work out if the frog was bait or a catch.

When Travis was still too young to drive, he was the worship leader for a local youth gathering. Every Monday night, I drove him up a road with many switchbacks to the barn where they met, on top of a mountain. Instead of simply waiting for Travis, or returning home, I took Dawson with me. This became our night out. Dawson always ran in with Travis for a few minutes to socialize with the high school kids (especially the girls—they loved him). But his main motivation was to pick up a fresh doughnut. When I finally got him back in the vehicle, we drove down to Baskin-Robbins, where we sat and licked a couple of cones, and hung out together until it was time to pick up Travis.

Kathy, a close friend of ours, is mother to eleven children. It takes ingenuity and insight to connect personally with each child, and she shared with me that sometimes the most obvious way is to look into their eyes. Eyes truly are the windows to the soul—they reveal the heart, and a child will know by our eyes that we can be trusted. Kathy and her youngest son have a morning "gazing time," when she looks deeply into his eyes with a lingering look of fondness, humor, and enjoyment. She has done this with all of her children since they were babies. She tries to catch each of her children's eyes when they approach, to let them know, uniquely, that they are the one she loves and wants to know.

We need to take advantage of every opportunity to relate one to one with each of our children. It is hard to romance a child's heart in a group.

THERE IS A COST

As I entered my teen years, I became increasingly involved in activities outside our home. New voices—attractive voices—were enticing me away from my family and the values I had absorbed and been taught through my upbringing. My parents, who for so many years had nurtured my passion for God and His creation, saw the danger I was in. They knew they could only shelter me for so long. So they became aggressive in their plan to out-romance the other suitors of my soul.

They had a literal "where the rubber meets the road" strategy. One of the things they did was let me pick out our new family car when I was in junior high. I'll never forget that ivory-colored 1963 Dodge slant-six. My criteria for choosing it were sleek looks, sleek looks, sleek looks—so I get no credit for the fact that it was the best car we ever owned. I used it in college, as did one of my brothers, and we drove it well over a hundred thousand miles.

Allowing me this much freedom came so naturally to Mom and Dad that today they hardly recall it. *But I do.* And it means as much to me today as it did then. They wooed my heart by listening to me, believing in me, trusting me, and then following through by putting their money—literal, hard-earned cash—where their respect was.

I still use the dictionary my parents bought me for college in 1966. Both covers are gone and it is barely holding together, but whenever I look at it I think: *They worked hard for the money they used to buy me that dictionary.* It is a symbol of the sacrifice they made to ensure that my brothers and I got college educations.

My brother Mike married into a family that has lived for generations on a beautiful island in Lake Michigan. The island is thirty-six miles around, a fact he knows because he once ran the perimeter in a single day. Mike and his wife, Linda, know everyone on the island, where friendships and relations run deep and strong, and there is a strong sense of community. They gather for music Friday nights in an old red barn, and sometimes have "Door County fish boils"—a famous community tradition.

Mike's expertise with computer software means that he has many business opportunities that would require a move to another part of the country. He is also a gifted Bible teacher and speaker, and has had attractive offers in fulltime ministry. But he has chosen to sacrifice career and ministry opportunities in exchange for staying close to his family. In fact, Linda and Mike chose the town that they live in based on its location—halfway between the homes of her parents and ours. Mike has not regretted it, and his children have greatly benefited from the deep roots they enjoy with family and friends. In his case, this sacrifice has had a significant role in the winning of his children's hearts for God.

Another brother, Skip, has hunted elk for several years with a bow and arrow. The hunting has not been "successful" in the normal definition of the word. But Skip has been successful in a much more important way, because he has exchanged the likelihood of bagging an elk for the pleasure of taking along his oldest son on almost every hunt.

Bringing anyone along in this sport greatly decreases your chances—but it increases your collection of stories, as each participant experiences each challenge uniquely. Together, Skip and his son have called in giant bulls, but always something happened to spoil the shot. Once, a bull was tearing up a tree with his antlers, bugling right in Skip's face, but he was on the wrong side of the tree trunk for a shot. Another time, Skip shot and a pinecone happened to fall from the tree at that particular instant, deflecting the arrow—or so he claims.

Together, father and son have camped in rain, snow and fog, miles from nowhere. Once they had to "swim" out through four or five feet of snow. But my brother has told me, "I don't care if my freezer isn't full. I won my son's heart."

Skip and his wife, Cindy, have applied this same principle in relation to sharing life with all their children. My niece wrote down some of her recollections:

> The Suburban was silent as the snow fell outside. My dad looked at my mom. What is there to say when you slide across a bridge and over a cattle guard on the ice? Even less when the cow on the other side totals the vehicle! We were stranded five miles from home on a back road in Wyoming, in the middle of December.
> "Well," Mom said, "we still need to get there."
> "There" in this case was one of a hundred events the eight of us kids participated in. Someone still had someplace to be and,

in my family, short of someone bleeding, we would manage to make it. The plan evolved. Dad was wearing dress shoes, as was Mom; my brother, who was wearing sneakers, was the same size as Mom. He elected to go stocking-foot for a time (rather than slip into her heels), giving Mom his shoes so she could jog the ice-covered gravel road in the dark back home to get our other vehicle. We were late, but we got "there."

When we first started homeschooling, Mom vowed that her children, while not having phys ed built into their school curriculum, would not be physical "morons"—a concept that won our hearts as we began trying and excelling in every sport (every sport quite literally meaning every sport that exists). I don't know how many times she must have regretted uttering those words. With at least half of us in different sports at any given time, she got creative. Coaching soccer teams means you can set the practice schedule, which in turn means you just might be able to coordinate with baseball. Coordinating with baseball means you only have two trips to make into town daily, rather then three, and only one meal a day to eat in town rather then two. Of course, all is null and void when the all-star season begins.

Ten thousand bratwursts and burgers later, we know every park in town that has BBQ grills where we can eat "family meals" between practices. Add an equal number of miles to the Suburban, resurrected after the near-fatal brush with the cow, and the hours my mother spent playing "super soccer-baseball-softball-swimming-football-basketball-(you get the picture) mom," and they begin to add up to astronomical proportions. We never felt unsupported. And my twenty-one-year-old brother still calls home to ask, "Mom, are you coming to my game?"

11

THE SENSE OF WONDER

If I've lost my sense of wonder,
What's the sense in living at all?
When the child in me can't remember,
Or hear my little boy's call?

At a conference that was drawing to a close, I wandered over to a window to relax and enjoy the scenery. The verdant green of a well-tended soccer field stretched out before me in the Colorado summer sun. Gazing at the restful scene, I noticed a mud puddle near the sidelines. A little boy sat in the middle of it, wiggling his barely-visible toes in the chocolate water. Applying some secret logic that only little boys can understand, his shoes and socks lay at the edge of the pool, completely clean and dry, while the rest of his clothes were being soaked as he splashed and laughed his way to paradise.

A knowing smile crept across my face as I watched him. After a while, I realized that a woman was standing beside me, watching the boy too. I assumed she was his mother, but no hint of disapproval or reprimand clouded her face.

I turned and asked, "Who taught you how to romance your son's heart like this?"

She remained quiet for several moments, gazing out of the window. During this time, what I had hoped was a profound question lingered in the air and seemed to wither. But then she responded as if I had asked the most natural question in the world. "Ever since his little brother died from leukemia last year, I see things differently."

Her voice trailed off. A shadow of painful memories crossed her face. "I have learned the difference between things that matter and those that are incidental. He is with me and we love each other—that matters. A little dirt and water don't. He is just a little boy loving God's creation in a way that makes God smile—in a state of innocent wonder. Who am I to rob them both of this pleasure?"

As she walked away, she implied with a whimsical shrug of her shoulders, "After all, you can always wash a pair of jeans."

A temporal perspective would see dirt, germs, and inconvenience. This wise woman's viewpoint tells the larger Story—that eternity intersects time when a little boy wonders that his toes can wiggle even when he can't see his legs. From an eternal perspective, we see a child's fascination, curiosity, amazement, and breathless enchantment at a creation with God's fingerprints and brush strokes all over it. With all that at stake, why would we rush to extricate our children from muddy puddles or syrup spills?

When children smell, touch, feel, hear, and see nature, it is as if it were creation's first morning. Eternity and the sense of wonder are connected because nature originated in the eternal creative heart of God. This single fact alone should arouse our sense of wonder as well as our children's, as they instinctively sense that the world is not ordinary, but a work of art. They are drawn to it as to a huge captivating drama—and for good reason, because creation constantly shows us the divine fingerprint. It is a book written by God, showing us glimpses of the larger Story, and eternal mystery.

Wonder is only a heartbeat away from worship.

Of all creatures, only humans are capable of wonder, of feeling excited by something unknown or miraculous that is beyond our comprehension, our grasp, our control—beyond the comfort and safety of our rational adultish world. To "halt in amazement" is the way Cornelis Verhoeven describes wonder. He suggests that the event of wonder is inserted into the middle of movement and brings a momentary pause to thought—a cessation of movement and a break in our normal stream of consciousness. When we halt in wonder, we instinctively "hold our breath"—which then "catches in our throat." This pause, for a Christian, is in actuality a form of worship.

According to Plato, wonder is the beginning and cause of philosophy. Wondering at the changing nature of things led Plato to assume the existence of the eternal, imperishable, and transcendent. This perspective implies that philosophy is something that is "done" rather than simply "known." Socrates said, "The sense of wonder is the work of the philosopher. Philosophy indeed has no other origin."

Verhoeven, in his book *The Philosophy of Wonder*, gives larger meaning to the word than is traditionally embraced. His definitions include many biblical elements, when he writes that wonder is not "a quasi-romantic, wide-eyed passivity" but "an aggressive action, an exciting adventure, an exercise in free fall." Wonder is "the principle, the basic structure...not only the beginning, but also the end." Wonder "guides and accompanies thought....It has not only the first but also the last word.[123]

Wonder is only a heartbeat away from worship. It is the natural reaction to belief in God and the fact that He is the Creator of time, space, and matter. Wonder is a prerequisite to worship. Scripture tells us that Almighty God is worthy of worship because He is the Creator of all things.[124] We honor Him when we live gladly in a state of wonder because of His works, the most wondrous of which is that humans can have an eternal relationship with Him.

Children wonder naturally, but adults soon teach them to end this esoteric pursuit. Most children's sense of wonder is crushed or lost by the time they reach third grade, through a secular culture that brings futile and cynical despondency into their once wonder-filled lives. When they become adults, they tend to fall into routines, grow complacent, and lead pragmatic lives. They grow up, and as they get bigger, everything else gets smaller. Words like blasé, worldly-wise and sophisticated describe grown-ups who have become adultish, and have stopped asking "silly" childlike questions.

Mike Storkey says "the effects of the sixties' libertarian revolution [loss of wonder] were a little like bludgeoning Santa Claus to death in order to get at the presents immediately...."[125] This is the natural consequence of a generation living out the secular worldview of our culture. Without God there is no big Story. Without Story, wonder is quixotically absurd, leading nowhere. Our culture has lost its sense of wonder because it has lost God.

The closer we are to God's absolute truth, goodness, and beauty, the more we wonder, regardless of our age. Charles Dickens, writing of his love for children, said it is not a slight thing when those who are "fresh from God" love us. But the Enlightenment narrowed our vision through its fragmented microscopic view of the world. According to Peter Kreeft, it was as though they "screwed down the manhole covers on us so we became squinting underground creatures."[126]

Einstein felt that anyone who could no longer feel the sense of wonder was as good as dead. Often, when I make a discovery in my field of science, I am left stunned with wonder. All I can say is, "God is here!" I sometimes feel like a child playing on the beach, as described by Sir Isaac Newton, looking for pretty pebbles while there is a whole ocean of undiscovered truth lying in front of me.

Children are spontaneously and naturally drawn to things that make them wonder, especially God's creation. The exploration of the creation is a satisfying process for a child. Because children naturally live in the present, they savor the moment and the sheer sensory experience. Perhaps this is why Christ spoke of the ideal of childlikeness. When children wonder at the world around them, they may be the closest of all people to comprehending the reality of God. Often this is expressed by a wide-open mouth. They believe in Story—in the sky, in the rocks, in the water, in the trees, and in the animals. This captivates them, draws them, and romances their hearts.

Childlike wonder is also characterized by trust in the order of things, because God is almighty and has a good heart. These assumptions are the foundation of childlike faith, for without them wonder degenerates into helpless bewilderment. Astronomer Jean Picard said that wonder is fatal if it is not assimilated. Wonder must be connected to the larger Story or it will lead nowhere, leaving the wonderer to despair.

Wonder is the essential instrument of the poet, artist, scientist, and any other creative thinker. It incites the mind to organize information, observations, data, and ideas into pattern and form. Perhaps adults cease to wonder simply out of fear. They do not wholly trust that God will provide a happy ending. They were taught to trust in their rational logic. This sophistication short-circuits their wonder, and they are afraid to be carried away into the unknown. They would rather hold their own flashlights, instead of holding God's hand and following Him through the darkness.

Wonder runs through Scripture, leading us to one reality—the worship of God. "Stand still and consider the wondrous works of God."[127] "Lift up your eyes on high, and see Who has created these things."[128] "When I consider Your heavens, the work of Your fingers, the moon and the stars, which You have ordained," David, the shepherd-king says to God, "what is man that You are mindful of him, and the son of man that You visit him?"[129]

David's son Solomon was a naturalist. "God gave Solomon wisdom and very great insight, and a breadth of understanding as measureless as the sand on the seashore....He described plant life, from the cedar of Lebanon to the hyssop that grows out of walls. He also taught about animals and birds, reptiles and fish. Men of all nations came to listen to Solomon's wisdom, sent by all the kings of the world, who had heard of his wisdom."[130]

Clearly, God's creation is far more than just a pretty backdrop to life. Getting to know the creation firsthand, and searching for truth as we walk the way of wisdom, should be one of the most natural pursuits of believers.

For many of us, the most vivid memories we have from childhood involve nature. Ask little children what they like most and it will usually be things like dirt, flowers, rocks, horses, water, volcanoes, dragonflies, earthquakes, dinosaurs, and thunderstorms. As children, most of us had a natural attraction to the earth—an insatiable desire to explore and to have adventures. This force drove us and filled each day with newness and wonder. Nature's stories wooed and romanced us to God, even if we had not been taught about Him and it was only an indefinable longing. Our natural awareness grew, fueled by the fascination we had for God's handiwork.

A lot may have changed in us and in our world since we were young, but children haven't changed. Our children probably also have an insatiable desire to experience and to explore nature. We can help them with a "sense of wonder" curriculum.

EXPERIENCING NATURE

Hands-on experiences allow our children's sense of wonder to thrive and grow. Children who touch rocks, catch butterflies and watch clouds become naturalists in the whimsical sense, whether they choose science as a vocation, hobby, or simply as a vehicle to deeper worship of God the Creator.

The activity of wonder will romance that child's heart—if we avoid sermonizing.

We can feed our children's sense of wonder through a systematic, hands-on exploration of the earth. How simple or varied this will be depends on where we live, our ability to dovetail the exploration into family vacations, our willingness to travel, the age of our children, and, to a lesser degree, our finances. But we can all begin where we live, in our own backyard or the local park. What is essential is that parents and children experience nature together.

A "curriculum" to cultivate a child's sense of wonder must be centered around all five senses. Children need to see, smell, hear, touch, and taste God's creation. In this phase, our goal is experience, not analysis.

As an earth scientist, I recommend a curriculum organized around the spheres of the earth: the atmosphere (air), the hydrosphere (water), the lithosphere (crust), the athenosphere (mantle), and the biosphere (life). This will give a broad and balanced coverage of creation, while sparking ideas for other areas of study.

To experience the atmosphere, consider: a hot air balloon or airplane ride; watching a sunrise or clouds; flying paper airplanes or a kite; photographing lightning; chasing a thunderstorm. The hydrosphere can be experienced through canoeing, fishing, watching waves, wading, swimming, and walking in the rain. Discover the lithosphere by spelunking (cave exploration), mountain climbing, rock collecting, and backpacking. Dig a hole, build a snowman, visit a quarry, or ride a bike. To learn about the athenosphere, visit a volcano, visit the Yellowstone geysers or lava flows, or soak in a hot spring. The biosphere is probably the most readily approachable wherever we live: keep a pet; go hunting or bird watching; climb a tree; pick raspberries; garden; cook a meal.

These activities, and many more like them, bring parents and children together into direct contact with nature. Unless children ask for facts about what they are experiencing, these are not the times for scientific lectures. Our primary role is to participate in a childlike way, by engaging our own five senses, and our hearts, in a shared, uncomplicated experience.

This is not always as easy as it sounds. Last winter, Dawson and I were driving past Evergreen Lake when we saw some ice fishermen. Dawson begged me to stop, and we walked down to the edge of the lake. I felt conspicuous without any fishing equipment, so I sat on a bench while Dawson stepped onto the slushy ice. To my surprise, he didn't walk up to the fishermen. He just wandered around on the ice, poking sticks down abandoned fishing holes, sliding, and examining the textures in the ice.

Finally, when he had talked me into joining him, I understood what was going on. The fishermen were secondary to his fascination and wonder that were focused on the lake. He then asked if we could try ice fishing sometime, and I said I had great plans to take him to a lake about an hour's drive away, where I knew there were huge northern pike. He said with a sigh, "Papa, let's just fish here."

I had missed the point. He didn't need a special lake with giant fish; he just needed a lake. All I had to do was let his agenda become mine, and let his sense of wonder resuscitate mine, and we would have a great time—as we always do when I allow this to happen.

As we cultivate our child's sense of wonder, our own sense of wonder will be stimulated too. We will become like children, enjoying again those things that the responsibilities of adulthood have crowded out of our lives.

Thomas Carlyle said that the tragedy in life is not what we suffer, but what we miss. We need to learn how to see, how to sense, how to be aware of what is going on around us—the small, simple, ordinary, everyday things. If we are doing that, we will be able to answer questions like:

- What types of clouds were in the sky the last time I was outside?
- What weather did they indicate might be approaching?

- What smells were carried by the wind?
- Which way was the wind blowing?
- What flowers were in bloom?
- What birds were singing?

If the answers are all a mystery, we need to get reacquainted with our senses. We can only enter our child's world if we are tuned in to our surroundings. Dawson prefers to sleep outside for most of the summer, and he would in the winter too if we let him. He wants to be engulfed by, and immersed in, nature—luxuriating in the mosquito-free, fresh Colorado night air.

Modern culture and society have lured many of us away from nature and from using our senses. Television, computers, the four-walled comfort of our houses, our luxurious cars—all have dulled our senses. Distinctions that were sharp to us as children are now but a blurred background for our stark, pollen-free, scentless adultish reality.

The most fascinating aspect of Y2K (besides it being the most significant non-event of the twentieth century) was its function as a wake-up call to people who had come to rely nearly completely on society and technology for their needs. Many had forgotten that a loaf of bread begins in a wheat field; that clean drinking water is not a luxury, but an everyday necessity; that apples on the supermarket shelf come from a tree, the milk from a cow that receives good feed. Forgetting these realities has weakened our connection to the earth. We are divorced and disconnected from true creation, as we live in a world we think we created.

Most of us have a vast knowledge of our popular culture, which we consume in earnest, but we are embarrassingly ignorant of the world God created. While nearly everyone can name those famous cereal characters—Snap, Crackle, and Pop—few can walk down the street where they live and name the flora and fauna that make their stroll so enjoyable. John Muir inspired his daughters to learn the names of the trees in their garden by saying, "Don't you like to be called by your first name?"

Participation with a child in the activity of wonder will romance that child's heart—if we avoid sermonizing. "Billy, see the pretty bird God made just for us to see" forces a dutiful response to our dutifully given theological explanation. On the other hand, a spontaneous expression of genuine wonder and curiosity excites a child's interest and points inevitably to God in a way that woos rather than repels a young mind. "Wow! Look at that hummingbird!"—as it dive bombs past your heads—"I wonder how it can fly like that—up, down, sideways, any which way it wants. I wonder if it can fly upside down?"

These comments may lead you to read descriptions in guidebooks or to visit www.hummingbirds.net on the Internet, where you can learn any number of things about the seventeen species in North America, or the three hundred and twenty species worldwide, of the bird family Trochilidae. For now, however, the "Wow!" will suffice.

While we're encouraging our children to touch the creation, they are bound to want to sit in a mud puddle from time to time. If we really want to impress them, we'll jump in with them. It's worth doing just to see the look on their faces, and to feel the camaraderie in the chocolate water. Mud, dust, sap, sand, bugs, soot, and plain dirt don't hurt anyone. In fact, a recent *Science News* issue promoted the idea that dirt is good for children—which every kid knew all along.

The article, "Germs of Endearment," reported that, by raising barricades against deadly scourges such as smallpox, typhoid fever, and polio, we have shielded people from microbes and parasites that do not harm us. Scientists now suspect (keep in mind that this is preliminary and the problem is extremely complex) that stamping out innocuous organisms and separating people from dirt with modern antiseptic environments is weakening some parts of children's immune systems while other parts grow unchecked. This, they theorize, causes an imbalance triggering asthma, allergies, and even autoimmune diseases such as rheumatoid arthritis and the most severe type of diabetes.

Studies have found that hay fever is less common in children raised on farms than in urban areas. Also, children in large families, particularly the younger siblings, have fewer allergies than children from smaller families. This suggests that germs brought home by older siblings may protect younger children from allergies by strengthening their immune systems. Antibiotics—especially when administered before age two—may be killing off beneficial bacteria, spurring some immune disorders. [131] So, a little dirt—even a moderate amount of dirt—is important to the health of children.

Had we known this, we might not have hindered two-year-old Travis's attempt to strengthen his immune system. We were living west of Tucson, Arizona, in the desert mountains. It was spring, and I was tilling some manure into our garden. I had brought Travis down from the house and set him under a Palo Verde tree in an open area away from the manure pile. The sandy and gravely ground was dry, and he seemed content to watch a covey of quail walking around with their newly hatched chicks.

I was preoccupied with the garden, but suddenly noticed how quiet Travis had become. When I glanced over I saw that his mouth was full of something. I ran over and, to my shock, realized that his little hands and mouth were packed full of rabbit droppings. They were well seasoned and dehydrated, and I hadn't noticed them when I set him there. I had kept him away from my manure pile, but he had found his own. Poor Travis—the next few minutes must have been bewildering for him as I scooped him up, and ran with him to the house, all the time pulling rabbit droppings out of his mouth. And then he had to endure having his mouth washed with soap—not once, but three times.

There is an irrepressible attraction between little children and dirt. Dawson enjoys dirt even more than I did as a child. Once, we flew to Florida from Denver via Dallas. In the Denver airport, when Dawson stood up to board the plane, we noticed that the seat he had been sitting in was covered with sand. We could not understand where so much sand had come from, especially since he had taken a bath the night before and he was wearing clean clothes. Then in Dallas he sat down waiting for our connecting flight, and when he stood up there was more sand—a lot of sand. By the time we got to Florida the sand was appearing in smaller quantities. To this day we don't know where it all came from. It would have been more understandable if we had been traveling back the other way, from Florida to Denver.

Tools of all sorts—nature guidebooks, rock hammers, hand lenses, butterfly nets—all help our children in their exploration of the spheres of the earth. If they learn, through our participation and guidance, to become good observers, skilled in the collection of specimens and data, then they will rise naturally to the more technical level of pattern recognition. When they want to go beyond merely experiencing the earth, it is time for unit study.

EXPLORING NATURE

Unit study can come in a variety of shapes and sizes—the best being delight-driven, because these flow from our child's natural inclinations and curiosities. When children's passions are ignited by some interest, then the study is personalized. They own it, and end up investing much more energy in the study than they otherwise might. Unit studies can be called special projects, hobbies, extracurricular activities, research, or play. In one case, we called ours "The Flowers of Evergreen."

When my mother was a young girl in northern Wisconsin, she was enthralled by the song "Springtime in the Rockies," and the vision it brought to her of Colorado mountains, meadows, and flowers. Little did she know that someday her eldest son would raise his children in Colorado. I love to call my mother when the snow is almost gone and springtime comes to the Rocky Mountain meadow that is our front yard, and tell her the first flowers of the year have bloomed. Her girlhood dream has come true through her son.

One spring, our family decided that, instead of just casually looking at the flowers in our meadow, we would study them, photograph them, smell them—get to know them firsthand. This experience was like examining the brush strokes of a master Artist, Who over the next few months painted our meadow with delicate, extravagantly beautiful flowers—some of which bloomed for just a few days until, to paraphrase the psalmist, the Chinook winds blew and they were gone and their place remembered them no more.[132]

But we remembered them—more than two hundred in all. Our study began when Travis (eight at the time) informed us that a purple pasqueflower had pushed its way up through the melting snow. I grabbed my camera, Karey and Heather, and brought along several flower guidebooks and a notebook. We then followed Travis through scattered snowdrifts to the first flower of the year.

Artistic photos of wildflowers generally emphasize color. But form and texture are also important because they are the keys to identification. These are captured best in black and white photos or by sketching. This is why many flower experts take great pride in their ability to draw flowers. Some even downplay the role of photography as an aid in flower identification.

Travis carefully sketched the pasqueflower, as Heather recorded information in our notebook, including date, location, and flower name. With camera in hand, I ended up lying down and crawling around on my elbows on the wet, gravely ground until I had framed several pasqueflowers in my viewfinder. We soon learned that, in order to examine and photograph a flower properly, you must contort your body into myriad uncomfortable positions for agonizing periods, to get the flower positioned just right for its portrait.

By the end of the spring, there was an amber haze of pollen hovering over our meadow. But not until green clouds of pine pollen began to drift by did anyone feel any hay fever symptoms. The pollen can become intense when you spend day after day eye to eye with flowers.

Something we noticed immediately was that bees were often interested in the same flowers we were photographing. It is a good idea to consult your doctor before embarking on a study like this, to ask if you should have a dose of epinephrine on hand for possible allergic reactions to bee stings. These are rare, but they can be deadly. Somehow, we escaped bee stings, even though we had ten beehives of our own at the edge of the meadow.

In these intimate studies of nature, we must always be prepared for the unexpected. One afternoon, we discovered endangered Colorado orange-red wood (tiger) lilies blooming around our spring. As I knelt down to photograph a flower, I was interrupted by a loud squeaking sound, which came from a very large mouse being swallowed by a very small snake. One of the strangest and funniest sights we ever came across was a stump sporting a crew cut— hundreds of golden hair-like strands sticking out of its top, which turned out to be a squirrel's hoard of grass seeds, stored in an amazingly orderly way for the winter.

Age level and natural science aptitude determine how sophisticated your study will be. Since our children were under ten when we did the flower study, we limited information collection to identification and the time of the first flower's appearance. Had they been older, we would have included such things as temperature, rainfall, length of blooming time, and flower color. The more information that is recorded, the more patterns we will see, and the more science we end up doing. Science is simply the pursuit of knowledge through observation and experience, pattern recognition, and the organization of this information into a story.

During a study like this, we will naturally be led down occasional rabbit trails. For us, one of them was the gathering and preparation

We can't, and shouldn't try to write the script for them—God already has.

of wild greens for a salad, which is a custom in France. We recommend doing this one in moderation—we found that our family's digestive systems were not accustomed to so many vitamins and nutrients in such a concentrated form.

This experience did not discourage us. Tasting edible flowers and plants became one of the highlights of our study, and gave us great respect for Native Americans and early settlers, who relied on wild plants as an important part of their diet. It also gave us a sense of self-reliance, since understanding what is edible in the wild is a practical survival skill.

Travis learned that one bowl of kinnikinnick berry soup for breakfast curbed his hunger for the whole day, and although the concoction tastes like green apples, it is not half bad if you pretend that you are starving. Although most wild plants are edible, a few are poisonous; therefore, the ability to identify them is all-important. When in doubt, don't eat. If young children are involved in the study, clear and careful instruction is advised.

Another highlight for us was collecting and drying the flowers. About the middle of the summer, when our meadow had become a kaleidoscope of colors, Karey began carefully picking flowers to dry. Approximately ten percent of flowers are considered rare or endangered and are protected by law, so we picked only flowers that were abundant, while avoiding uprooting any flower.

We discovered that there are two traditional drying methods. The first requires a drying agent such as silica gel or smooth beach sand. Mortar sand is too abrasive. We used silica gel purchased from a craft store. Flowers are placed in a box and the sand (which must be dry) is gently poured around and over the flowers. In a few days the sand will dehydrate the flowers. Once the sand is gently removed we are left with a perfectly dry preserved flower. In most cases the color is also preserved. We made some beautiful arrangements of dried flowers with these.

Flowers can also be dried in a flower press, which is two nine-by-twelve-inch pieces of wood with wing nut screws at each corner. Place the flower between the boards along with some cardboard to absorb moisture, and tighten the screws. After a few days the dried flowers can be mounted behind glass in a picture frame for wall hanging, or mounted on heavy paper as a page in a notebook of flowers.

Karey also gathered flowers and other plants, particularly seedpods, and hung them in bunches to dry. These were beautiful works of art in themselves, and added a nice aroma to air in the house. She used the dried flowers to make wildflower wreaths, which she hung on our porch and throughout our home.

Our family persisted in documenting flowers through late spring snows, monsoon thunderstorms, hot and dry summer days, and finally September frosts. We rarely missed a day. Although our goal was to complete the study, our greatest joy came during the process of search and discovery.

After the last flower—a showy aster—had caught the frost and withered in late September, we began organizing our slides and flower information, grouping the more than two hundred flowers we had identified according to the month in which they first appeared. It was fascinating to research the origin of a flower's common name, and the folklore attached to it. This gave us a wealth of material for a colorful slide presentation. Karey and I helped with organization, while Heather and Travis wrote the text. They eventually presented the show to their grandparents, friends, and local community groups. Encouraged by the positive responses, we contemplated publishing a flower guide for Evergreen, but the cost of doing it in color was prohibitive.

The key to successful, and fun, unit study is to recognize that each child has unique interests. We can't, and shouldn't try, to write the script for them. God already has.

A few years after Heather and Travis completed our first flower study, I suggested to Dawson that we do one with him. "No thanks," he said. "I've already started my own study."

"But you don't understand," I argued. "We will learn all about edible plants, and we can collect specimens."

"Papa, I know all about the study Heather and Travis did," Dawson replied, "but I want to do one on bugs."

Today the main attraction for guests in the Swan home is Dawson's insect collection. It is a work of art. All the insects are professionally mounted and labeled. He uses a black light and white sheet to attract moths at night. He sets his alarm clock to wake himself up at certain times to check the sheet. One summer our family drove from Denver to the West Coast, then back across the continent to the East Coast before returning home to Denver. Every night, we went to sleep with swarms of insects landing on the black-light-illuminated sheet.

Dawson collected and collected. One night, I drew and colored a huge moth on cardboard, then cut it out and pinned it to the sheet while he was asleep. He got the surprise of his life when he checked his sheet the next morning. I loved the grin he had for me when I asked him if he had caught anything during the night.

Recently, Dawson scheduled us to spend three nights in southern Arizona with his entomologist mentor and colleagues. They use powerful mercury vapor lamps to attract insects at night. Dawson had to obtain a permit for this world-class collection area, so that he could pursue his treasures night after night. I could fill a book with the experiences from that expedition. Insect nightlife is spectacular and mysterious. The first night Dawson and a gargantuan long-horned beetle collided. Dawson was knocked down and the beetle knocked out. The same night hundreds of huge silk moths came to Dawson's sheet—*Eacles imperialis oslari*, *Citheronia splendens sinaloensis*, and *Automeris pimina*—some of them sporting seven-inch wingspans. We were both enchanted as they silently came to the light, and spellbound as bats periodically snatched one out of the air. The next day we joined a professor and his students hiking and collecting reptiles and amphibians in a remote Arizona canyon. Incidentally, I never pictured myself carrying a butterfly net until this trip. Now I never leave home without one.

TREASURE HUNTING

Peter Hiett, our pastor, who has a degree in geology, wrote in a letter to me: "In Proverbs 25:2 we find these words: 'It is the glory of God to conceal a matter, but the glory of kings is to search out a matter.' Does that mean creation is like a treasure hunt arranged by a loving father? I think that's what the fathers of the scientific revolution thought....Science at first was worship. I think worship is wonder, and wonder is the obvious response to glory."

I am sure God experiences joy when we explore and search His creation, because I know the joy that I've experienced in creating treasure hunts for my kids and then watching them follow the clues.

One day when Travis was about ten, he came up to the house with an ancient axe. The handle was weathered to a thin skeleton. "I was building a fort next to the ledge when I found this!" he exclaimed. "You said that Jesse James used to hang out around here. Do you think this might have been his axe, Papa? Do you?"

We were living on part of an old Colorado ranch located in an area that had been one of Jesse James's old haunts. At that moment, an idea crystallized in my mind—to design a treasure hunt and keep this excitement of discovery and imagination alive as long as possible, while at the same time teaching Travis and Heather a little history, orienteering, biology, logic, reading, and research.

I shook my head slowly, pondering the possibilities. "I don't know, Travis," I replied. "But it sure looks like it's old enough to have been here when he was alive."

To make a long and wonderful story short, I spent the next three days secretly placing leather map fragments, antique bottles, artifacts, and a sealed wooden box containing pre-1900 coins wrapped in an old canvas bag, in various places near the spot where the axe had been found. I chipped clues into cliff faces and then glued moss back on to give the clues the appearance of age. When I was finished, there was a hand-sculpted bear track at the spring hole and a bottle carefully placed under the roots of a tree, among the clues and along the trail to the treasure.

As the day of the hunt approached, the sense of anticipation I experienced was intense. I suggested that Travis and Heather invite two friends over and the stage was set. When the children arrived we had a lunch together and then I nonchalantly said to Travis, "Why don't you see if you can find some more relics under that rock ledge where you found the axe? Here's a shovel you can use."

In a moment, the four children were transformed into explorers, archaeologists and adventurers, as they set off to see what they might find. I followed at a distance, not wanting to miss a thing. When they discovered the first old bottle with the map fragment in it, and an Indianhead penny, they entered another world. They truly believed for several days that they had found the treasure of Jesse James. They had a wonder-filled day, and mine was just plain wonder-full.

There isn't room to tell you the rest of the story here. In fact, they had such a great time that we began writing a little book together, telling the treasure hunt story complete with maps and illustrations. Then the little book started to grow, as if it had its own life. All that's missing now for this story to become a historical novel for children is some research on nearby gold-mining towns. Now, doesn't that romance your heart a little and tap into your sense of wonder?

As far as I'm concerned, anybody can design a treasure hunt for kids. Start by discovering some local lore with a little mystery (or invent some through storytelling), and then develop a hunt that will test the participants without frustrating them. Success depends on the combination of just enough suspense and difficulty to keep them wondering, plus an increasing set of rewards that will keep them motivated to reach the final goal—the treasure.

The last time we did a treasure hunt, since Dawson had caught on, I surprised him with a comical twist. The "treasure" at the end of the hunt was a case of Rawhide root beer (a special locally brewed beverage) that I had buried carefully, remembering to replace the sod over the hole. "Papa!" Dawson exclaimed when he discovered it, and I said, "Let's go up to the house and make root beer floats."

Two to four children is just about the right number to keep them working together to find a prize that none of them might be able to find alone. If they can learn this valuable lesson about creative cooperation early, who knows what they will be able to discover or achieve as their sense of wonder encounters God's treasures over a whole lifetime.

We as parents have the responsibility and privilege to protect and cultivate our children's sense of wonder. Fortunately, God has made this easy through the beauty and intricacy of His creation. Our role is to provide the opportunity for them to experience and explore it—and to share these endeavors with them as fellow treasure hunters (sometimes called "scientists"). God will do the rest—for us, and in us.

> With a quiver of arrows, a dog at his side,
> The sun on his shoulders, a gleam in his eye,
> The whimsical wisdom he shares with me,
> Paints a picture of life, it's somethin' to see.
> He builds forts in the trees and forts underground,
> And some out of old aspen logs.
> His goal's in the making, the building, creating,
> And not in what's finished and done.
> And when the fires of his wonder warm my soul,
> His honest brown eyes let me know.
> I'll hold this moment as long as I can,
> For it may never come 'round again.[133]

12

THE CREATIVE IMAGE

Holy, Holy Wind,
Let Your passion rise again;
Lover of their souls,
Set a fire in them.

There is a place, an enchanted place, down near our spring, cradled by a granite ledge. It is where an aspen grove meets a stand of giant blue spruce and Douglas fir. In this small, secluded meadow, edged with a raspberry patch and carpeted with purple violets, we found the name for our home—Singing Springs. Often I have dreamed of building a log cabin there, with a porch for sitting and songwriting, creating, and contemplating. I put it off partly because I have so many projects on the go, but partly too because I did not want to disturb the pristine beauty God placed there. But every time I walk down the path that takes me to the forest beyond, I design and construct this cabin in my imagination.

So when I heard about the newest fort that Dawson was building "down by the spring," I went to investigate.

The most delicately beautiful part of "my" little meadow was a big mess. Scrap lumber, even particleboard, had been dragged a long distance from some construction site, and was strewn about, crushing the tender spring grass and wildflowers. The beginning of a frame was taking shape. The design was "pole barn, circa 1970." It was not square or level. Sixteen-penny nails, painstakingly driven, held it together.

At first, shock and disgust froze my heart with anger. But soon the ice melted, as the reality of my little boy's passion swept over me like a sweet storm. He had begun construction with the best materials he could find, following his own original design. He had placed it not just anywhere in my meadow but in *the best spot* in my meadow—the spot that even the designs in my imagination refused to consider because of its "sacredness."

As the fires of his wonder warmed my soul, tears welled in my eyes, and it dawned on me—this is the creative image of God incarnate in my little boy! He had made this pristine place a holy place. I joined in God's joy, and smiled and smiled and smiled.

Dr. Paul Brand and Philip Yancey, in their book *In His Image*, tell us the image or likeness of God in which we were made is not our physical shell of bones, muscle, and skin. Our body is simply a vessel or repository for God's image, which is non-material. Although there is no consensus among theologians, the image of God in us is probably a combination of attributes, including our ability to reason, spiritual facility, capacity to make moral judgments, and the capacity for relationship.[134]

Dorothy Sayers has stated, "When we turn back to see what He [God] says about the original upon which the 'image' of God was modeled, we find only the single assertion, 'God created.' The characteristic common to God and man is apparently that; the desire and ability to make things [creativity]."[135]

God's creativity is the central theme of the first chapter of the Bible. God created time, space, and matter out of nothing—*ex nihilo*. Then He created us, "in His own image."[136] Both Old and New Testaments emphasize that we are God's "workmanship."[137] The Greek word, *poeas*, is the root of our English word "poetry." Thus, in a sense, we are God's poetry, which is just another way of saying that the image of God in us conforms in part to God's attribute of creativity—the desire, ability, and need to create. If we are created in His image then we *must* be creative.

The creative image of God in us is difficult to define absolutely, because it is, at best, but a poor reflection of an infinite reality—an attribute of God. What we do know is this: to be creative is to have the ability to bring into existence, to cause, or to make. This power is expressed in designing, inventing, shaping, and organizing through imaginative skill and ingenuity. This ability is innate in humans—transmitted to us from God. The creative image is a representation, likeness, or copy of the original—a similitude of God's creativity.

In a very real sense, discovering and developing this attribute is central to finding success and fulfillment in life, because most things that are interesting, important and human are the results of creativity. Burning curiosity, wonder at mystery, and delight at finding a solution that makes order visible—all these accompany creativity. Our fullest happiness, greatest passions, and deepest satisfactions on earth come during the creative act.

Creativity causes the spirit to sing because it brings relief from the fear that no one is out there. The discovery of order—cosmos out of chaos—floods us with peace, hope, and joy. Order is evidence for God's existence. This reality slices through the veil of despair and boredom that shrouds our fallen nature, giving us a lightning-flash glimpse of true reality—the larger Story. Creativity is a powerful tool for us to wield in the competition for our children's hearts.

Cultivating the creative image of God in them will draw them to the true Source of what delights them most.

Creativity is present even in the "hidden art" of everyday life. Where it stands out is in the fine arts, performing arts, literature, and crafts. Although not traditionally acknowledged, it is also present in such things as science, engineering, athletics, business, and politics.

The creative image of God in us demands expression. When we create we comprehend God better—even feel a holy camaraderie with Him. We own the process. This is a powerful reality. Children long for this ownership when they say the revealing words, "Let *me* do it."

As I see it, the process of creating is as much the goal as the product of the creative effort. The journey is actually the destination. The story told by the process gives our creativity value, purpose, and ultimate meaning. The mere fact that we can create at all is evidence that there is a divine blueprint, not only for each of us personally, but for all humanity.

CREATIVITY AND CHRISTIANITY: DISAVOWING THE DIVORCE

The creative aspect of the image of God in man was laid aside and largely ignored by Christians during the twentieth century. What attention it did receive usually revealed an awkward and estranged relationship. The roots of this tension can be traced to the Enlightenment, when art and religion began to separate. Eventually, there developed a split—the marriage between art and religion that had once produced great works ended in divorce. Christian culture, in response to the separation, began viewing functionality as its highest aspiration. In reaching for that end, creativity in every sphere was neglected.

With Christianity no longer the driving force and inspiration behind music, art, literature, science, and social reform, marginalization of Christianity in our culture was inevitable. Today, our efforts are centered primarily in the humanitarian and moralistic arenas. We have invested our resources and focused our creative imagination on mass evangelism, and have become watchdogs of the moral conscience of the culture. These are legitimate endeavors, but where is the witness to God's creative nature and His passion for beauty, in a world that was made to be dazzled by these aspects of His character?

The first persons recorded in Scripture as being filled with the Holy Spirit were the artisans and craftsmen God ordained to fashion the holy vessels and furniture for the tabernacle. Aaron's priestly garments were to be designed for "beauty and holiness." Beauty thus bears witness to the character of God, and art is an ordained way to bear this witness. Art lifts us beyond the physical world, building a bridge to the spiritual realm. Since all our thoughts of God by definition are analogical, the creative imagination provides a blueprint for building this bridge.

But where beauty is viewed as non-essential by many Christians—a worldly extravagance that believers do not have time to indulge in as they work for God's kingdom—the secular world, particularly in the powerful arenas of the arts, science, entertainment and the media, is largely devoid of Christian influence. To the degree that we boycott involvement in these areas, the competition wins by default. We forfeit our children's creative desires to the adversary because we offer no appealing alternative.

Our children's hearts are naturally drawn to the challenge and fascination of creating, and to the beauty that the world deceptively presents. How can we romance our children if we are not in the contest? God is the Creator, Artist, and Author. All we need to do is show up. We have the advantage in this arena, but if we abdicate the romance of our children's hearts in the name of pragmatism and a misguided sense of morality, in the end we will essentially hand the prize to the competition.

PROTECTING THEIR CREATIVE IMAGE

Often Christian parents do not recognize the need to protect the creative image of God in their children, who are then left unprotected as cultural noise bombards them from all sides, assaulting and corrupting their imaginations. The noise desensitizes, calluses and robs them of their innocence, and then misdirects their creativity. I have already mentioned how it seeps into our homes through television, videos, videogames, popular music and music videos. Many of these electronic entertainments leave children mesmerized and, curiously, bored yet hyperactive. They bypass consciousness, inducing a trancelike, passive state—the opposite of the state of mind required for God-honoring creative activity.

Earlier, I addressed—in the context of sheltering and protecting our children's hearts—the physical, emotional and moral battering children suffer from the media and from their peers. The same principles apply to protecting the creative image of God in them. We need to be diligent guardians of their creativity, so that beauty, drama, happiness and adventure remain in their lives as they grow, and can someday be a witness to the world.

If our children's creativity points them to God, revealing Him as its source, it will play an important role in the romance of their hearts. But if they grow up entertained by cartoon characters, superheroes, videotapes, videogames, toys, electronic gadgets, and amusements provided by profit-hungry third parties, our children will become creatively constipated, their minds and hearts stagnant receptacles instead of fountains of creative energy bringing joy to themselves and to those around them.

I do not enjoy reading or writing about these dangers or dwelling on them. There are many books on this subject, and for good reason—our children are under assault. I particularly recommend:

Saving Childhood by the Medveds, *The Hurried Child* by David Elkind, *Endangered Minds* by Jane Healy, *Children Without Childhood* by Marie Winn, and *The Disappearance of Childhood* by Neil Postman.

Our children need to know that we approve of and value their creations.

Ironically, the most dangerous threat to the creativity of children may come from their own parents, who have the power to build up or tear down. Children who are ridiculed, put down, or ignored may eventually stop creating, or never begin. As their emotional tank drains down to dangerous levels, the creative image in them may eventually shut down. In contrast, affirmation strengthens a child's creative image. Our children need to know that we approve of and value their creations. Setting them up with the tools to pursue their interests sends a message that we believe in them and are willing to invest in their creativity, giving them a sense of security and the freedom to be themselves. Encouragement protects—in a sense immunizes—them against the negative messages they will inevitably receive from the culture around us.

Maintaining a Creative Atmosphere in the Home

Perhaps the greatest gift we can give our children to protect and nurture the creative image of God in them is the freedom to be themselves—unafraid to create, uninhibited to imagine, to feel, and then to find God's calling for their lives.

The atmosphere in a home originates in the hearts of the parents. When children are secure in knowing we will not ridicule or reject them, but will accept them for who they are, the creative image in them flourishes. When we treasure their creativity and their creations, we not only bring them joy, but also the confidence and freedom to discover the expression of God's creative image in them.

Creating this kind of environment takes time, energy, and willingness to invest our resources. It also requires commitment to the process of romancing our child's heart to the One Who is the source of all creative endeavors.

One project that Karey and I worked on with our children was binding their stories into books. When they were young they dictated their stories to us, and we wrote them down. Taking that time, valuing their words and their stories, sent a clear message to their hearts. One particularly unusual book that Heather, who was age seven at the time, wrote and bound is entitled *The Pond's Puns*. It's a great example of what can happen when we turn off the television, limit other amusements, and encourage a child to let her creativity flow:

Once upon a time there was a pond: a clear, cool pond fed by several springs. He had lots of friends, mainly kids, who would just sit around talking to him, eating their picnic lunch, and figuring out what to do. Lots of kids liked to swim in him in the summer or ice-skate on him in the winter. He was so popular that kids from all over, from different states, and even different countries, came to visit him to keep him company and to learn what ponds do.

One day in the spring the pond was visited by some men who had robbed some houses and decided to rob the pond's bank, but they got into an argument during the robbery. Suddenly...the pond sloshed its icy cold water all over the men. In shock they ran downhill toward the mouth of the pond. To their amazement the pond opened its mouth and said, "I'll give you a head start to that tree over there and then I'll be after you." Hearing a voice come out of the mouth of the pond made them run even faster.

Nobody knew that the pond could also walk, and when the pond stood up with its fish, frogs, and cattails showing and walked after the robbers everyone looked at the pond in astonishment and said, "What are you doing?" The pond didn't stop to tell them, since it was obvious.

The little stream that ran out of the pond's mouth ran after the pond as he chased the robbers. The pond soon caught the robbers, who by now were so scared that they began looking for a jail just to get away from the walking and talking pond and the stream running out of its mouth. When the pond grabbed the robbers they nearly drowned and they were so cold and wet by the time they were put in jail that they built a fire to warm up and dry out. The jail soon caught on fire but luckily the pond was still nearby and put out the fire by just standing on it. The only trouble now was that he flooded the jail, but all the prisoners got a bath. He then decided he better walk home and become a normal pond again.

This type of project cultivates the creative image in children by taking them step-by-step through the creative process, while also producing a tangible result. But they don't have to come up with the first (or even their umpteenth) story by themselves—we can find a good book that's on their level and let them copy it. Educator and author Dr. Ruth Beechick recommends copying the work of a master as one way to develop the creative image of a child. Teachers used this approach during the Renaissance—art students in particular spent years copying the compositional techniques and brushstrokes of the great masters. Technique and skill taught in this context develop taste, appreciation, and a vision for excellence. The best way to excel in any endeavor is to be mentored by masters, whether personally or through study of their great works.

ENCOURAGING CREATIVE PLAY

Play is a state in which a child (or a childlike adult) is unselfconscious—completely enthralled. Energy flows. The body, the emotions, the intellect are all coherently focused, driven by burning curiosity and caught up in the mystery of what is going to happen next. Play is an ego-less state, since there is no risk or possibility of failure and judgment. In this state, creativity flourishes.

Karey said in her book, *Hearth and Home*, "I believe children need long stretches of time to complete their 'play thoughts.' They need the free time to pursue and perfect them. Children at play have a concentration analogous to the concentration of an artist and sometimes this 'play' needs time to develop and come full circle, but we so often disrupt them for running here and there and they lose this concentration and with continual disruptions they may even lose the ability to play."[138]

When children play, they are exercising the creative image of God in themselves in the most natural way. Their creations will give us clues as to where their talents lie. When we have zeroed in on a talent, we can provide a child with tools to pursue that interest. Recently, I remodeled our older children's playhouse into a museum and lab for Dawson, since that is the direction in which his creative imagination lies. It is where he plays. This is his workplace and his creating place.

Through the years, our children have been perpetually in the process of planning, designing, building, making. They inspired the line from the song I quoted at the end of the last chapter: "His goal's in the making, the building, creating...and not in what's finished and done." Children engaged in these activities are truly alive, now, because they are telling their story in the present—the only point where anyone, young or old, touches eternity.

Travis designed and assembled an electronic combination lock for his bedroom door from paperclips, brads, and disassembled appliances. He also designed and built an extensive underground fort, and a log cabin with a loft and a shake roof. He animated cartoons on his computer using software that would be considered primitive today. Heather's imagination is unusual. Our house became the United States, and various rooms were regions or states where she took journeys with her matchbox cars. She imagined that clouds hug mountains and wash them clean—which is not far from the truth—and she loved to sit in the driver's seat of vehicles for hours pretending she was driving.

Dawson's creations are in progress as I write this. Day after day, from morning to night, he's in nonstop motion like a busy beaver, making or planning something—except when he is sick. When he was seven years old, he caught a flu bug and ended up with an ear infection that kept him in the house for over a week. During that time he slipped a note to me:

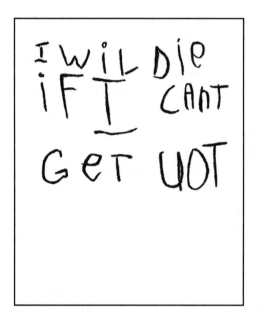

His frustration wasn't from squelched garden-variety hyperactivity. The creative image of God in Dawson demands physical expression.

Over the past several years, Dawson has made an oven out of bricks and mud, a six-foot-long swing that you lie down on as you swing, and a thirty-five-foot-long daisy chain to decorate our porch. He made a major addition to Travis's underground fort, complete with architectural plans and a scale model, and he created a city of three billion people on his Simm City computer program. We have responded to all of these projects with enthusiasm, acknowledging the ideas and encouraging the children to continue by supplying them with tools and time to create more things.

My friend Jim has never really known where his play ends and his work begins. He lives in the old mining town of Victor, Colorado, and is one of the most gifted people I know. Though he never went to college, he received an honorary doctorate from a college for a paper he presented. He is an expert in all aspects of mining—from drilling to handling explosives to assaying the ore—a master mechanic and electrician, a theologian and inventor, and he has served his little town as mayor while also serving his church as pastor. Jim remembers a very real burning desire in his heart to design and build from about age three, when he built ramps so he could steal the sap from his father's maple sugaring buckets in the spring in New Hampshire.

By age five, Jim was building go-carts, racing them with no brakes or steering, until they disintegrated against a tree—usually with him driving—or just fell apart. When he was about seven, he moved to bigger things—getting under the hood of his father's De Soto one day. Before he knew it, Jim had taken the thing half apart. He intended to put it back together—except that he couldn't precisely recall which wires had been connected where. You can imagine his father's surprise when the car wouldn't start.

Not long afterwards, Jim constructed a helicopter from scrap lumber, with a rope and pulley to spin the propeller, hooked up to an electric motor. He fully expected the contraption to fly. His father just smiled as he plugged in the extension cord for Jim, with the words, "Hold on. Don't let it get away from you!"

Years later, Jim designed a single-person helicopter propelled by hydrogen peroxide, and this one flew. I'm not kidding. There's a video to prove it. The only thing that killed production was that his investors backed out when the stock market crashed in 1987.

Shortly after that, Jim got into gold mining, and he's been at that ever since, not to become wealthy, but so he can support the work of missionaries and pastors around the world.

SUPPORTING EARLY PASSION AND OLDER DESIRE

My dad was an exceptional baseball player in his youth, so he expected that I would excel in the sport, starting with Little League. A number of problems interfered with that goal—the first being that I was benched and excluded by the locals because my religion was different from theirs. And, although I was a good pitcher, I could never learn to hit the ball well. I could see the pitcher's release, but by the time the ball was near the plate, it had become a blur, and then it disappeared.

Football was out, as my parents wanted to protect my knees. I tried running cross-country, but was plagued with side cramps. At one meet, I came in second to last out of three hundred and fifty-seven runners—the only guy I beat broke his leg during the race. So my participation in athletics seemed doomed to failure until I tried basketball. A young coach stuck me into a varsity game during my sophomore year in high school and, to everyone's surprise, I scored eleven points and pulled down an unusually high number of rebounds. "Coach" believed in me, and this had a major impact on my high school years and beyond. I began training year-round.

Mom and Dad gave me their complete support. They sent me to basketball camps they couldn't really afford. And Dad helped me build a basketball court in our backyard, after I shared my dream of having a regulation court, totally to spec, so that, when I played in the gym, it would be exactly the same.

At his insistence, I hand-dug down two feet through clay soil for the foundation of the asphalt pad he poured. This took weeks of backbreaking work, hauling the dirt away with a wheelbarrow. The court was equipped with lights, and an official backboard and rim that hung ten feet out from the vertical support—a classy oil derrick-like structure Dad had designed. Our team practiced there all summer long. In the winter, I practiced wearing fingerless gloves, shooting a hundred free throws every day along with about the same number of jump shots.

"Coach" called me recently. We had lost touch and hadn't talked for many years. He said, "It's kind of funny that when we are back in the Milwaukee area and I go past your old home, I check to see if you guys are shooting baskets in the back yard." The romance is mutual, and the faith invested in a child or young person can bring lifelong dividends—a truth wonderfully illustrated in the film *Mr. Holland's Opus.*

It is not uncommon for children even as young as five to express the specifics of their creative image. Their innate creative talent often comes with an uncommon passion for exercising and pursuing it, as though they know intuitively that this is how God has designed them. During these early, experimental years, parents should respond with support and encouragement—tempered with caution—plus wisdom, since each child's script is unique.

The lives of gifted individuals who were child prodigies often are characterized by burnout related to the loss of childhood and a loss of balance. Parents may make matters worse by trying to push, manage, or control such a child, but I am careful not to condemn, for who knows how to parent such talent?

However, there is strong evidence that later childhood—from ten to fourteen—is the more natural time for the creative image of God to be manifest. A significant number of great musicians, specifically violinists, began lessons at about this age. This may be the ideal time to get serious about helping our children define their specific creative image. By that time, we hope that they have grown strong from a healthy, diversified childhood, and the world is just beginning to come into cognitive focus. Regimented training, lessons, goals, and practice are much more appropriate for an emotionally and mentally competent child of fourteen than for a five-year-old.

The primary expression of their creative image may not occur until age eighteen to twenty-four. Even then, it may evolve over time. The famous artist Grandma Moses began painting at seventy-six, and continued until her death at a hundred and one. She never

"My dad believes in me" protected and nurtured Kathy's creative image.

had an art lesson. I wrote my first legitimate song when I was forty-five. A friend of mine didn't start climbing mountains until he was in his late seventies. He had a heart attack in his sixties, and had never been athletic before then. Once, when I was out hiking with friends, all of us laden under full packs, we met him seven miles from the trailhead at ten thousand feet. He was in his mid-eighties by then, "just out for an afternoon stroll" without a backpack or canteen— just his necessary pills in his pocket.

These stories should inspire us by dissolving the illusion that the creative part of life is only available to the young, or to those with special credentials in a specific creative area.

My friend Kathy is one of the most amazing women I know. The creative image of God in her was first manifested in her relationship with peers when she was a child. She always ended up in charge— the leader and problem solver. Kathy grew up in Michigan, and received Christ as her personal Savior when she was a child. From the start, it was apparent that she was not going to be successful in school. Due to complex eye problems and symptoms of attention deficit disorder, she struggled with academics, and her leadership ability went unrecognized. Fortunately, when she was just a little girl, her father told her, "Kathy, you can do anything you put your heart to." But as a result of her failure in school, she began associating with the wrong crowd, which led her down a pathway to heartache.

With no education or training, a failed teenage marriage, and enough drama to fill several novels, this single mother then struggled with alcoholism, drugs, and poverty. When she had sunk to a point of desperation, she cried out to God, Who at that moment miraculously reached down and saved her life. She asked God never to let her forget what she had gone through, so she would always be sensitive to others. By sheer determination she started a dress shop business, which was successful. The creative image of God—stymied in her youth—was reappearing.

Then her second husband's brother and partner was killed in an auto accident, putting their company in crisis. After much discussion, Kathy was asked to come in and help out. With a national recession, and the company deep in debt, Kathy—at age forty-two—took on the task of learning all she could in applications of fire-rated commercial construction. She had no education in this arena, and no idea what spray fireproofing was, other than something she continually had to wash out of her husband's clothes.

Against all odds—including being a woman in an all-male field—she obtained a commercial contractor's license, pulled the company out of debt, and built it into the largest and most successful specialty subcontractor in its field in the country, and possibly the world. Beyond managing several companies, industrial park development, and a golf course, she is busy now with national trade organizations, and lobby and code bodies. She sits on several boards and chaired the committee that wrote the standard manual of practice for fire-stop installations.

How in the world did she do this? She says, "It was only through God's grace and my father's belief in me." She discovered inside herself a brilliant business sense and executive mind, an insatiable desire and ability to solve problems and bring order from disorder, and a unique entrepreneurial spirit that inspires all around her. This is the creative image of God in Kathy. It first showed itself when she was a child and, against tremendous odds, it survived and developed within her over time—an irresistible force set free to create. "No one," she says, "taught me to do what I do—I just do it."

The plot of her story is a familiar one, and never fails to inspire. I believe that the key ingredient is the creative image of God. Although she could now retire, she is most happy and satisfied meeting challenges, solving problems, and leading the company.

If we want to help our children, as Kathy's father encouraged her, we need to let them know that we believe in them. This single inner conviction—"My dad (or my mom) believes in me"—will do more to protect and nurture the creative image of God in a child than anything else, even if our encouragement takes years to bear fruit.

13

CREATIVE DOMAINS

It seems like just yesterday he stood at my knee.
His little fingers tuned my guitar.
He looked up at me with those big brown eyes,
And strummed me his first little tune.[139]

At seven years of age, Ben had never seen an artist's picture, until he himself made one. He was born into the eighteenth century Quaker faith, which frowned on "needless gaudy images." But this ordinary Quaker lad suddenly developed a strange urge and a stranger gift for drawing pictures. With a goose quill pen and black ink he drew a portrait of his sleeping baby sister, which his mother discovered. She said, "Memories grow old, but this picture of my darling will hold the memory." However, she did not show the picture to Ben's father for a time.

Ben grew tired of only black ink, so one day his Native American friends taught him how to make colored paint from the earth. Still, he had no paintbrush. So the budding artist made his own paintbrush from hair clipped from his cat, Grimalkin. Within a few weeks the family began to notice the cat's deteriorating condition, so one night during family prayer time Ben's father prayed for poor Grimalkin, who was losing his hair.

Ben then confessed. He showed his pictures to his father, who said, "Tell me why it is that thee must draw?" Ben was at a loss. How could he explain the need for putting things on paper? How could he explain how his fingers ached to draw? With reservation, his father gave him permission to continue his painting, when he wasn't doing chores—which was rare. His father believed that the boy would outgrow this fancy.

Eventually, however, Ben's father acknowledged that his son had a special gift, and the church elders gave the lad their consent to pursue painting instead of a "useful craft." Ben received a scholarship from an art academy in Philadelphia, and went on to become "the father of American painting." He was also the only American honored to be the president of the English Royal Academy of Arts. Even as an aged man, Benjamin West spoke nostalgically of the cat that had been the constant companion of his boyhood and had supplied him with hair for his first paintbrushes. You can read his story—one of my kids' favorites—in the book *Benjamin West and His Cat Grimalkin*, by Marguerite Henry, illustrated by Wesley Dennis.

Creativity spans a broad spectrum. It is actually a way of thinking, or even a way of living—so the creative image of God may find expression in any number of arenas. Mihly Csikszentmihalyi refers to these arenas as "domains." Examples of domains include: art, baking, calligraphy, canoeing, computers, conversation, cooking, dancing, decorating, design, fencing, fly fishing, flying model airplanes, football, forestry, gardening, mechanics, music, nature studies, piano, polo, publishing, reading, sailing, skiing, teaching, tennis. There are thousands of domains that make life interesting and meaningful. Each domain has its own special rules, skills, knowledge, boundaries, and procedures.

Too often, we assume that most domains are off limits. This habit of thought is frequently established during childhood, and has stifled and impoverished many lives. However, the creative urge is strong in children. Like steam in a boiling kettle, it will find a way to express itself, even in the face of withering suppression—not out of defiance, but out of deference to the One Whose Spirit is empowering the child in question.

Benjamin West's creative domain was obviously painting. For many, their creative domain starts as an interest, develops into a hobby, and then over time becomes an avocation that blossoms and bears fruit as a lifelong vocation. I love that word, because it means "calling," which is the whole point I'm trying to make: God calls each of us to fulfill some purpose in life. His calling is consistent with the creative image of Himself in us, which is most effectively exercised within a particular creative domain.

DISCERNING CREATIVE DOMAINS

My mother not only studied my brothers and me—she acted on what she learned, using her creativity to win our hearts. One thing she did was teach her boys how to cook—in her own kitchen! And she laughed, rather than scolded, at the horrendous messes we made. My favorite creation was a variation on sponge candy. It is made by cooking down corn syrup and sugar with a little vinegar, until the mixture becomes brittle when dropped into cold water. The fun starts when you add in a little baking soda, and the candy erupts from the bowl like golden lava. I think my fascination with magma and volatiles started in Mom's kitchen, and led me to co-found a geologic company called MagmaChem.

My parents provided exposure to a wide range of activities chosen to harness the talents and energy that they saw in me. Looking back, what I appreciate most is that they kept trying, regardless of the financial and personal sacrifices required, so that I could discover and develop my particular creative domains.

We can help our children discover their creative domains by exposing them to a variety of arenas where creativity is required—arenas they like and in which they may even be especially gifted. The key here is broad exposure. To specialize and focus on one area too soon may overlook the child's primary area of creativity, and may throw them out of balance. But at some point it will be time to zero in on at least one domain. The most challenging part is keeping abreast of the changing abilities and desires of a growing child. It's like shooting at a moving target, since creativity is by nature dynamic.

Not every child is a prodigy. Unusual talents, gifts, and abilities are not a prerequisite for creativity. The script God has written for each person is only revealed as it is lived. What we can do is protect and cultivate the qualities necessary for creativity, which are innate in most children—a keen curiosity about one's surroundings, awe about the mysteries of life, and an insatiable passion to solve them.

There is a story of a famous scientist who was walking in the woods near his home as a youth when he noticed a large beetle scurrying to hide under the bark of a tree. Because he did not have this beetle in his collection, he ran to the tree, peeled off the bark, and grabbed the insect. That's when he saw that there were two similar beetles under the bark. He wanted to collect these, too, but the creatures were so large that he could hold only one in each hand. In desperation, he popped the third beetle in his mouth, and ran all the way home, trying to keep it from escaping down his throat! A truly creative person will endure almost anything for the pure joy of pursuing and developing their particular bent, which ultimately finds expression in the way that water from an underground thermal will always find its way to the surface. For such people, the entire endeavor is not work, no matter how challenging; it is recreation in the truest sense of the word—"re-creation." Some would even call it play.

We can easily miss this process of discovery and growth if we are constantly distracted by matters of lesser importance.

My friend Dave, who helped me write this book, shared with me how, at age eight, he borrowed some of his father's mimeo cushion sheets and produced a little newspaper, which he peddled around the neighborhood. In his mind, he's always been a writer. Creatively speaking, when he was eight he looked in the mirror and saw not a child, but a writer. Gazing back at him was not a third grader missing a couple of teeth, but the creative image of God. It was almost as if he had met his own soul and discovered his destiny. He knew who he was, and that writing would be his way of co-creating with the One Who had created him. Today he edits a major Christian medical magazine and has produced eleven books, including this one. As we work together, it is obvious that he has a gift. I feel God's image in him as he wades through my manuscripts, straightening out the logical flow and helping me find the right words. He knows the truth of William Buckley's often-quoted statement that the difference between "the best word and a right word" is like the difference between "lightning and a lightning bug."

FACILITATING THE PROCESS

Mom is an excellent pianist, so when I was in junior high she enrolled me in piano lessons for several months. It soon became obvious that I was not interested in or programmed for the keyboard. But studying music led me to the trumpet, which I loved. My parents bought me a quality instrument, and arranged for lessons with a professional jazz musician. Later, they transported me many miles weekly so that I could study with a concert trumpet player. My goal was to become a professional trumpet player, until I had an allergic reaction to the metal of the mouthpiece and was forced to quit playing.

At about the same age, I started woodcarving. My parents bought me *How to Do Wood Carving,* by John Lacey. Now, as I thumb through its yellowed pages, the old-book smell and finger smudges connect me with a wonderful boyhood of whittling. My parents equipped me with German-made knives and quality pieces of wood. First I used pine, but soon advanced to hardwoods—my favorites being walnut and maple. I still love the smell of freshly sanded walnut. I carved in my bedroom, on the workbench Dad had built, taking as long as three days to make a whitetail deer. Over time my hobby produced piles of wood chips and sawdust that I tracked all over the house. Mom and Dad ignored the mess, because they knew it was temporary, and focused instead on my creations—and my creativity, which they knew would be a life long pursuit. Their encouragement and praises taught me to do the same for my own children, and now I smile when I find wood chips leading from all parts of the house to Dawson's bedroom.

We can easily miss this process of discovery and growth in our own child, if we are constantly distracted by matters of lesser importance—such as paying the mortgage, advancing a career, attending committee meetings, or just keeping the floors spotlessly clean. Worse, we can put out the fire by critiquing instead of encouraging, or by dictating instead of enjoying the script.

In the film *Dead Poets Society,* a young man with a passion and gift for acting is denied the opportunity to pursue his dreams by his father, who insists that he must go to medical school. The boy commits suicide, because he cannot live within the script his father has written for him. This character was an adolescent, but when younger children are controlled by their parents in the same way, denied the opportunity to explore their creative domains, they die inside.

Our role as parents is to facilitate. It is God Who is at work in our child "both to will and to do for His good pleasure."[140] Hindering

His will and work dishonors God, Who has gifted our child in a particular, unique way. We must not limit them to what we can imagine, but try to discover their passions, and then follow those passions where they lead. If we don't, they will become discouraged. If, through God's grace, they do develop a creative domain without our help, we will have forfeited the great joy of romancing them through our relationship.

Allen, a master mechanic who grew up in New Hampshire, lives near us. He is the son of a minister who comes from a long family tradition of ministers and missionaries, so people probably assumed that he would also "go into the ministry." But from a very early age, Allen's joy was taking things apart and putting them back together. Since this wasn't up his father's alley, his father more or less ignored Allen's interests in favor of tending his "flock." So Allen built models, moved on to cars, then to bigger things—much bigger, as in the Air Force—before settling back to maintaining our county's vehicles, which includes fixing snowplows on snowy nights. Although he has not gone into the ministry officially as a preacher, he does have a ministry, one I believe is even more dynamic than many official ministries. He is out in the midst of the battle, caring for the wounded, lost, and heartbroken. He works with widows, single moms, and hurting people, repairing their vehicles for little or no pay. Like an old-fashioned doctor, he makes house calls. Allen is, therefore, a minister, even though the tools he wields are those of a mechanic.

When we consider our child's creative image and the domains in which it might be best expressed, we should try to see the horizons of possibilities as broadly as God sees them. Just as the body needs all its parts, so the body of Christ, of which we—adults *and* children—are members, needs all the creative gifts God has given in order to function most effectively.[141] Not everyone can be a painter, poet, politician, or pastor. We all have lofty dreams for our children, but the crucial issue is not our vision, but theirs—or more importantly, God's vision for their creative role in His Story— mechanic or missionary, or both, it's His calling that counts.

DEVELOPING CREATIVE DOMAINS

A child needs our help to develop skills, abilities, and talents in a particular creative domain. We should provide proper equipment and seek out coaches or mentors. Creative domains are found in work and play, vocation and recreation, occupation and hobby, career and ministry.

One summer, after working three days whitewashing an Oscar Meyer stock pen, I invested my entire pay of seven dollars, not in candy, or even fishing gear, but in a book entitled *Prehistoric America*. The book described how the discipline of geology had begun. I read it myself, and then my mother read it aloud to me. My fascination with this book, added to the rocks I found along the crick, was the beginning of my career as a geologist. Mom was as interested in the earth as I was, and sharing that book with her gave us a bond that I treasure to this day.

Seeing this new passion in me, Mom and Dad took me to museums, lectures, and even on a family trip through the Rocky Mountains. Once Mom arranged for me to meet with a paleontologist, to help me conduct a carbon 14 test for a science fair. The scientist, delighted that I would attempt such a project, generously supplied me with a piece of a mastodon tusk and some ancient charcoal from an anthropological dig for my age-dating project. Although the experiment produced little more than some pure white smoke, it took first place in the science fair and started me thinking seriously about science as a career.

But science took a back seat to athletics until my sophomore year in college, when I switched my major from civil engineering to my childhood love, geology. As I studied geology, I became more and more enthralled with "out west," because that is where rocks are well exposed. Mom and Dad encouraged me to go out west, even though it meant that I would be living far away from them. They knew that my love for God's creation, adventure in the mountains, and the profession of geology were all calling me.

The youth subculture competes determinedly for the hearts of our children.

For ten years I roamed the western United States, four-wheeling and backpacking in search of gold, copper, zinc, and uranium. It was a life filled with startling beauty, breathtaking vistas, and high adventure. There was my first desert hike into the Superstition Wilderness without water, and the time a "Teddy Bear"—jumping cholla cactus—stuck my legs together and I thought I had been bitten by a rattlesnake. There was an emergency sixteen-mile-trek out of the Glacier Peak Wilderness, and the time I was treed by a bear eight miles from camp, not to mention a terrifying, but hilarious, experience involving a mountain lion, a bear, and a pack of coyotes, in a deep, dark canyon in the Santa Teresa Mountains.

One summer, I lived on the crest of the North Cascade Mountains, sixteen miles from the nearest road. I explored the Wyoming Buttes for a summer, looking for uranium, every day opening sixteen gates just to get to my field area. For five years I covered most of Arizona's mountain ranges, searching for giant faults and copper, four-wheeling and hiking ten hours a day. During all that time I was reading the story God had written in the rocks, and getting paid to do so. The little boy in me who had hugged the pine stump was now completely immersed in God's creation—enchanted, spellbound, captivated by the Lord's continuing romance of my heart. This happened because my parents released me, with no strings attached, to follow my calling.

Ideally, the creative image of God should be expressed in our life's work. If it is, work will be more enjoyable and successful because our heart will naturally be in it as well as our talents. Some creative interests that could potentially become our work develop early in childhood, but most, as I have suggested, develop between ten and fourteen years of age. This is when we as parents should consider making it a point to arrange a variety of trial flights from the "nest" for our children, in the company of trusted mentors who will teach, guide, and befriend them.

First, we must know the passions of our child. Second, we need to find a Christian older than our child, usually an adult, who shares one of their passions and has time to be a kindred spirit. This could be a plumber, musician, doctor, rancher, computer engineer, carpenter, or homemaker. If we can show our children someone who is "cool," who also embraces our values, principles, and beliefs, this will both draw and woo their hearts, and reinforce our training.

Our daughter, Heather, seems to have found her niche, after help from several wonderful mentors. She has attended a community college and a Bible college, as well as graduating from a culinary arts school. Her vision was to work in the hospitality industry on dude ranches and camps. Reality, however, turned out to be not exactly consistent with what she had pictured in her dreams.

First, the food was seldom made from scratch, and in some cases was trucked in, pre-cooked and frozen. Heather has learned home-style and gourmet cooking skills from Karey—she even grinds her own flour. The other surprise was the multitasked, high-pressure working environment. Most head cooks are unusual women—they could probably have been CEOs of major corporations or drill sergeants, had they wished to be. Heather is sweet and gentle, and this was not a good fit.

Along the way, several women who had mentored Heather in a variety of arenas all said—more than once—that Heather's gifts are special, ideally suited for working with children or the elderly. I believe that they were seeing the creative image of God in Heather. It was through following their counsel that Heather began her work at a life-care center. Her Mother Teresa-like bedside manner, sweet smile, and gentle personality are a huge hit with the residents. They naturally confide in her because they are drawn to her and trust her. Consequently, she shares Christ with them in the same way that a chaplain would, with gentle compassion. She has told us that it feels so good to have found her place of work and ministry. Her mentors were instrumental in this process.

The youth subculture competes determinedly for the hearts of our children. Many parents have felt this competitive wedge being driven between them and their children. By contrast, mentors who are kindred spirits and have childlike hearts give our children a genuine alternative.

It is a mentor's responsibility to walk alongside and pass on knowledge and skills, while romancing the child to God through the shared experience. The key is that they view what they do as a calling, and are excited and passionate about it.

Travis began working with an inventor when he was thirteen. This person inspired Travis's heart, and opened up the world of small business and risk-taking to him. To Travis's surprise and delight, the mentor also had a wonderful sense of humor. Travis was the youngest senators' aide working in the state capitol at age fifteen. Through this experience, he learned much about protocol and the legislative process, as well as how to feel comfortable wearing a suit.

For several years, Travis worked with a Denver University professor and his entrepreneurial son, manufacturing micro-dissection surgical needles. Daily exposure to the adult culture was valuable, as were the research and problem-solving skills he acquired. He also joined a small worship band at a local weekly youth gathering when he turned sixteen. The worship leader trained Travis in the basics of worship leading, and he discovered that he had leadership and musical production gifts. Now, while still in college, Travis has been the worship leader for a large church on campus, and it appears that "worship minister" may be his vocation.

When he was in senior high, Travis gave a presentation during a workshop at an educational conference. Part of his speech went like this:

> Most high schoolers think of their first job as just a way to make some extra spending money. They typically end up flipping hamburgers with like-minded high schoolers at the local fast food

establishment. It is not that this is an undesirable job, but few high schoolers will ever own a fast food restaurant. For me, the workplace is more than just a place for making money—it is a laboratory where I test my talents and education, and gain real-life knowledge and experience working with adults who do what I think I might like to do for my life's work. If you can't find a paying job, find a volunteer position doing something you are interested in. Don't worry about the pay. In a short time, if you do a good job, chances are that they will begin paying you anyway. It's a great way to find a high-quality job and build a résumé of experience. I know, because it happened to me.

CATALYZING DOMAINS—FOUR EXAMPLES

1. Competitive Sports

Our culture is obsessed with competitive sports and athletics—and some of the reasons are valid. Sports develop teamwork, discipline, leadership skills, character, and healthy, strong, coordinated bodies. From personal experience I have tasted the challenge, the pure joy, the pain, and the glory because I ate, drank, slept, and played basketball for seven straight years. When I gave it up, it took me months to re-equilibrate emotionally. Was I out of balance? Yes and no.

Balance is a complex concept. Great feats and defining moments in history are generally not thought of as the product of balance. In fact, balance is generally thought of as a rather boring concept. But it is not! Balance is a dynamic state of perpetual moving, compensating, calculating, shifting—in a sense it is like a dance. If we try walking across a rushing river on a narrow log, we will find that balance is both an exciting athletic challenge and a test of intellect, emotions, and character.

Balance depends on our most deeply held values and vision, which provide our reference frame and plumb line. Without them, balance is impossible. When I ate, drank, and slept basketball, I was actually in balance with my deepest desires and dreams. If I had known then what I know now—that archery, music, and writing would one day be my passions—then my reference frame would have been different, and the way I balanced everything would also have been different.

What is the purpose and objective of sports in our child's life? Are these consistent with our child's values and vision, and with ours? Is our focus long or short-term? Some athletic activities can only be done when a person is young. Should we allow children to sacrifice their knees for a few short years of pleasure and glory, and the opportunity to develop specific character traits and a strong, coordinated body? Or do we help them preserve their knees for a full life of other physical pursuits, without the strength that early years of competitive sports develop? Many of my athletic friends face knee replacements and shoulder reconstructions, now that they have reached middle age. Do we encourage our children to invest their young lives in a lifelong sport such as golf, or a temporary sport such as gymnastics? Should they learn how to ski or how to tackle a quarterback? How to ride a bull or a bicycle? Are individual sports a better lifelong investment than team sports? Or do we want our child to do them all?

These questions need to be handled with care in light of our knowledge of sports and of our child. Every child is unique, and there is no simple formula. Their interests may change from week to week, day to day, or even from moment to moment—which means we must keep an open mind about any sports commitment. In an earlier chapter, I mentioned my friend Ray. He and his wife, Trish, have five children—four boys and a girl. Trish told me how their family has flexed with the interests of each:

We have always felt it was crucial to expose each of our kids to various athletic experiences. Since the first three children were boys, the fall sport activity of choice was soccer. When nearly four seasons had gone by, our youngest, Caroline, was to make her debut on the four-to-six-year-old team with her brother Patrick. One game into the season, her desire to play soccer seemed to wane. She had been in the game only a short time when she said, "Mommy, please take me out of here. I don't like soccer."

Since I was the coach, I said, "Well then, just hang out with Mommy." She preferred sitting on the sidelines, either coloring or playing dolls. Since we like to take videos of all our kids, we begged her to just go in for one minute, so Daddy could get a little footage. The big moment came and the footage Ray took is a treasure. Every time the ball rolled toward her, Caroline ran in the other direction. When it was kicked toward her, she bent down and covered her head with her hands. As she came out of the game, her comment was, "Mommy, can I try ballet instead?"

Now, two years later, ballet, gymnastics, swimming, and tennis have all been part of Caroline's sporting activities. She has had a great deal of enthusiasm for each of these and has commented that she might even try soccer once more. Exposure and variety have been keys in our children's development—always having an open mind and never closing doors. Development involves a complex and dynamic interplay of motor and cognitive skills, as well as success and failure. This makes our children physically, emotionally, and spiritually well rounded.

Caroline still is our precious princess, as the only girl among four brothers. She continues to prefer dolls, dress-up, and ballet, but she steps up to all the challenges we hand her, and completes the tasks whether they're her "bag" or not. She is God's wonderful, unique creature, so we look forward to seeing what she may become.

2. Outdoor Sports

Nature-related activities or outdoor sports comprise another creative domain. In these, the activity itself is what brings happiness and pleasure, involving suspense, danger, adventure, challenge, patience, and skill. The competition is not usually another person or team, but nature, and ultimately ourselves. In 1887, Sioux Chief Yellowlark summed up this challenge with these words, "Make me strong, not to be superior to my brothers, but to fight my greatest enemy—myself."[142] Native Americans certainly knew the reality of the challenge to survive. Worldwide, many people groups are still engaged in this same endeavor.

For most of us, however, the closest we can come is through activities such as fishing and hunting, mountain biking, rock climbing, shooting the rapids of a river, backpacking in the wilds, trekking on cross-country skis, or mountain climbing. Those words make me think of such adventures as being surprised, near the top of Mount Evans, by a thunderstorm passing overhead. The static electricity buzzing all around—my hair literally standing on end—was terrifyingly wonderful. Any of these outdoor sports can put us to the ultimate test—against nature, or against ourselves.

I enjoy following in the footsteps of Native Americans with my friends, as we bowhunt for big game in the Rockies—bear, mountain lion, moose, elk, deer. The quarry does not matter as much as the experience itself. The most memorable experiences are the most hair-raising, such as when two of my friends (both pastors) spent the night perched on a semi-flat spot about five feet long and six feet wide. By some miracle they found this place while lost in the dark trying to climb a cliff face to reach a trail they thought was just ahead. At a critical moment both sensed that they should not continue climbing. They didn't sleep too well that night, because there wasn't enough room on that promontory for them to lie down side by side next to a log that was wedged against a tree. In the early morning light, they were stunned to discover that the log had prevented them from rolling down the two-hundred-foot cliffs that dropped off on three sides.

It is at times like these that we face our fears and our faith.

As I mentioned earlier, when I was twelve years old I contracted a severe case of "muskie fever" that lasted several years. I still have periodic relapses. My grandfather told me a story of a thirty-seven pounder he had shot with his rifle up on Hay Creek when he was a boy. Back then, fish were looked at more as food than sport. That stretch of creek was nearly impossible to fish because it meandered through a swampy forest of tag-alder and tamarack. I finally talked Grandpa into taking me to the spot where he had shot the fish. After what seemed like miles of bushwhacking cross-country through clouds of mosquitoes, we reached the creek, which was much smaller than I had imagined. Much to my dismay, my grandfather told me he could walk no further, and that I should head up-creek to the spot—an oxbow bend where the creek ran slow and deep.

This area was legendary bear country. I had heard many stories—most of them embellished—and they caused my imagination to run wild. Up until that moment, I hadn't worried about the bears, because Grandpa was with me. But now, I would be alone—something I had not anticipated. Apprehensively, I waded on, sometimes up to my armpits in the dark water. Tall grass and brush grew right up to the water's edge and I feared that a bear would appear at any moment. I felt vulnerable, and helpless. But the "fever" forced me to face my fear and fish, promising all the while that if God would deliver me from the bears I would go to deepest, darkest Africa as a missionary for life (maybe that little lie is why I didn't catch the monster muskie that day). I did catch a small muskie, and I saw the water boil one time as a big fish swam by.

When I turned back, I decided to take a shortcut, so I climbed out of the river. Soon I was on a game trail, but rounding a corner I stopped dead in my tracks as I spied a fresh steamy pile of bear "sign." I almost panicked, but continued on my way until I heard a rustle in the brush next to me. Then I saw a patch of black fur. I envisioned a huge bear and death's yawning gate swinging open. But soon the sweet aroma of skunk wafted through the air. What relief! Wonderful, joyous palliation somehow connected with this perfume of the north country and worked a miraculous electrochemical reaction in my brain. To this day, because of that experience, I still love the smell of skunk.

Situations like this are common in the wilderness. Do we panic, or do we embrace the challenge and face our fears? Participants in wilderness survival programs such as "Outward Bound" attest to the feelings expressed in my story. Part of their training is a solo time without the modern equipment a camper would normally take along. We should all have the experience of being alone in the wild overnight with only a knife. We can't experience the outdoors simply by reading or watching movies. We have to go there, and stay long enough to become part of it.

The outdoors offers activities for the young, the old, the weak, the non-athletic, and the strongest of the strong. There is something for everyone, which is why it is so appropriate for children. You don't, of course, have to start in bear country. A local park will do. But for some there is a genetic predisposition to the more earthy activities such as hunting and fishing, and even camping. I have seen this in many families. One child naturally gravitates towards nature, and the others may participate in outdoor activities, but they do not go out of their way to collect deer antlers, capture small animals, collect butterflies, and shoot bows and arrows. For parents, as always, the key is to be students of our children's hearts.

3. The Fine Arts

Our children need to experience personally the texture, colors, and hues of original paintings, because brush strokes of the artist speak volumes that are lost in reproduction. In museums, we can see the grand scale of the canvases of the masters. These firsthand experiences allow us to sense and witness the creative image of the artist, which may connect on a soul-mate level with God's creative image in our children.

A friend and watercolor artist, Beth Thurow, once wrote:

The brain's tools are language, intelligence, reason, and creativity (ability to be innovative with principles). These, combined with conscience, free will, emotion, and self-awareness, define the human soul. Some paintings may be intellectual exercises, others driven by sheer emotion. Nevertheless, whether profound or silly, your state of soul meets the artist's at the art piece. If two souls sublimely agree, then Emmanuel (God with us) can incarnate. We weep.[143]

We do not judge art; it judges us.

Involvement in the arts is often considered purely a leisure activity, frivolous and entertaining, but not practical. This attitude misses the point of God's creative image within us. God created because it brought Him joy. We create because He made us like Himself. Too often, modern "Christian" artists create their works out of good intentions, around sermonettes and the retelling of Bible stories. Their creations carry meaning in concrete, not abstract form. A non-Christian would label it propaganda. Where is the soul of the artist in Christian "elevator music" or in the knick-knacks that cram the shelves of Christian bookstores? As secular investors control more and more of the business that has grown up around Christian "art," its soul seems to be further impoverished. Perhaps our children will help to change all this. But only if we support them, the way my parents supported me.

After high school, I played two years of college basketball, before an injury—the first in my career—changed my life forever. Since I was laid up, the next weekend I accepted an invitation to a ski retreat, during which I found myself seated at a table in a ski lodge with thirty-six girls—all beautiful in my eyes. One of the girls was leading songs on her guitar. I had not sung since sixth grade, which had been a disaster because my voice was changing and music was just not cool then. Well, the girls forced me to sing, and to my complete surprise I could. And as a result, a whole new non-athletic world opened up.

The next week, a guy in our dorm gave me a beat-up old guitar. Within a couple of hours I was playing and singing "They Call the Wind Mariah." That day, my passion for basketball began to be transferred to music, and in my junior year I dropped out of basketball to pursue music.

My parents were completely shocked when I broke the news, since it was a major change in direction. But, after talking it over, they supported me. They knew me, and recognized that this change reflected my heart. The next time I came home they bought me a good guitar.

Soon I started a singing group, called The Damascus Road. Our aim was to give churches a fresh vision for youth ministry. I enlisted college students as speakers and we had mini-crusades. It was a stretch for me to be on stage in a non-basketball mode, but it turned out to be preparation for future ministry. Along the way the members of our group taught me music.

I think the reason my parents adapted so well to this new direction was that they had no agenda of their own for me. For years, they had been praying this simple prayer: "Dear Lord: Grant our sons common sense, good judgment, and wisdom." As a result, they trusted me. During all the decision-making I had to do at that time, I never forgot my parents' trust, and I did my best to be worthy of it. It gave me hope that everything was going to work out—and hope, at that point, was as vital to me as air, food, and water.

Through the years, another key to the development of my music ministry has been the encouragement of others who believed in me. I hesitate to think of where I'd be with music had it not been for several church music ministers who mentored me, sharing and challenging me with their vision for music's role in addressing the needs of the church at any given time. They asked me to create. They were catalysts who stimulated me to produce musical dramas, original songs, and stage sets that were used in ministry with them. Nearly all my creative works can be traced back to a person's act of trust in me.

Music, a vital creative domain, is all around us. It has become the background static of life—the radio, boom boxes, phones, walkmans, in doctors' offices, in movies, everywhere. At least half the hours that teenagers are awake they are listening to music. There is no doubt that music stands apart from the other arts. Its power penetrates the heart, striking it directly with a message— whether truth or lie. Often its message is not in propositional form. It is incarnate in the rhythm and harmony of the music. It tells a story in a language that immediately communicates a message to our souls. How it does this is a mystery.

Karey and I have recorded several albums. Our experience has been that exposing our children to good music early, when their ears were still sensitive and life was relatively quiet, was key to helping them know what we value and treasure. Contemporary music that is complex to the point of sounding chaotic to young ears, with an unresolved structure and message, can overwhelm, destabilize, and confuse children. There is also a danger of addiction to some forms, not to mention possible evil that can seep into their minds through their ears. Music ultimately is an expression of the heart of the music's creator. I believe it is bordering on abuse to bring disharmony and despair into a child's life through music.

Listening to music is wonderful, but making our own music is even more wonderful. Music lessons are a part of many parents' strategies. A host of variables must be considered, including the child's talent, age, musical desire, and the practicality of a particular instrument—for example, tuba versus guitar. Our pastor, Peter Hiett, accurately expresses the feelings of many of us adults as we look back on our own childhood music lesson experiences. "I quit because none of my enlightened friends in third grade thought piano was cool. And, to be honest, I'd never listened to any great piano music."

I believe that maintaining strict control of our children's music as they move into their teen years is misguided. Some children are gifted with an ear that comprehends complex music that to a less

Computers, related technology, and the Internet are a double-edged sword for our children.

gifted parent's ear is noise. Of course a line must be drawn at the point where chaos, evil, and destruction enter in. There will always be debate about where we draw the line, but there is a line. In only a few short years our teenagers will be totally free to choose their own music. Communicating to them, while they are still at home, that we respect their freedom to choose, their personal opinion and taste, and even trust their judgment, places the responsibility on their shoulders, and makes them more apt to listen to us. Open communication, sharing our perspective and knowledge in a spirit of camaraderie, is our best hope. They will then be more inclined to do what is right—assuming they understand the difference between right and wrong in this context. Here's where earlier teaching and training pays off.

Plato said, "All learning which is required under compulsion has no hold upon the mind."[144] Battle lines drawn over music alienate children. Why are we battling anyway? We are supposed to be on the same team. Moral lectures and rigid rules can undo years of romancing, because values learned under compulsion have no hold on the heart.

Our best line of action is to expose our children early to good music, to develop their appreciation of it, and to help them develop a Christian worldview that will be reflected in their musical tastes. If we are students of our children, we can help them find the musical niche that fits best as we provide instruction in musical skills and techniques, and attend live performances together.

Karey's mother played classical music and opera, along with current popular adult music, when Karey was growing up. The music was simply there—no lectures, no talk, no expert commentary. Karey's current enjoyment of classical music (beyond her need for peace) is probably due to that exposure.

4. Computers and Related Technology

Computers have opened up an entirely new creative domain in the last generation—a literal "new age" that still makes some adults uncomfortable, while most kids jump in with both feet from day one. Nearly every home in America has at least one computer—some have half a dozen. My brothers are all PC experts, while I just commune with my friendly Macintosh. My business partner, who is a great earth scientist, will hardly touch a computer. Karey's brother, a systems engineer, uses his as an essential tool that he wields with great skill.

Early in Travis's education, I asked several computer scientists for their advice regarding how to acquaint him with computers. They said typing skills are essential and should be taught early (eight to twelve years of age). They also suggested I use computers as electronic "flash cards" for Travis's memory work. They said to wait until junior high before I introduced him to the more cognitive applications such as computer programming. This advice was consistent with the childhood development patterns I had researched, so I took their advice. The results have been fascinating.

After years of typing training, Travis started, at age twelve, animating with the simple program HyperCard. He moved quickly into programming with BASIC. I remember buying "Fox Pro" and arranging time for him with an accountant and a data base manager, but it turned out to be a dead end, so I backed off. At fourteen, he worked for a small computer company where a couple of passionate entrepreneurial computer scientists provided opportunity for extensive hands-on experience with computer hardware. He took computers apart, cleaned and rebuilt them, learning a wide range of practical skills in the process.

During this time, Travis literally grew up with the Internet, which in itself was a unique opportunity. He experienced history in the making, and feels privileged to have witnessed the whole process. In fact, he gets philosophical about it. There were tense times when we knew that he could get around any computer filter designed by man. It came down to a matter of trust at one point. I prefer having the computer our children use with Internet access not to be in a closed, private room, but in a more open family room. The FBI came knocking on our door looking for him one day. This sobered him up considerably. He had not done anything wrong, but he had witnessed a hack, and they wanted to know the details. He was amazed how little they actually understood about the hacking world.

Eventually, Travis decided not to pursue computer science—the hardware, software writing, or networking career tracks. Instead, he chose art and computer graphic design. I have heard him use this analogy: "Instead of designing, building, or servicing the vehicle, I wanted to drive it."

Although Travis is a Macintosh man, he serviced most of the PCs in his dorm at college—working on the hardware and software for the students, including helping computer science majors solve their computer-related problems. His broad understanding turned out to be unique among his classmates. His computer talent was obvious to us early on, so we opened many doors for him to walk through. Although most computer talent lands in software writing or networking, he took his talent into the arena of music and art, which, he has discovered, is not that common a combination.

Computers, related technology, and the Internet are a double-edged sword for our children. Though some Christians condemn these relatively new creative domains, I prefer to view them as more or less neutral. Yes, they can be addictive. Yes, a computer screen can have the same mesmerizing effect on a child as a television screen. Yes, there are dangers lurking around every corner on the Internet, from pornography to pedophiles. But if our children are going to function effectively in their new world, knowledge of computers and related technologies is essential. Common sense and open communication are keys to successfully guiding our children through this maze.

If our child expresses a creative interest, as Travis did, we can provide good equipment and programs, and connect them with trustworthy, likeminded mentors who can take them to the highest level possible. We cannot control completely what our son or daughter does with a computer when we are not around. We need to give our fears to God, and to trust our children with this charge: "I am allowing you access to this technology as my investment in your future. I'm not going to be looking over your shoulder or worrying every minute, because I trust you. I believe in you. And I know that when you encounter situations involving right and wrong, you will try to choose wisely, because you are who you are—not just my child, but a child of God, Who will give you all the wisdom you need whenever you ask."

Every child is unique, and creativity by definition produces something novel and different. We should expect to break new ground with each of our children. As we do, we need to remember that God has placed some unique aspect of His creative image in every child, as if He had implanted the score for an instrument in a cosmic symphony. Our role as parents is to help our children discover what part they are to play in this grand orchestra.

This runs in the face of the pressure for conformity that so often drives opinions and decisions in the Christian church today. When we play the wrong instrument or note we are in discord and the symphony is out of tune. If God wants my son to be a choreographer, or your daughter to become a waste management engineer, it is to their own Master, and yours—and not any modern-day Pharisee—that we all must answer.[145] The same goes for domains from sewing to surgery, pie making to photojournalism, homemaking to hockey, movie making to missionary medicine.

God didn't design us all, nor does He want us all, to play the same note. He wants us to find our "instrument," develop our talents, discover the Score, and then to make great music together with all the others who are following the right Conductor. There is a faint memory of the sound of the symphony within us all, and when we hear the music it brings joy. It is a celebration of truth and beauty, an echo of Eden and a prelude to the Master's piece.

Today, reading a good book and then discussing it with Karey or the kids is every bit as exciting for me as basketball ever was. I feel the same way about communing with my friends over supper or around the campfire about matters of mutual interest, from skiing to storytelling, eschatology to piscatology (my favorite is muskie-ology), ornithology, entomology, cooking, architecture, mechanics, mining, ministry, or making ice cream—whatever the topic of the moment may be. Although I still challenge myself with things such as pursuing elk in the mountains with a bow and arrow, or wild trout with a fly rod, hunting ideas and thoughts that lead me to God's truth is the creative domain that especially brings me joy these days.

After pursuing so many physical challenges throughout my life, it surprises and excites me to think that I've never had more fun than during the creative journey that has produced this book. It has been all the more enjoyable with the company and camaraderie of Dave Biebel, as we have worked through it word by word. Here I am in a whole new creative domain after passing age fifty. It makes me wonder what's next.

High and Far

With the bow bent, the arrow anchored,
We released our little boy,
Now he flies into his future,
To a place we may not see.

Early one spring day several years ago, a crew of concrete workers was pouring the walls for a root cellar under our kitchen. We live at an elevation of eight thousand feet, so there was still quite a bit of snow on the ground, but it was warm and sunny. The owner of the company had brought his little boy, Bronson, along. I was practicing shooting my bow below our house in our meadow when Bronson walked up to me and said, "Mr. Swan, will you teach me how to shoot a bow like you do?"

I said I'd love to, if he promised to work hard and listen to my instructions. With his father's permission, we began.

I led Bronson through all the steps—choosing a target, assuming the proper stance, gripping the bow, bending the bow arm slightly, nocking the arrow, using correct back tension. As I guided him, Bronson followed the steps until he was at full draw, ready to shoot his first arrow. He had done everything perfectly and was intently focused on the target as I reminded him to think of one thing—aiming. I can still remember seeing his little fingers gripping the bowstring and his blue eyes riveted, with all the passion his ten-year-old heart could muster, on the bull's eye.

Just as Bronson released his first arrow, we heard a swishing sound behind us. We turned to see a red plastic sled streaking down the hill with Dawson, then four years old, lying in it on his stomach with his head facing downhill. In that position, even had he known how to steer, steering would have been impossible. Dawson had just missed a fence post and a tree and was headed toward our wooden beehives and aspen grove. If he happened to miss the hives, there was no way that he would miss the trees.

I dropped my bow and sprinted down the hill, mukluks and all. After a thirty-yard sprint I became Superman for a moment, diving through the air to catch the sled. With arms fully extended I was able to grab it by the left rear end, stopping Dawson one foot from the beehives. The snow cushioned my landing and I rolled to the side of the beehives with Dawson and the sled in hand. Dawson tumbled out of the sled and turned over in the slushy spring snow. He sat up with a big smile, rosy cheeks shining with melting snow, and exclaimed, "Hey Papa—that was fun! Let's do it again!" He had enjoyed the ride more than anything because his papa had participated with such extravagant passion. I had not only jumped into Dawson's metaphorical "mud puddle," I had rolled in it! But he remained oblivious to the danger and to the fact that he had aimed his sled in the wrong direction. On top of that, he had no idea that he had distracted Bronson.

Bronson was hanging his head in disappointment. His arrow had missed the target, glanced off a tree, and careened end-over-end into an outcrop of granite, which abruptly ended its flight. As a result, the arrow's nock broke off, and the point was smashed and shoved up the shaft, which was bent. It was repairable, but would be an inch shorter, scarred and dented, and never again be truly straight.

He had done everything right, except that he had moved the bow before the arrow cleared the arrow rest. It only takes a split second for an arrow to be free of the string and the bow, but that last split second is critical to the success of the shot.

Psalm 127 says that our children are like arrows in our quiver, and for almost two decades that is where they stay as we prepare them to fly straight and true when they leave us.

AIMING YOUR CHILDREN

As I began writing this chapter, my mother called and shared with me this old letter she had recently come across. She and Dad had just had a great laugh as they read it again.

dear Grandpa and Grandma
thank you for the jack knife.
thank you for thinking that I'm
old enough to have it I cut myself
3 times. I got a glider made of
compressed styrofoam.
Iit's wingspan is 53 inches.
Love
travis

For some parents, releasing a child into the world feels like handing them a knife before they are prepared to use it properly. We can become obsessed with the fear of little cuts, only to miss the essential truth that our children desperately desire and need our encouragement, belief, faith, and trust. Travis was thanking his grandma and grandpa for their trust in him. Through this simple gift, they were helping me aim him in the right direction.

Like Travis, I also experienced my parents' investment of trust in me. Trust usually is conditional, earned or built on a history of behavior. But my parents' trust had an unconditional twist, because they saw something in me that I did not see, and they knew something about me that I did not know. Their trust gave me hope, and hope for a child is as vital to life as air, food, and water. If they believed in me, then it was okay for me to believe in myself. Yes, I was being aimed—but with my informed consent. I was not coerced, but inspired, to find and fulfill my unique destiny as a child of theirs, and of God.

A friend of mine told the story of a college student he was discipling. The young man had dabbled in drugs and had run around with the wrong crowd, but his heart now desired God. My friend asked him, "Why did you come back to God?"

The young man said, "When I was in high school, every morning my father, who you know is a high-powered businessman, drove me to school. And as I opened the car door he never failed to reach over, put his hand on my arm and say, 'Son, remember, I believe in you.' This one statement more than anything else kept me from getting into serious trouble. It has wooed me back to God. Those words haunted me as I strayed. They reached something deep inside me and called me to be better. I have finally begun living up to the faith my dad had in me. He saw something in me I didn't see—his son conformed to the image of Christ."

The way this father saw his son is parallel to the way God views all who trust in Christ for salvation—as already made perfect through

His grace. He is saying, "I love you. And there's nothing you can ever do or say that will change that." The Greek root for belief simply means "to give one's heart to." This is how perfect love casts out fear—and the need to prove anything. The question for the child—whether in physical or spiritual terms—becomes: "How can I honor (and not disappoint) someone who has such faith in me?"

What if our child has not earned our trust, or has squandered it in the past? Trust may be conditional, but faith is not. This is risky, but it is also where grace comes in. A parent who has faith in a child who seems unworthy of trust may be surprised by the response. Of course there are no guarantees where humans are concerned. But I do know that conditional, controlling "love," which demands payment before it takes the risk of faith, will never succeed. Philip Yancey said, "Doubt always coexists with faith, for in the presence of certainty who would need faith at all?"[146] And Kathleen Norris shares this statement from a monk, "Doubt is merely the seed of faith, a sign that faith is alive and ready to grow."[147]

There is a fine line here between grace-filled faith and false faith. In either case, our approach to our child during the final phase of parenting clearly indicates whether we are involved in a romance, or a business venture. A parent who operates with bookkeeping logic is basically selfish—probably engaged in self-protection, which so often seems justified. After all, what will the neighbors, the larger family, or church members think of parents whose children seem to be crooked arrows?

Real love—the kind that God expressed for us through Jesus—is risky and sometimes very costly. The apostle Paul wrote that love "bears all things, believes all things, hopes all things, endures all things."[148] In Matthew 25, where Jesus tells the parable of the talents (a unit of currency), I believe we find biblical support for investing faith (even as we doubt) in our child, in the form of unconditional grace.

In the parable, one servant did not invest the talent given to him, because he was afraid that he might lose it. Instead, he hid the money in the ground. His lord called him a "wicked and lazy servant." This appears on the surface to be a somewhat harsh judgment for being conservative. But Jesus was saying that faithfulness requires using or investing what God entrusts to us, for His glory.

Within the context of parenting, the "talent" entrusted to parents by the Lord is the faith we can either invest or withhold from our children. To hold back is an act of self-protection motivated by fear and a lack of trust in God. Larry Crabb has said that the sin of self-protection is very difficult to recognize and acknowledge, and then to deal with, because change must come from the inside out.[149] Self-protection seems at face value justified, as in the case of the wicked and lazy servant. We do not want to play the fool, be disappointed, or have our investment in our children return void. The choice not to risk has a wise, frugal ring to it, which in another context might be noble. To react defensively when doubt arises seems—and may even be—rational. But to invest our faith unconditionally, even though the venture appears risky, is an act of courage and grace. Without an eternal perspective, this appears foolish, naïve, and unwise. Supernatural logic always seems this way to the secular mind. But "the wisdom of this world is foolishness with God."[150]

Jesus gave His life for undeserving, wayward sinners—including us, and our children—because He believed that the will of His Father was good, and that His Word was trustworthy. Our Savior is our model. Incarnating His character is the central issue of properly aiming the arrows that we hope will honor Him. By faith, we can proceed, trusting not in our own abilities, or even in our children's character, but in Christ, Who will persevere with them more than they with Him, or we with them. We can, therefore, release them with confidence, hope, and joy.

RELEASING YOUR CHILDREN

Releasing—an arrow or a child—is not an event, but a process involving a series of events. In archery, this series of events happens in the blink of an eye. In parenting the process is much longer, although when we look back it will seem to have been but the blink of the eye.

As our children near adulthood, they begin testing what we have taught them through the years. It is a suspenseful time for parents, because everything is up in the air, pending our children's decisions. As Christians, we wonder if they will make God the object of their passion. They stretch our patience and our finances, go on to college, or start a job. We wonder—even sometimes worry—about their careers, their calling, their future spouses, and as they become more independent we realize that soon they will be completely on their own. It is natural for parents to become preoccupied with these events, sometimes to the point where the process that has already happened is forgotten, and the continuing process is ignored.

Recently, I spoke at a conference where a woman told me that she was at a loss as to what to do with her daughter, who was about to go away to college. She said, "Our relationship is crumbling. My daughter is not in rebellion against God, but she is rebelling against *me.*" This bewildered the mother, since her daughter had been a model child through her entire life, including high school.

"Give me an example of your conflict," I said.

"She won't keep her room clean," the distraught mother replied.

As far as I could see, the conflict was mostly inside the mother. But for her, the crisis was real enough, and it was threatening to cause a major relational disaster. She was trying to stand by her principles, and the daughter was trying to make her own choices.

"Most eighteen-year-old females are preoccupied with major life changes and choices," I reminded her. "If ever you err on the side of grace it should be now."

"But she knows the rules," the mother said. "I feel that to change them just because she won't keep them anymore would violate everything I've taught her. And it would be a bad example for her younger sister. All we need is for the house to become a pigpen for the next three years."

Over several weeks of coaching by phone, I tried to encourage this mother to raise her sights. She was looking only at the daughter's newfound sloppiness. I encouraged her to try to look past the dirt to her daughter's heart. "In the process of releasing," I said, "we do best when we major on the majors and overlook the minors."

The lady was experiencing what archers call "target panic." At the instant the arrow is released, while the shaft is moving along the arrow rest, the archer flinches, deflecting the arrow, causing it to miss its mark. Target panic is responsible for up to ninety percent of misses under twenty-five yards in range, since most serious archers can become quite proficient up to that distance. Why this panic happens in a person normally confident in their aim is difficult to determine, because most archers with this problem blank out mentally and cannot recall the small details of what actually happened. The issue, as far as I can see, is again a matter of belief and faith, or trust. Even an archer with good form and good equipment properly set up can miss, if they allow fear, anxiety, or worry to creep in as distractions at the last split second. The strange thing is that, for most who experience target panic, the focus becomes the equipment or the set-up, or too much or too little practice, when the remedy is faith that follows through, holding the bow steady until the arrow has completely cleared the bow.

FOLLOWING THROUGH

Archers differ in their shooting styles. Some close an eye, some cant the bow, some use a mechanical release, and some use fingers to pull back the string. Anchor points and methods of gripping the handle vary. Some archers shoot with bent arm; others shoot straight-armed. Techniques vary in archery—as in parenting—but no archer or parent can hope to hit the target without proper follow-through.

When we finally let them fly, there is no higher joy than knowing their trajectory is fixed on Christ.

As I finish this book, Travis is in his third year of college. He is still partly supported by us; he has not totally settled on a vocation, nor is he married. He does not own a house; he has told us that his home is now at college. This arrow is pulling away from the bowstring. We spent a lot of time together as he was growing up. We homeschooled him all the way—even through high school. But I am currently spending more time with him by phone and email in heart-to-heart discussion about crucial issues and watershed decisions than I did at any time when he was home.

It is not that I am having a hard time letting go; we are simply close friends—best friends. It is a wonderful relationship. I often think of the words of young Teddy Roosevelt, who wrote to his father while attending Harvard, "I am sure that there is no one who has a father who is also his best…friend as you are mine."[151]

Right now, I am trying to hold the bow perfectly still as the arrow named Travis is launched into the world. Travis has not quite cleared the bow yet, but he will very soon. It seems like just a few moments ago we pulled him out of our quiver, placed him on the string, focused on the target, and drew the bow. My main concern now is not to lose my concentration by getting distracted by anything other than following through as he leaves. For an archer, even the blink of the eye will interrupt the aim. The analogy to faith is well made by novelist Doris Bett, who said it is "not synonymous with certainty" but "is the decision to keep one's eyes open."

My parents did not lose their concentration as they released their four sons. To make sure their "arrows" would clear their bow without being deflected, they went so far as to wait until my youngest brother was settled in his career, and married, before they sold the family house and moved on to their next season of life. It was a great sacrifice, those last few years of waiting, but nothing distracted them from their determination to follow through as their last arrow was launched. I see now that I had radical parents. Until their parenting responsibilities were completed, they were intent on protecting that physical symbol of family roots embodied in the family house where they had raised their sons. After the youngest one was established in life, they built a house in northern Wisconsin on my father's grandfather's homestead, where they now grow Christmas trees and enjoy the periodic visits of their grandchildren—and one great-grandchild so far.

The unconditional sacrifice my parents made, combined with their faith and trust, was a combination I could not resist. They won my heart, as well as my brothers' hearts. This book has flowed directly from their lives. I pray that I have communicated what they taught me well and accurately.

The fifth commandment, which is the first commandment dealing with human relationships, is directed at children, including adult children: "Honor your father and your mother, that your days may be long upon the land which the Lord your God is giving you."[152] These words bind children to parents in a multigenerational community of faith. This command is unique among the Ten Commandments, for it is both a promise and a warning. Disrespect for parents is a serious matter, for it also dishonors God.

I have always taken this command seriously. Honor to me means giving credit, recognition, decoration, deference, and reverence. The practical side of honoring parents includes gratitude for their monetary sacrifice. When I graduated from college, started my career, and began graduate work, I took out a term life insurance policy on myself with my parents designated as the beneficiaries. If I had died, they would have had at least some return on their investment in me. I don't believe they ever knew I did this.

I also committed to sharing my life with them through ongoing communication. I have had a long phone conversation with my parents at least once a week since I left home in 1966. This comes to nearly two thousand phone calls. I have asked for their counsel, and considered their advice with all seriousness. I have shared just about everything significant in my life with them. They have known my plans and dreams since the day I left for college. They are not dictating my life or interfering. I am simply sharing my story with them as it unfolds. I am quite independent. I believe that the commandment to honor our parents applies after we have grown up and left home as much as, or even more than, when we were children. Only as adults can we fully comprehend what honor means. And then we have more appreciation when it is returned to us.

I can see this happening now with my own children, and I trust that it will happen for you with yours.

Sometimes, we are privileged to see, and hear, the results of our efforts firsthand. Remember the weeklong family camps I mentioned earlier, that we hosted at our home? Ten families attended who had made the romance of their children's hearts a priority. Each year's camp was rich with relationship, but one night stands out. It was still and moonlit. Our children, then of high school age, were talking and singing around a campfire as we parents lay in our beds listening to their conversation and observing a page of their story unfold. We could hear every word they said. They were passionately sharing with each other how to protect a girl's heart. They discussed free will and election. They sang in harmony accompanied by violin and guitar. They discussed making their way into the world—"planting their fields and building their houses." We shed tears of joy that night as we realized that we had reached our highest objective in romancing our children to God—we had won their hearts.

When all our training, discipling, mentoring, shepherding, and romancing is said and done, when our children have outgrown mud puddles next to soccer fields, when we finally release our arrows into the world and watch them fly away into the future toward eternity, there is no higher joy than knowing that their trajectory is fixed on Christ. Although there will be nothing then between us and the target but air, our prayers will have the wings to fly with our arrows, even though we may not be around to see all of the flight.

For as long as I can remember, I've been enchanted by the flight of an arrow. I am still enchanted, because the flight of an arrow is a mystery, and mystery causes me to wonder. The launched arrow is free to fly, to cut through the air into the far-flung future. It is the risk and danger of the journey into the unknown that now draws my attention. I am enthralled with it, fascinated—spellbound.

John Eldredge wrote about a breakfast table conversation he once had with his son Luke, who asked, "Are there any great adventures anymore? Are there any great battles...and are there any dragons?"[153]

Like us, children need an adventure to live. In their dreams they wonder: *Are there any adventures left to live? Is there a place reserved for me?* Inside of them burns the desire, the longing to be the hero or the heroine. No one else can be who our child is meant to be. They have the lead role in the script God wrote for them. According to the secular worldview, few adventures remain; the battle is a myth and the dragon is make-believe—just a fairytale. Ecclesiastes says of this worldview, "I have seen all the works that are done under the sun; and indeed, all is vanity and grasping for the wind."[154]

The Christian's view is different. We are guaranteed adventure— high adventure—when we walk the way of wisdom, passionately seeking wisdom as a treasure. We are personally written into the larger Story—the great adventure—by the hand of God. This is what we were made for. It captures our souls with a transcendent vision beyond our mortal selves. We are not some kind of gods building our own little kingdoms—we are warriors winning the kingdom of God. This higher purpose will propel our arrows to places beyond our imagination. This is why I am enchanted by their flight.

"Like arrows in the hands of a warrior, so are the children of one's youth. Happy [blessed] is the man who has his quiver full of them...."[155] This passage usually brings to mind the comforting vision of a parent enjoying the pleasures of a full quiver of children and the security they provide in old age. But the context is war— the spiritual conflict of the ages being waged even as you read. The quiver belongs to a warrior whose desire is to obtain as many arrows as possible to shoot into, through, and even behind enemy lines.

To imagine our precious children involved in a direct D-Day style spiritual attack, penetrating Satan's stronghold, is startling. To envision them as Special Forces infiltrating the most dangerous territory of all is almost too much to bear.

At the beginning of this book, I said that Travis, when he stood on stage and was questioned by an audience of parents, was already in college—a balanced arrow, strong and sharp. He was also involved in a daring ministry that has penetrated the frontlines of the secular campus culture. He and several other leaders started a church, using the language, music, and philosophy of the campus to take on hearts for Jesus, just as they would do in a foreign country. I can still see Travis on the first Friday night of the school year, singing to thousands of tattooed and pierced bodies in the city square. He is a winsome warrior among the enemy, and sometimes he flies so high and far that I am uncomfortable and thrilled at the same time. I never bargained for this much drama. But this is the purpose of parenting. Romancing our child's heart is all about lifting our sights above our human vision, to the context of the larger Story.

Our daughter Heather's flight may have seemed less dramatic on the surface, but it has led her just as deeply into the battle. Only she serves on a different front—one most of us would rather avoid. Heather has a special gift, a rich ministry bringing hope and joy, love and dignity, to the elderly who are overwhelmed with loneliness and despair as they face their last days on earth. She is Jesus in disguise, holding the hands of people as they die, singing to them, comforting them with the warm sunshine of her smile. She gives as Mother Teresa did—not only her care but her heart as well.

And Dawson—well, at the moment he's out on the porch hammering together a cage for the caterpillars he carried home in his tee shirt. In the morning they will probably be all over the house, and Karey will have to pick them out of the breadbox. But the Robin Hood days of my childhood have come full circle, and I know that Dawson himself is now the arrow balanced on my string. For all of us as parents, the moment when our children are ready to be released comes much sooner than we think. But the quiver is God's, and on His bow they will fly according to His good purpose and pleasure.

Scripture tells us that Jesus loved His children "to the end." He never faltered in His direction or the intensity of His purpose, and neither must we. I remember when Dawson shot his arrows on stage—he never wavered in the power of his concentration, and he hit gold. As parents, we too need to keep our focus, to romance his heart every moment so that when we release him he will fly, not only straight and true, but high and far, winning other hearts for Jesus as his has been won, with the Sacred Romance of God's love. It's up to us not to blink—even if we have to smother our laughs as he digs into his bowl of cereal and says, "I've been thinking about collecting tarantulas—just like you used to...."

NOTES

STRAIGHT AND TRUE

1   Monte Swan, "Arrows," from the album *Straight and True* (Loyal Publishing, Inc., 2002).

1. ONCE UPON A CHILDHOOD

2   Charles Pellegrino, *Unearthing Atlantis—An Archaeological Odyssey* (New York: Random House, Vintage Books, 1993), dedication.

2. FINDING THE SILVER BULLET

3   Karey Swan, *Hearth and Home—Recipes For Life* (Sisters, OR: Loyal Publishing, 1996), 167.
4   Steve Randazzo, "Fairytale Romance." Used by permission.

3. THE WAY OF WISDOM

5   See Philippians 4:8,9.
6   See Hebrews 11 and 12
7   Elisabeth Elliot, *Shadow of the Almighty: the Life and Testament of Jim Elliot* (New York: Harper and Row, 1956), 15.
8   See 2 Kings 6:15-17.

9   C. S. Lewis, *The Last Battle* (New York: Macmillan, 1956), 173-174.
10 *The Heart of George McDonald*, ed. Roland Hein (Wheaton: Harold Shaw, 1994), 417.
11 See Acts 17:22ff.
12 Brent Curtis and John Eldredge, *The Sacred Romance—Drawing Closer to the Heart of God* (Nashville: Thomas Nelson, 1997), 35.
13 *The Tempest*, 4.1.148.
14 G. K. Chesterton, *The Collected Works of G. K. Chesterton: Heretics, Orthodoxy, The Blatchford Controversies*, ed. David Dooley (San Francisco: Ignatius Press, 1986), 264.
15 Letter from John Keats to George and Georgiana Keats, 18 February 1819 (n.p.).
16 C. S. Lewis, *The Screwtape Letters* (New York: Macmillan, 1956), 76-77.
17 Luke 24:32.
18 Eleanor H. Porter, *Pollyanna* (Boston: L.C. Page and Company, 1913), 149.
19 *Macbeth*, 5.5.17.
20 James C. Dobson, *Parenting Isn't for Cowards* (Waco: Word Books, 1987), 49-50.
21 Proverbs 1:7.
22 Proverbs 2:4.
23 Proverbs 3:15.
24 Proverbs 2:1-5.
25 Proverbs 2:10.
26 Proverbs 2:11.
27 See Philippians 3:14ff.
28 John Eldredge, *Wild at Heart: Discovering the Secret of a Man's Soul* (Nashville: Thomas Nelson, 2001), 13.
29 John Bunyan, *Pilgrim's Progress* (1678).
30 Acts 17:28.

4. THE IDEA OF STORY

31 C. S. Lewis, *Of Other Worlds*, ed. Walter Hooper (New York: Harcourt Brace Javanovich, 1975), 24.
32 Vigen Guroian, *Tending the Heart of Virtue* (New York: Oxford University Press, 1998), 8,178.
33 Ibid., 10 (emphasis added).
34 Gladys Hunt, *Honey for a Child's Heart: The Imaginative Use of Books in Family Life* (Grand Rapids: Zondervan, 1978), 55.
35 Frederick Buechner, *Telling the Truth: The Gospel as Tragedy, Comedy and Fairy Tale* (San Francisco: Harper and Row, 1977), 81,90.
36 2 Samuel 11:27-12:7.
37 *Hamlet*, 2.2.641.
38 Joe Wheeler, comp./ed., *Dad in My Heart: A Treasury of Heartwarming Stories about Dads* (Wheaton: Tyndale House, 1997), xiii-xiv.
39 Norma Livo and Sandra Rietz, *Storytelling: Process and Practice* (Littleton, CO: Libraries Unlimited, 1986).
40 Joshua 4:6,7.
41 Exodus 12:26,27, NIV.
42 C. S. Lewis, *On Stories and Other Essays on Literature*, ed. Walter Hooper (New York: Harcourt Brace and Company, 1982), 47.
43 See Hebrews 4:12.

44   Kirk Webb, "Theology: System or Narrative? How Story Transforms the Soul," *Mars Hill Review* 7 (winter/spring 1997): 23.

5. ANOTHER SUITOR

45   Arnold Burron, *Discipline That Can't Fail: Fundamentals for Christian Parents* (Greeley, CO: Diamond Peak Press, 1999), 30.
46   1 Peter 5:8.
47   Ephesians 6:10.
48   Edith Schaeffer, *Hidden Art* (Wheaton: Tyndale House, 1971), 213.
49   See Ezekiel 1.

6. THE WATERSHED

50   Luke 9:51ff.
51   Psalms 42:1.
52   Proverbs 22:6.
53   See the note on this verse in the *New Geneva Study Bible*, ed. R. C. Sproul (Nashville: Thomas Nelson, 1995), 967.
54   See Acts 9:2.
55   Charles R. Swindoll, *You and Your Child* (Nashville: Thomas Nelson, 1977), 19.
56   S. Clark and J. MacRae, "You Can't Make a Heart Love Somebody" from the album *George Strait* (Universal City, MCA Records Inc., Victoria Kay Music/B.M.G. Songs/ Little Beagle Music, 1994).
57   Curtis and Eldredge, *The Sacred Romance*, 137.
58   1 John 4:10.
59   E. D. Hirsch Jr., "Romancing Your Child," *Education Matters* (spring 2001): 9.
60   Isaiah 54:5,10, NIV.
61   Exodus 20:5a; 34:14b.
62   Jeremiah 31:3.
63   Hosea 2:14.
64   1 Corinthians 13:13b.
65   Peter Kreeft, *Three Philosophies of Life: Ecclesiastes: Life as Vanity, Job: Life as Suffering, Song of Songs: Life as Love* (San Francisco: Ignatius Press, 1989), 104.
66   Philip Yancey, *What's So Amazing About Grace?* (Grand Rapids: Zondervan, 1997), 12,26.
67   John 17:21.
68   Ephesians 5:32.
69   John 17:11b.
70   John 17:24b.
71   Deuteronomy 6:6-9.
72   Deuteronomy 11:18-21.
73   Revelation 3:20.

7. PREREQUISITES TO ROMANCE

74   David Elkind, *The Hurried Child: Growing Up Too Fast, Too Soon* (Reading, MA: Addison-Wesley Publishing Company, 1992), 4.
75   Ibid., 71-93.

76 Jean Healy, *Endangered Minds: Why Kids Can't Think and What We Can Do About It* (New York: Simon and Schuster, 1990), 195-217.
77 Ross Campbell, *How To Really Love Your Child* (Wheaton: Victor Books, 1982), 32-33.
78 Gary Chapman, *The Five Love Languages* (Chicago: Northfield Publishing, 1995), 38.
79 Dr. James Dobson, *The Strong-Willed Child: Birth Through Adolescence* (Wheaton: Tyndale House, 1982), 76.
80 John Nieder, *God, Sex, and Your Child: What You Need To Tell Your Child About Sex* (Nashville: Thomas Nelson, 1988), 46.
81 Michael Medved and Diane Medved, Ph.D., *Saving Childhood: Protecting Our Children from the National Assault on Innocence* (New York: Zondervan, 1998).
82 Philippians 4:8.
83 Michael Martin Murphey and David Hoffner, "Once Upon A Time," from the album *Americana* (Warner Bros. Records, Inc., Timberwolf Music, Inc. and Hoffner Haus Music, 1987).
84 See 1 Thessalonians 5:17.
85 Monte Swan, "What They Need Even More," from the album *Straight and True* (Loyal Publishing, Inc., 2002).
86 Psalms 68:5a.

8. PARENTAL INCARNATION

87 John 1:14a,18.
88 Philippians 2:5-8.
89 John 14:9b.
90 Galatians 5:22,23.
91 See Ephesians 5 and 6.
92 See Luke 2:46-52.
93 *George McDonald*, xii.
94 See Matthew 28:19.

9. CHARACTERISTICS OF A ROMANCER

95 C. S. Lewis, *C. S. Lewis: Letters To Children* (New York: Macmillan, 1985), 5.
96 See Mark 9:33-39 and Matthew 18:1-5.
97 Brad Roberts, "Superman's Song," from the album *The Ghosts That Haunt Me* (Cha-Ching Records, 1991).
98 See Paul C. Vitz, *Faith of the Fatherless: The Psychology of Atheism* (Dallas: Spence Publishing, 1999).
99 Psalms 91:5.
100 See Revelation 21:1-5.
101 C. S. Lewis, *Present Concerns and Other Essays*, ed. Walter Hooper (New York: Harcourt Brace Jovanovich, 1986), 53.
102 See 2 Corinthians 4 and 5.
103 C. S. Lewis, *Screwtape*, 57-58.
104 John 15:11.
105 See Hebrews 12:2.
106 C. S. Lewis, *They Stand Together: The Letters of C. S. Lewis to Arthur Greeves (1914-1963)*, ed. Walter Hooper (New York: Macmillan, 1979), 311.

107 C. S. Lewis, *Letters of C. S. Lewis*, ed. W. H. Lewis (New York: Harcourt, Brace and World, 1966), 289.
108 Michael McLean, "The Curse" and "The Melody Within" from the Feature Films for Families film *Rigoletto* (Salt Lake City: Shining Star Music (ASCAP), 1994).
109 Fyodor Dostoyevsky, *The Gospel in Dostoyevsky—Selections from His Works*, ed. The Bruderhof Foundation (Farmington, PA: The Plough Publishing House, 1998), 3.
110 Matthew 18:6.
111 *The Dialogues of Plato*, tr. B. Jowett, M.A. (New York: Random House, 1937), vol. 1, 695-696.
112 Karey Swan, *Hearth and Home*, 188,191.

10. METHODS FOR ROMANCERS

113 Saxton Pope, *Hunting with the Bow and Arrow* (New York: G.P. Putnam's Sons, 1923), 66,73.
114 See Ephesians 5:15ff.
115 Richard A. Swenson, M.D., *The Overload Syndrome: Learning To Live Within Your Limits* (Colorado Springs: NavPress, 1998), 18.
116 Jay O'Callahan, verbal communication to author.
117 Livo and Rietz, *Storytelling*, 102-103.
118 Michael Martin Murphy and David Hoffner, "Once Upon A Time" in *Americana* (Warner Bros. Records, Inc., Timberwolf Music, Inc. and Hoffner Haus Music, 1987).
119 Healy, *Endangered Minds*, 91,102-103.
120 S. Dante and C. Dante, "So We Never Got To Paris" from the album *Out of the Gray* (Brentwood, Tennessee: The Sparrow Corporation, 1995).
121 Amos 5:21.
122 Romans 14:5,6, *The Living Bible Paraphrased* (Wheaton: Tyndale House, 1971).

11. THE SENSE OF WONDER

123 Cornelis Verhoeven, *The Philosophy of Wonder: An Introduction and Incitement to Philosophy*, tr. Mary Foran (New York: Macmillan, 1972).
124 See Revelation 4:11.
125 Mark Starkey, *God, Sex, and the Lost Sense of Wonder: For Those Looking For Something To Believe In* (Downers Grove, IL: InterVarsity Press, 1998), 26.
126 Ellen Haroutunian, "A Baptism of Imagination: A Conversation With Peter Kreeft," *Mars Hill Review* 5 (summer 1996): 60.
127 Job 37:14.
128 Isaiah 40:26.
129 Psalms 8:3,4.
130 1 Kings 4:29,33,34, NIV.
131 S. Carpenter, "Germs of Endearment—Modern Hygiene's Dirty Tricks: The Clean Life May Throw Off a Delicate Balance in the Immune System," *Science News: The Weekly Newsmagazine of Science* 156 (August 14, 1999): 108-110.
132 See Psalms 103:15.
133 Monte Swan, "Fires of His Wonder," from the album *Straight and True* (Loyal Publishing, Inc., 2002).

12. THE CREATIVE IMAGE

134 Dr. Paul Brand and Philip Yancey, *In His Image* (Grand Rapids: Zondervan, Judith Markham Books, 1984), 20-22.
135 Dorothy L. Sayers, *The Mind of the Maker* (San Francisco: Harper and Row, 1941), 22.
136 Genesis 1:27.
137 See Ephesians 2:10.
138 Karey Swan, *Hearth and Home*, 22.

13. CREATIVE DOMAINS

139 Monte Swan, "Daddy, What Is Her Name?" from the album *Straight and True* (Loyal Publishing, Inc., 2002).
140 Philippians 2:13.
141 See 1 Corinthians 12-14.
142 Dave Holt, *Balanced Bowhunting: A Guide to Modern Bowhunting* (Lakewood, CO: High Country Publishers, 1988), 149.
143 Beth Thurow, personal communication to the author.
144 *The Dialogues of Plato*, vol. 1, 796.
145 See Romans 14:4.

HIGH AND FAR

146 Philip Yancey, *Reaching for the Invisible God: What Can We Expect to Find?* (Grand Rapids: Zondervan, 2000), 41.
147 Kathleen Norris, *Amazing Grace: A Vocabulary of Faith* (New York: The Berkley Publishing Group, Penguin Putnam, Riverhead Books, 1998), 63.
148 1 Corinthians 13:7.
149 Larry Crabb, *Real Change Is Possible—If You're Willing to Start from the Inside Out* (Colorado Springs: NavPress, 1988), 184.
150 1 Corinthians 3:19.
151 Theodore Roosevelt, *A Bully Father: Theodore Roosevelt's Letters to His Children* (New York: Random House, 1995), 7.
152 Exodus 20:12.
153 Eldredge, *Wild at Heart*, 140.
154 Ecclesiastes 1:14.
155 Psalms 127:4.

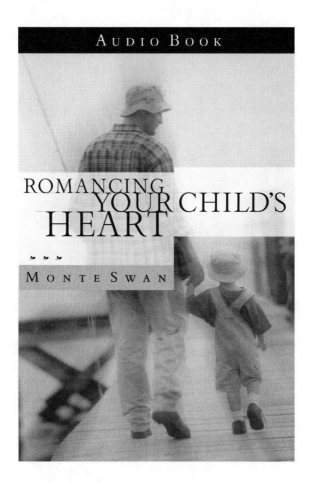

AUDIO BOOK

ROMANCING YOUR CHILD'S HEART

MONTE SWAN

ROMANCING YOUR CHILD'S HEART
AUDIO BOOK | MONTE SWAN
AVAILABLE BY CALLING 1-888-775-6925 OR BY LOGGING ON TO
WWW.LOYALPUBLISHING.COM
ISBN: 1-929125-35-6 | RETAIL: $12.99

STRAIGHT & TRUE

MUSIC CD | MONTE & KAREY SWAN WITH JERRY NELSON

AVAILABLE BY CALLING 1-888-775-6925 OR BY LOGGING ON TO

WWW.LOYALPUBLISHING.COM

ISBN: 1-929125-38-0 | RETAIL: $16.99

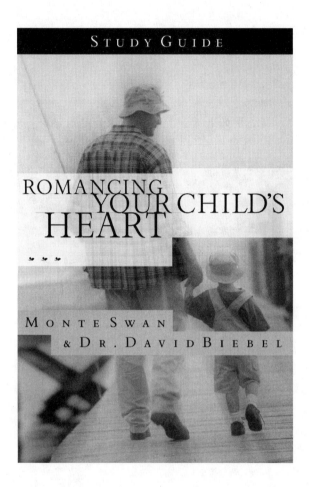

ROMANCING YOUR CHILD'S HEART

MANUAL FOR CRAFTING THE ROMANCE │ MONTE SWAN WITH DR. DAVID BIEBEL

AVAILABLE AT BOOKSTORES EVERYWHERE OR BY CALLING 1-888-775-6925

OR BY LOGGING ON TO WWW.LOYALPUBLISHING.COM

ISBN: 1-929125-36-4 │ RETAIL: $10.99